B. Tyndall
Christmas 1983

# GEORGIAN AND VICTORIAN BROADWATER

# Georgian and Victorian
# BROADWATER

## R.G.P. Kerridge
## and
## M.R.Standing

Phillimore

1983

Published by
PHILLIMORE & CO. LTD.
Shopwyke Hall, Chichester, Sussex

ISBN 0 85033 511 6

Printed and bound in Great Britain by
CAMELOT PRESS LTD.
Southampton, England

# Contents

# List of Plates

(between pages 52 and 53)

# List of Line Drawings

# *Acknowledgements*

The authors are particularly indebted to the following: Worthing Borough Council for permission to search and use material from the Town Hall archives; Messrs. H. Divall, D. Allen, K. Downer, and K. Bryant, as well as Dr. G. Shaw for their assistance with the collection of information and photographic material; Roy Downer for the use of his excellent photographs, both for reference and reproduction; S. Flitton for his assistance and advice on the geological text; Dr. T. Hudson, and Mrs. P. Gill and her staff at the West Sussex Record Office, Chichester; Mr. R. Elleray and his colleagues in the Local Studies section of Worthing Library and Wilf Page for his help, knowledge and use of photographic and other material.

Special thanks are due to Miss Sharon Phillips who typed the manuscript and gave so much of her time, patience and enthusiasm, to Mr. P. Langelaan for kindly allowing us to research the Company records and archives of 'Paine, Manwaring', and to Miss Hilary Hide for details of her family and other valuable material.

# Introduction

Broadwater's development between 1700 and 1900 can be summarised as 'Dominance to Obscurity', for in 1700 the Parish of Broadwater governed the three separate village communities of Broadwater, Worthing and Offington, all of which were within its ancient parochial boundaries. By the end of the 18th century, as a result of the increasing popularity of sea bathing, the roles of Broadwater and Worthing had, however, started to reverse. Throughout the 19th century the town of Worthing expanded, with the result that by 1902 Broadwater was totally engulfed, and became one of the residential suburbs within the urban sprawl that is today the modern Borough of Worthing. The former village community, centred on Broadwater Street, has therefore lost much of its distinct character and identity.

The authors have attempted to reconstruct its former character, by researching the people of Broadwater village and the history of all the properties that are known to have existed in Broadwater Street during the Georgian and Victorian periods. The task of recording both the development of the Street and the fortunes of the community resident there through the centuries has been like assembling a jigsaw puzzle, when many of the pieces are missing. Over the past ten years many of the scattered documentary sources that still exist have been researched, and this publication is a result of our collation and analysis of the information obtained.

It is our sincere hope that this book will contribute to the knowledge of Broadwater's history, and is dedicated to the many residents who have assisted and encouraged our research and, like us, find this ancient parish of interest. We also hope that it will be of interest to all those who are curious to know more about the life of earlier generations.

M. R. Standing
R. G. P. Kerridge
1983

*Chapter One*

# The Early History of Broadwater

*Prehistoric Times*

From the top of Cissbury Hill some 602 feet above sea level, (now owned by the National Trust), the whole of the ancient parish of Broadwater can be seen, the area of which in 1876 was recorded as 2,735 acres.[1] Included within its boundaries were both the southern slopes of the South Downs, and the fertile coastal plain of Sussex, on which the settlements of Broadwater, Worthing and Offington were all established. The parish was elongate and irregular in shape, being nearly 4 miles long, and 2 miles wide at the coast.[2] When man first settled in the area the view from Cissbury Hill was, however, very different from that of today. The Sussex coastline and topography, which seem so defined and stable, have been in a state of continuous change over the centuries.[3] The flatness of the Sussex coastal plain, which is so evident from Cissbury, is the result of events which occurred during the last two million years, when great sheets of polar ice advanced and retreated over much of northern Europe, Siberia and North America. With each glacial advance, ocean water froze to become polar ice and with each retreat the polar ice melted to return water to the oceans. Consequently the sea level fell and rose as the ice ages came and went, and in lowland coastal areas such as Sussex there were substantial lateral shifts in the coastline. At Worthing, for example, the sea once lapped the southern foot of Highdown. The Sussex coastal plain is a remnant of the flat floor of this sea, bevelled by the slowly-encroaching waves, and exposed after the eventual retreat of the water during the last Ice Age. The ancient beach may be located in boreholes.

After the Ice Age, about 10,000 years ago, the sea level has gradually risen in South East England, from about 100 feet below the present level.[4] During this rise, the mouths of rivers draining southward across the coastal plain became flooded to form estuaries. The Arun was a broad estuary as far upstream as Amberley Wild Brooks about 2,500 years ago, and it is probable that the mouths of minor streams had become tidal creeks by this time. Thus the mouth of Broadwater stream may have already become the broad expanse of brackish water from which Broadwater perhaps took its name[5] (See Fig. 2.[6])

According to Dr. Frederick Dixon, a mid-19th century Worthing geologist, the extent of the tidal creek could easily be discerned by its level, the character of the soil, which in some places was mere shingle, and by the presence of marine shells of existing species.[7] On the 1:63,360 Ordnance Survey geological map the strata in the area of the old creek is Alluvium, Coombe Deposits and Woolwich and Reading Beds. Modern soil investigation prior to development in the area substantiated both these statements. The site–indicated on Fig. 2–revealed the ground conditions to be a very shallow covering of Alluvium over a fine pale grey, silty clay. The Alluvium consisted of soft estuarine soils that represent infilled creeks, resulting from a change of sea level relative to land in fairly recent geological time.[8] Over the years, the creek slowly diminished in size and by about 1250 the eastward drift of the channel tides had gradually formed a shingle bar across its mouth which cut off its direct access to the sea.[9]

1

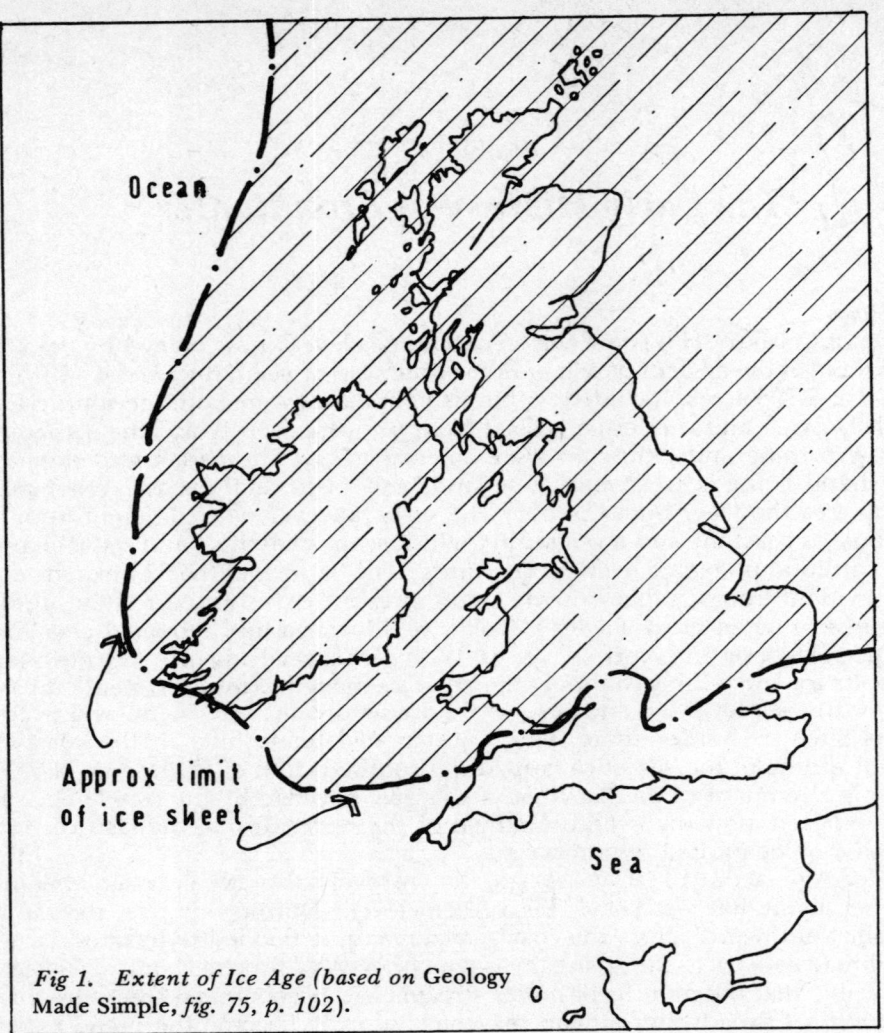

*Fig 1. Extent of Ice Age (based on* Geology Made Simple, *fig. 75, p. 102*).

It is impossible to be sure when man first settled in the area, but archaeological evidence clearly shows that flint mines were established between 3,000 and 2,000 B.C. during the Neolithic Period on the western side of Cissbury Hill.[10] From the abundance of archaeological finds, it is evident that Cissbury was the location of one of the largest flint mining industries in this country, second only to Grimes' Graves in Norfolk. The mining operation appears to have been very intensive; within a radius of a few hundred yards there were approximately 150 mines, each being 15 to 20 feet deep and approximately the same width. Once obtained, the flints were used in the manufacture of axes, arrowheads, scrapers and other implements. Flint mining provides possibly the most interesting feature of Neolithic culture, for Neolithic man already knew that mined flint made better tools and weapons than flint found lying on the surface.[11] Towards the end of this period the

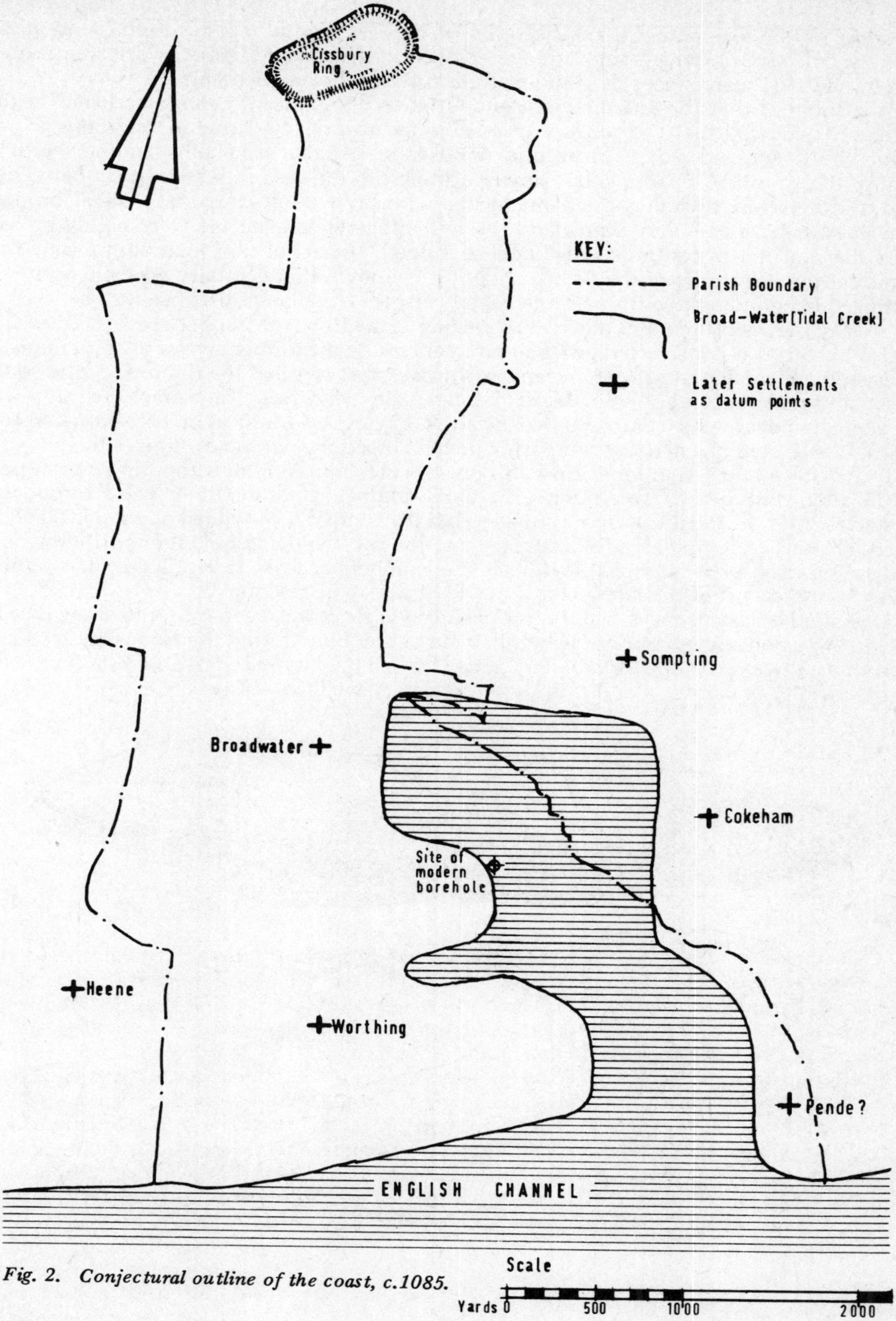

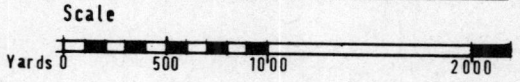

KEY:

—·—·—  Parish Boundary

⎯⎯⎯  Broad-Water [Tidal Creek]

+  Later Settlements
as datum points

Cissbury Ring

+ Sompting

Broadwater +

Site of
modern
borehole

+ Cokeham

+ Heene

+ Worthing

+ Pende?

ENGLISH  CHANNEL

*Fig. 2.  Conjectural outline of the coast, c.1085.*

Scale

Yards 0          500          1000                    2000

grinding of flint axes was also practised, but to date no ground tool has been found in the vicinity of Cissbury, which supports the conjecture that this additional work was carried out by the purchaser rather than the manufacturer of flint implements.

It is thought that the Neolithic era ended when a significant change occurred in the climate. It appears that the country was subjected to drier and colder conditions which made the Downland slopes bleak and windswept. At the same time another cultural group, the so-called 'Beaker Folk', slowly drifted into the area in search of copper. They had discovered that when copper was heated with tin it resulted in a new metal–bronze. However, bronze was very scarce and the few implements available were highly prized; thus the flint mines continued to function. Indeed, the art of flint knapping reached its zenith at the beginning of the Bronze Age.[12] It is known that Cissbury was still occupied during this period as two Bronze Age burial barrows have been discovered close to it.[13]

Most of the visible remains at Cissbury belong to the Iron Age, for between c.400 and 250 B.C. a hill fort was constructed on its summit, enclosing the former area of the flint mines.[14] It was one of the long chain of ancient earthworks that fortified the hill tops of the south coast, and ranks second only to Maiden Castle in fame and size. The plan of the camp was an elongated oval, which enclosed over 60 acres, having its entrances on the south and east sides. It consisted of a massive rampart, which followed the natural contour of the hill, and a ditch with a small counter-scarp bank on its outer lip. Although the ramparts appear small after centuries of weathering, in their original condition they were formidable obstacles.[15] Dr. E. Cecil Curwen estimates that the ramparts contained about 35,000 cubic yards of chalk weighing some 60,000 tons, and the revetments to hold it in position would have comprised between 8,000 to 12,000 stout timbers at least 15 feet long, all of which gives an indication of the labour force needed for its construction.[16]

Despite the vast size of Cissbury, no positive evidence has been found to show that its interior was densely or continuously inhabited at any time during the Iron Age. Traces of Iron Age cultivation in the form of 'lynchetts', (raised field boundaries) still, however, exist in the vicinity of Cissbury and it is known that pit-dwellings also existed.[17]

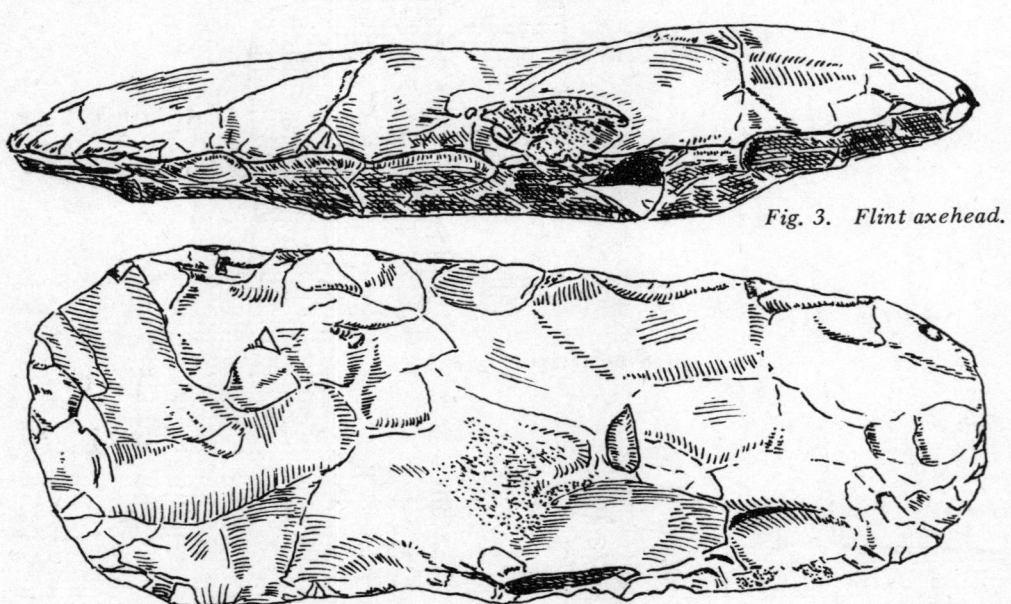

Fig. 3.   Flint axehead.

*Fig. 4.   Flint axehead.*

### The Roman Period

Although it is known that the South of England was rapidly conquered by the Roman Legions, it is impossible to say much with certainty about the Roman occupation of Broadwater–if, in fact, it was occupied. Archaeological finds show, however, some evidence of a Roman presence. The Roman road from Chichester to Brighton crossed the parish to the north of the modern Upper Brighton Road, through what were later to be the grounds of Charmandean House.[18] In 1845, five perfect and three broken funeral vessels were discovered during the construction of the railway line between Brighton and Worthing. This revealed the existence of a Roman cemetery, which was substantiated by a further find in 1881 of urns, together with pieces of Roman pottery, at a site on the East Chesswood estate, between the railway and Chesswood Road (see Fig. 5).[19]

During the closing years of the Roman Occupation, Saxon pirates began to raid the Sussex coast with increasing regularity, and the eventual withdrawal of Roman forces left Sussex vulnerable to their invasion.

### Saxon and Norman Broadwater

With the arrival of the Saxons, the character of settlement again changed, for the Saxons, as farmers, chose the fertile coastal plain rather than the Downs on which to live and work. They established small compact communities under the folds of the Downs. It is therefore highly probably that the village settlement of Broadwater was established in its current location during the Saxon period, for it is recorded as 'Bradenwaetere' in A.D. 946-955, the earliest known reference (see R. G. Roberts, *The Place Names of Sussex*, (E.P.N.S.).

The earliest reference to the inhabitants of Broadwater occurs in Domesday Book (1086), and as such provides a fascinating insight into the medieval community that had become established. The entry in the Domesday Book for Broadwater (as translated in *Domesday Book: Sussex*, Phillimore, 1976): 'Robert holds Broadwater from William. Wigot held it from King Edward. Then it answered for 29 hides. Of these, 9 hides are in William of Warenne's Rape and William of Braose has 2 hides in lordship. What Robert holds paid tax for 6 hides.

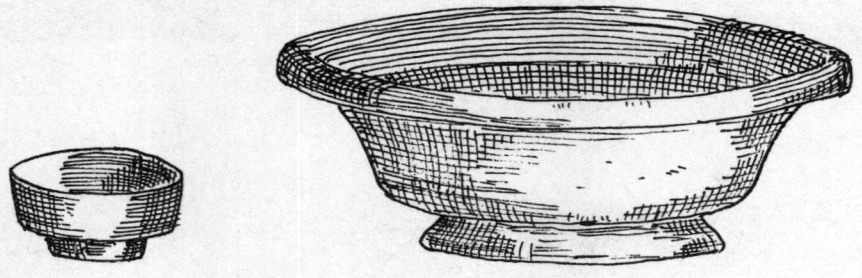

Fig. 5.   *Roman pottery.*

Fig. 6.   *A Samian-ware urn.*

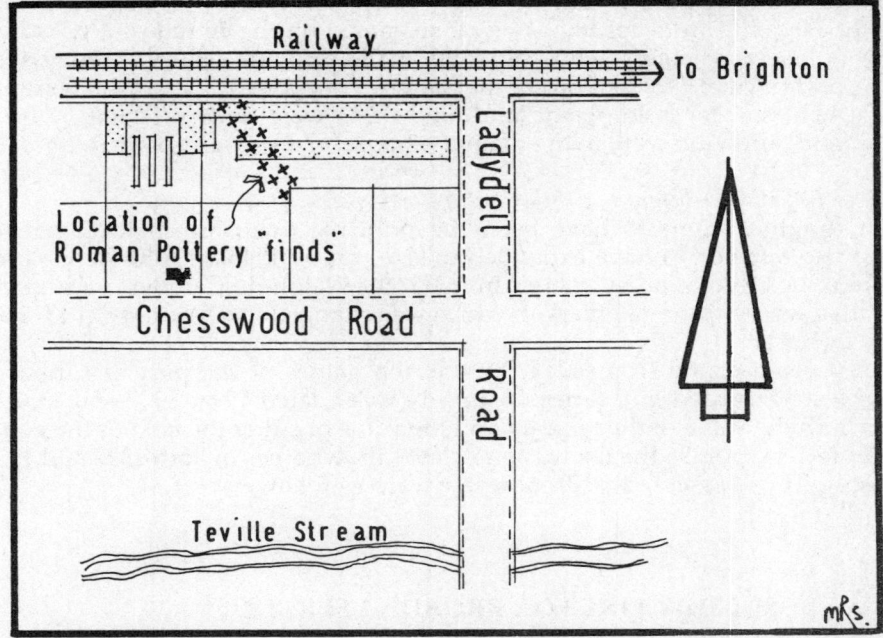

*Fig. 7. Location of Roman pottery 'finds'.*

Land for 7 ploughs. In lordship 2 ploughs; 30 villagers and 4 smallholders with 10 ploughs. A church; 3 slaves; 1 mill at 7s; meadow, 60 acres; woodland, 20 pigs. A man-at-arms holds 1 hide of this land. Total value before 1066 and later £15; now £14.'[20] From this it can be seen that the estate of 29 hides that later became the Manor of Broadwater, was held in 1066 by the Saxon Wigot of Wallingford.[21]

Following the Norman Conquest, the County of Sussex was subdivided into six administrative areas called Rapes, in order that both the coast and the vital communication routes with Normandy could be adequately protected. Broadwater was situated in the Rape of Bramber, which was under the control of William de Braose. He established a fortress at Bramber to protect the wide estuary of the Adur and the Port of Steyning.[22] Of the 29 hides recorded for Saxon Broadwater, only 20 were located in the Rape of Bramber. The remaining nine hides were a detached portion of the manor situated at Aldrington in the Rape of Lewes, which was controlled by William de Warene.[23] Of the hides under the control of William de Braose only two were held directly by him, the remainder being held by Robert-le-Savage, from whom a knight held one hide.[24]

It is generally considered that a 'hide', the basic unit of land-measurement in Saxon England, was the area of land upon which an individual could support his household. Its size varied according to soil conditions but it appears to have been, in Broadwater's case, the equivalent of 125 statute acres. This therefore suggests that Broadwater Manor (recorded as 20 hides) was approximately 2,500 acres in area, which is some 300 acres less than recorded by the Ordnance Survey in 1876. Our research strongly suggests that this 300-acre deficit was represented by the area of the Brodewatre at the time of Domesday.

No finite statistical approach can, however, be applied to the Domesday Survey, for 37 individual households are recorded as being sustained on the 20 hides of Broadwater. Of these 30 were *villeins*–villagers–who held land in the common fields, and owed in return both service and payment to the Lord of the Manor. Four were *bordars*, who were similar to villeins, but held smaller holdings of land, and three were *servi*, or slaves, who held no property or land, and who were in the main the household servants of the manorial lord.[25]

### The Growth of Broadwater before the 18th Century

Although Offington seems to have been the principal township in the area in 1282,[26] Broadwater also appears to have expanded in size, for by 1245 Sir John-de-Gatesden was holding an unlicensed market there. In 1312 Sir Ralph-de-Camoys was granted (or confirmed in) a weekly Monday market, which was changed to a Saturday in 1375 and back to Monday in 1383.[27]

Within 200 years of the Domesday Survey, the names of the principal inhabitants at Broadwater were recorded in a series of subsidy rolls, dated 1296, 1327 and 1332.[28] These rolls record both the value of the tax paid and the value of either the land or the goods upon which it was levied. In 1296 the tax was one-eleventh, whereas in both 1327 and 1332 it was one-twentieth. Those assessed at Broadwater were as follows:

## SUBSIDY LIST FOR BROADWATER, 1296[29]

| Villat' de Bradewatere | £ | s | d | Villat' de Bradewatere | £ | s | d |
|---|---|---|---|---|---|---|---|
| Willmo Paynel | 2 | 19 | 4 | Ricro le Dynkere | | 1 | 5¼ |
| Henr' de Lyons | | 12 | 8 | Robro Arnald | | 2 | 9 |
| Johanne Blaunchard | | 2 | 0½ | Willmo atte Wythye | | 1 | 9½ |
| Relicta Brian | | 1 | 11 | Robro Mayne | | 1 | 7½ |
| Rogero Bolay | | 2 | 1½ | Ad' le Knyt | | 1 | 8¾ |
| Rado le Cook | | 1 | 6½ | Rado le Eueske | | 5 | 4¾ |
| Godefro Porear' | | 1 | 7¾ | Willmo le Rede | | 1 | 4½ |
| Willmo Carl | | 4 | 1½ | Lucia Relicta Godefri | | 2 | 6 |
| Ricro' Jop | | 1 | 7½ | Robro Marescal | | 1 | 4½ |
| Johanne le Trinne | | 1 | 7½ | Waltero atte Wyke | | 7 | 5 |
| Johanne ater Puttes | | 3 | 0½ | Galfro de Pechewyke | | 6 | 5½ |
| | | | | Sm<sup>a</sup> 6 | 6 | 5 | 6½ |

## SUBSIDY LIST FOR BROADWATER, 1327[30]

| Villat' de Bradewatere | £ | s | d | Villat' de Bradewatere | £ | s | d |
|---|---|---|---|---|---|---|---|
| Egidio de Gousill | | 4 | 0 | Willo atte Wyk | | 1 | 6 |
| Wille atte Whithie | | 1 | 8 | Rogo Melkere | | 1 | 6 |
| Rado le Vesqe | | 2 | 0 | Galfro Lamnel | | 1 | 3½ |
| Johe Reynold | | 3 | 0 | Johe in the Hale | | 1 | 0½ |
| Godefro le Fauconer | | 1 | 3 | Robto le King | | 5 | 9 |
| Johe Forbench | | | 9 | Sm<sup>a</sup>istius villat' | 1 | 3 | 9 |

## SUBSIDY LIST FOR BROADWATER, 1332[31]

| Villat' de Bradewatere | £ | s | d | Villat' de Bradewatere | £ | s | d |
|---|---|---|---|---|---|---|---|
| Epo Elyens' | | 12 | 5½ | Willo Badion | | 3 | 0 |
| Pho. Seer | | 8 | 4 | Robto Joup | | 1 | 0 |
| Willo atte Wyke | | 2 | 0 | Galfro Laumval | | 1 | 6 |
| Rogo Melker | | 2 | 6 | Rado Bristrych | | 3 | 0 |
| Dulcia atte Wyk | | 2 | 0 | Walto Phelyp | | | 10 |
| Symone Coteman | | 1 | 6 | Robto atte Halle | | 1 | 9 |
| Robto Tourner | | 1 | 0 | Thom Poynaunt | | 3 | 4 |
| Rogo Foray | | 2 | 0 | Thom Bernard | | 2 | 0 |
| Oliva Shephurd | | 5 | 8 | Johe Waryn | | 2 | 0 |
| Willo Androu | | 1 | 0 | Thom Willam | | 1 | 6 |
| Robto Jan | | 1 | 0 | Robto Ricard | | | 8 |
| Robto Phelyp | | | 8 | Willo Elys | | 1 | 0 |
| Johe in the Hale | | 2 | 0¾ | Gilbto Gervays | | | 8 |
| | | | | Sma istius villat | 3 | 4 | 5¼ |

The next recorded list of inhabitants is included in the Lay Subsidy Rolls of 1524 and 1525, when 34 households are listed.[32] In 1641, all the male members of the parish over the age of 18 were required to sign a 'protestation' of loyalty to the Church of England, following a resolution passed in the House of Commons on 30 July 1641 which declared 'that what person soever shall not take the protestation is unfit to bear office in the Church or Commonwealth'. This was designed to exclude Catholics from holding any influential positions. Within the parish of Broadwater, 132 inhabitants complied, and no person is recorded as having dissented, which suggests no declared Catholic families existed.[33] By the 1660s there were approximately 42 households at Broadwater.[34]

From these lists of inhabitants a crude assessment of the population can be made. For each male recorded we can assume there was an equal number of women, and that 40 per cent of the recorded population were children. (See W. B. Stephens, *Teaching Local History*.) The various population totals are shown below.

| Source/date | No. of Principal inhabitants recorded | Equivalent No. of Females | No. of Children (40% of Adults) | Assessed Population |
|---|---|---|---|---|
| Domesday Survey 1086 | 37 | 37 | 30 | 104* |
| Subsidy 1296 | 22 | 22 | 18 | 62 |
| Subsidy 1327 | 11 | 11 | 9 | 31 |
| Subsidy 1332 | 26 | 26 | 21 | 73 |
| Lay Subsidy 1524/5 | 34 | 34 | 27 | 95 |
| Protestation return 1641 | 132 | 132 | 106 | 370* |

*Overall parish including Worthing and Offington

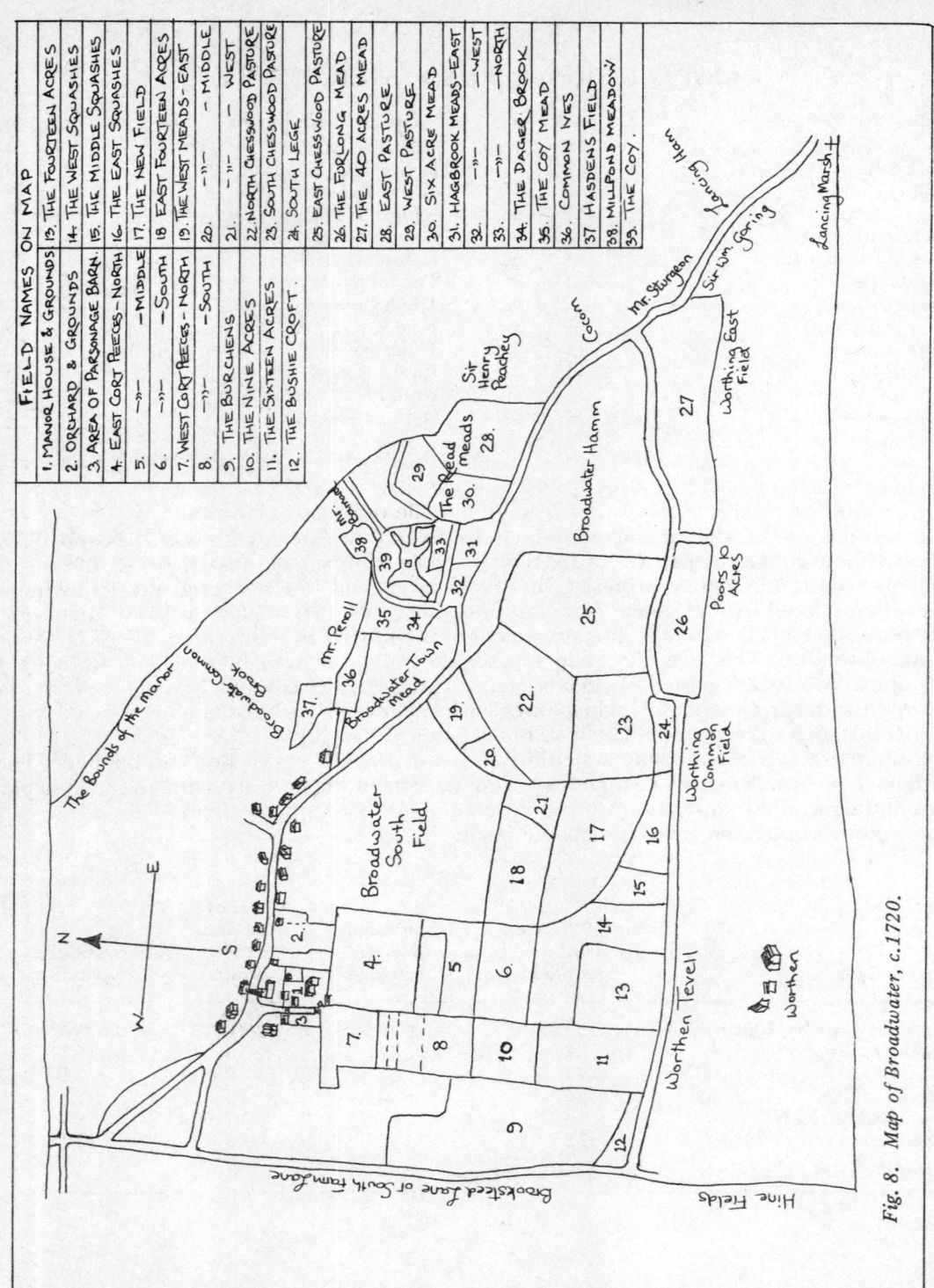

| FIELD NAMES ON MAP | |
|---|---|
| 1. MANOR HOUSE & GROUNDS | 13. THE FOURTEEN ACRES |
| 2. ORCHARD & GROUNDS | 14. THE WEST SQUASHES |
| 3. AREA OF PARSONAGE BARN. | 15. THE MIDDLE SQUASHES |
| 4. EAST CORT REECES – NORTH | 16. THE EAST SQUASHES |
| 5. " – MIDDLE | 17. THE NEW FIELD |
| 6. " – SOUTH | 18. EAST FOURTEEN ACRES |
| 7. WEST CORT REECES – NORTH | 19. THE WEST MEADS – EAST |
| 8. " – SOUTH | 20. " – MIDDLE |
| 9. THE BURCHENS | 21. " – WEST |
| 10. THE NINE ACRES | 22. NORTH CHESSWOOD PASTURE |
| 11. THE SIXTEEN ACRES | 23. SOUTH CHESSWOOD PASTURE |
| 12. THE BUSHIE CROFT. | 24. SOUTH LEGE. |
| | 25. EAST CHESSWOOD PASTURE |
| | 26. THE FORLONG MEAD |
| | 27. THE 40 ACRES MEAD |
| | 28. EAST PASTURE |
| | 29. WEST PASTURE |
| | 30. SIX ACRE MEAD |
| | 31. HAGBROOK MEADS – EAST |
| | 32. " – WEST |
| | 33. " – NORTH |
| | 34. THE DAGER BROOK |
| | 35. THE COY MEAD |
| | 36. COMMON IVES |
| | 37. HASDENS FIELD |
| | 38. MILLPOND MEADOW |
| | 39. THE COY. |

*Fig. 8.  Map of Broadwater, c.1720.*

Chapter Two

# The 18th and 19th-Century Community

For many, all that is needed to create a village is a church, a green and a public house, all of which could be found in Broadwater from the beginning of the 18th century. This, however, leaves out the most important feature, the community of *people* which congregated together through the centuries.

By 1700, the village settlement at Broadwater had become firmly established across the 25-ft. contour, at the head of the shallow but marshy valley of the Broadwater or Sompting Brook, formerly the area of the old tidal creek. The topography of the village is clearly shown on the earliest known map of Broadwater, which was a survey of the Broadwater, Chantry and Decoy Farms *c*.1720. (See Fig. 8.) In shape the village was long and narrow, with all the properties being situated on either side of Broadwater Street, which ran first south-east from Broadwater Green to the church and then east for a quarter of a mile, until it forked into what are now the modern Sompting and Dominion Roads. To the south-east of the modern Dominion Road lay the two common meadows or pastures–the 'Town Mead' and 'The Ham'. The focal point of the village was the church, which lay centrally between the settlements of Worthing, Offington and Little Broadwater, all of which were within its parish. The village inn was recorded as early as 1690,[1] but its precise location is not known. Broadwater Road was then only a short lane that existed solely as the approach from the North to both the Manor House, and the Rectory.

At the beginning of the 18th century, Broadwater was typical of most village communities, in that the majority if not all of the inhabitants were illiterate or semi-literate. They did not, therefore, write diaries or make speeches that recorded everyday events. The development of the community was, however, recorded by the Parish Vestry, and these vestry documents have, fortunately, survived.

One of the other early 18th-century documents for Broadwater is a Poll for knights of the Shire for the County of Sussex, contested on 24 May 1705, which reveals the following as freeholders of land in the parish:[2] Holden, Thomas; Alford, John, Esq; Sendall, George; Barker, Robert; Johnson, Charles; Bender, John; Hunt, Richard; Boundy, Thomas; and Barnden, John. This list, however, is for the entire parish and the freehold land recorded could, therefore, have been located in either Broadwater, Worthing or Offington, as all were within its parochial boundaries at this time.

A written declaration dated 13 May 1712 is of particular interest. It is contained in an early volume of the vestry minutes,[3] and defines the eastern bounds and limits of the parish. The list of witnesses (reproduced below) reveals both their ages, and the period of time they had lived at Broadwater.

#### The Parish of Broadwater in the County of Sussex

1. *William Wade* Rector of the said parish aged 72 years, who hath lived there 42 years.
2. *John Martin*–aged 62 years who hath always lived there.

3. *Wm Easton*–aged 52 years who hath lived there 40 years. (Yeoman[4])
4. *Daniel Avery*–aged 64 years who hath lived there 50 years.
5. *Walter Humphrey*–aged 62 years who hath lived there 40 years.
6. *Edward Stocker*–aged ? years who hath lived there ? years. (Yeoman[5])
7. *Richard Hunt*–aged 52 years, who hath lived there 30 years.
8. *John French*–aged 50 years, who hath lived there 40 years. (Yeoman[6])
9. *Richard Lidsey*–aged 30 years, who hath lived there 18 years.
10. *Ferdinando Lindup*–aged 29 years, who hath lived there 29 years. (Husbandman[5])
11. *Peter Price*–aged 69 yeares who hath lived there 50 years. (Yeoman[7])
12. *John Parrot*–aged 56 yeares who hath lived there 56 years. (Blacksmith[8])
13. *Thomas Parrot*–aged 60 yeares who hath lived there 60 years. (Husbandman[9])
14. *Thomas Bagshall*–aged 38 yeares, who hath lived there 26 years. (Cordwainer[10])
15. *Edward Hardham*–aged 58 years, who hath lived there 32 years.
16. *Thomas Geary*–aged 55 years, who hath lived there 30 years.
17. *Walter Lee*–aged 46 years, who hath lived there 20 years. (Yeoman[4])
18. *John Budd*–aged ? years, who hath lived there ? years.
19. *Thomas Martin*–aged ? years, who hath lived there ? years.
20. *William Turner*–aged 37 years, who hath lived there his life time.
21. *James Walker*–aged 58 years, who hath always lived in the said parish.
22. *Richard Maundy*–aged 45 years, who hath always lived in the said parish.
23. *John Deane*–aged 45 years, who hath always lived in the said parish.

Another Poll Book dated 1734 provides the following list of freeholders for 'Broedwater':[11] Robert Barker; William Cheal, Bramber; Jeremiah Dodson (Rector); Peter Burden, Lauceing (Lancing); John Ffrench; William Haynes (Gentleman);[12] John Howell; Charles Johnson (Cordwainer);[13] Thomas Lindupp (Husbandman);[14] Henry Newland, Hove; John Penfold (Yeoman);[15] William Pain (Blacksmith);[16] Ayling Shephard, Arundell; William Whitebread (Gentleman).[17]

By comparison with the earlier Poll for knights, it is of considerable interest to note that although the number of freeholders had increased, only one person–Robert Barker– appears on both lists. When the 1734 list is compared with the list of inhabitants for 1712, only John French appears on both lists. This suggests that, contrary to popular belief, most of the population of Broadwater was already very itinerant prior to 1800; most people were not born and buried in their parish of origin. In substantiation of this, a further list of inhabitants dated 1752 (which follows) reveals a similar pattern as only three names occur on both this list and the one for 1734.

## 'A TAX FOR 1752 AT 1/- PER POUND'[18]

| £ | s | d | | £ | s | d |
|---|---|---|---|---|---|---|
| 4 | 0 | 0 | *Robert Ford* for his house & land | 0 | 4 | 0 |
| 4 | 10 | 0 | *Mr Norton* for Mr Wades house | 0 | 18 | 0 |
| 5 | 0 | 0 | *William Humphries* for his house | 0 | 5 | 0 |
| 4 | 0 | 0 | *Mrs Cooper* for Mr Carltons house | 0 | 4 | 0 |
| 5 | 0 | 0 | *Henry Harwood* for Coates house (Yeoman[19]) | 0 | 5 | 0 |
| 2 | 10 | 0 | *Thomas Knight* for his house (Glazier[20]) | 0 | 2 | 6 |
| 2 | 10 | 0 | *Widow Backshell* for her house | 0 | 2 | 6 |
| 1 | 10 | 0 | *Mary Walder* for her house | 0 | 1 | 6 |
| 1 | 10 | 0 | *Thom. Peryer* for his house (Shoemaker[21]) | 0 | 1 | 6 |
| 2 | 0 | 0 | *Wm Tribe* for his house | 0 | 2 | 0 |
| 2 | 0 | 0 | *Edward Pannel* for his house | 0 | 2 | 0 |
| 2 | 10 | 0 | *Ayling Shepherd* for his house | 0 | 2 | 6 |
| 2 | 10 | 0 | *John Hide* for his house | 0 | 2 | 6 |
| 2 | 10 | 0 | *Wm Pain* for his house (Blacksmith[22]) | 0 | 2 | 6 |
| 2 | 0 | 0 | *Tho. Thorn* for his house | 0 | 2 | 0 |

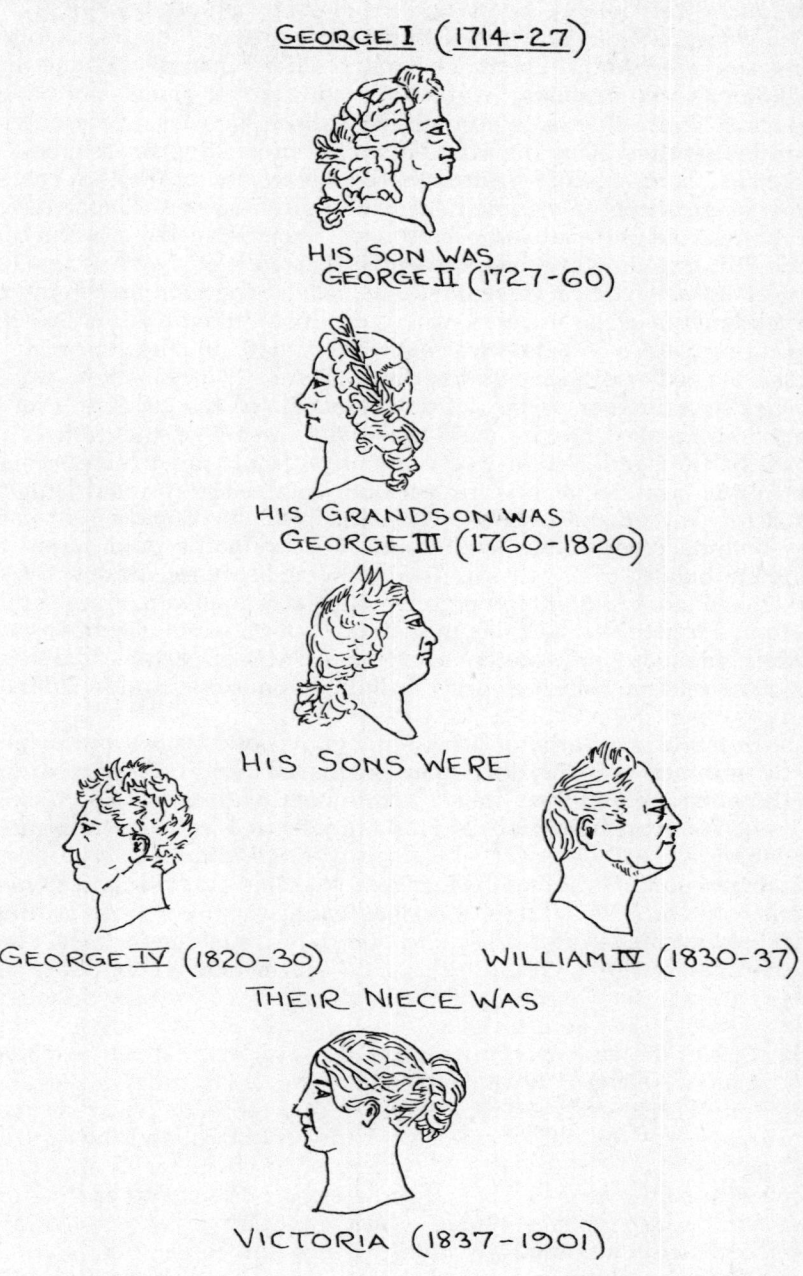

GEORGE I (1714-27)

HIS SON WAS
GEORGE II (1727-60)

HIS GRANDSON WAS
GEORGE III (1760-1820)

HIS SONS WERE

GEORGE IV (1820-30)          WILLIAM IV (1830-37)

THEIR NIECE WAS

VICTORIA (1837-1901)

*Fig. 9.  George I to Victoria.*

This list also reveals a further interesting fact about the development of Broadwater, for it suggests a marked decline in the number of inhabited properties. Only 15 are recorded, whereas 23 are recorded in both the 1712 list and on the 1720 map. Only fragments of information have been found about the size, building materials, style and ages of the houses recorded in the foregoing lists. It is assumed that some may have been timber framed, similar to those that have survived in Tarring, and were therefore very old. It is highly probable that the inhabitants could not afford to maintain or rebuild the houses that fell into disrepair, for it is clearly evident that by the middle of the 18th century the village community was retracting in size. Although buildings had in 1720 extended over most of the land on either side of Broadwater Street, by 1780 most of those in the central part had disappeared. Probably they had become so dilapidated that they had totally collapsed.[23]

This established pattern of 18th-century decline, also found at Brighton,[24] and indeed all the coastal settlements of Sussex, was not to continue in the Parish of Broadwater, for the era of the fashionable seaside watering place was on the horizon. Doctors had recommended sea-water drinking and bathing prior to 1700, but there was little interest, for the wealthy continued to partake of the waters at spa resorts as an established part of their annual routine. It was not until the middle years of the 18th century that the institution of the 'English Seaside' really emerged. Sea bathing then became fashionable among the middle and upper classes, possibly as a reaction against the formality and expense of the spas, and the exaggerated claims made by doctors for the virtues of spa waters. Sea bathing received further impetus following the publication in 1750 of Dr. Richard Russell's book *A Dissertation concerning the use of sea water in diseases of the glands*. Its appearance coincided with an upsurge of interest in such matters, and the medical profession soon adopted sea-water as the new cure for a variety of diseases and disorders that had hitherto defied their primitive treatments. Thus was established the habit of going to the seaside, a place which had previously been considered rather damp, windy and smelly.

In its early days the popularity of sea bathing grew slowly. Visitors only invaded seaside resorts for therapeutic reasons, and in consequence conditions for bathing were very primitive. The gentlemen bathed naked from a boat or from the beach, while the ladies disrobed in a little hut and plunged into the sea wrapped in voluminous and nondescript garments.[25]

The initial impact on hamlets and villages like Worthing and Broadwater was, therefore, minimal, but following Dr. Russell's move to the fishing village of Brighthelmstone (Brighton) to supervise the practical application of his remedies, which coincided with an increasing patronage of that village by royalty, the fashion for seawater cures began to affect adjacent areas in the County, and the advantages of Worthing's sheltered beach was discovered.[26]

Worthing was, in the early part of the 18th century, very similar to Broadwater, albeit smaller and far more isolated. The only access for wheeled traffic was by way of Brooksteed Lane (today South Farm Road) and for those on foot, a footpath known as the Squashetts or Quashetts provided the only link between Broadwater Street and the centre of Worthing. The greater part of the village was still very rural in character. It was typical of ribbon development with all the farmsteads and cottages being clustered either side of the single road or track known as Worthing Street, which wandered its way down towards the sea. Narrow enclosed fields adjoined Worthing Street, the remainder of the hamlet being divided into three large common fields. The 'West Field' extended from the Heene Boundary to the west of Worthing Street. The middle or 'Homefield' (from which Homefield Park and Homefield Road derive their names), extended from the homesteads

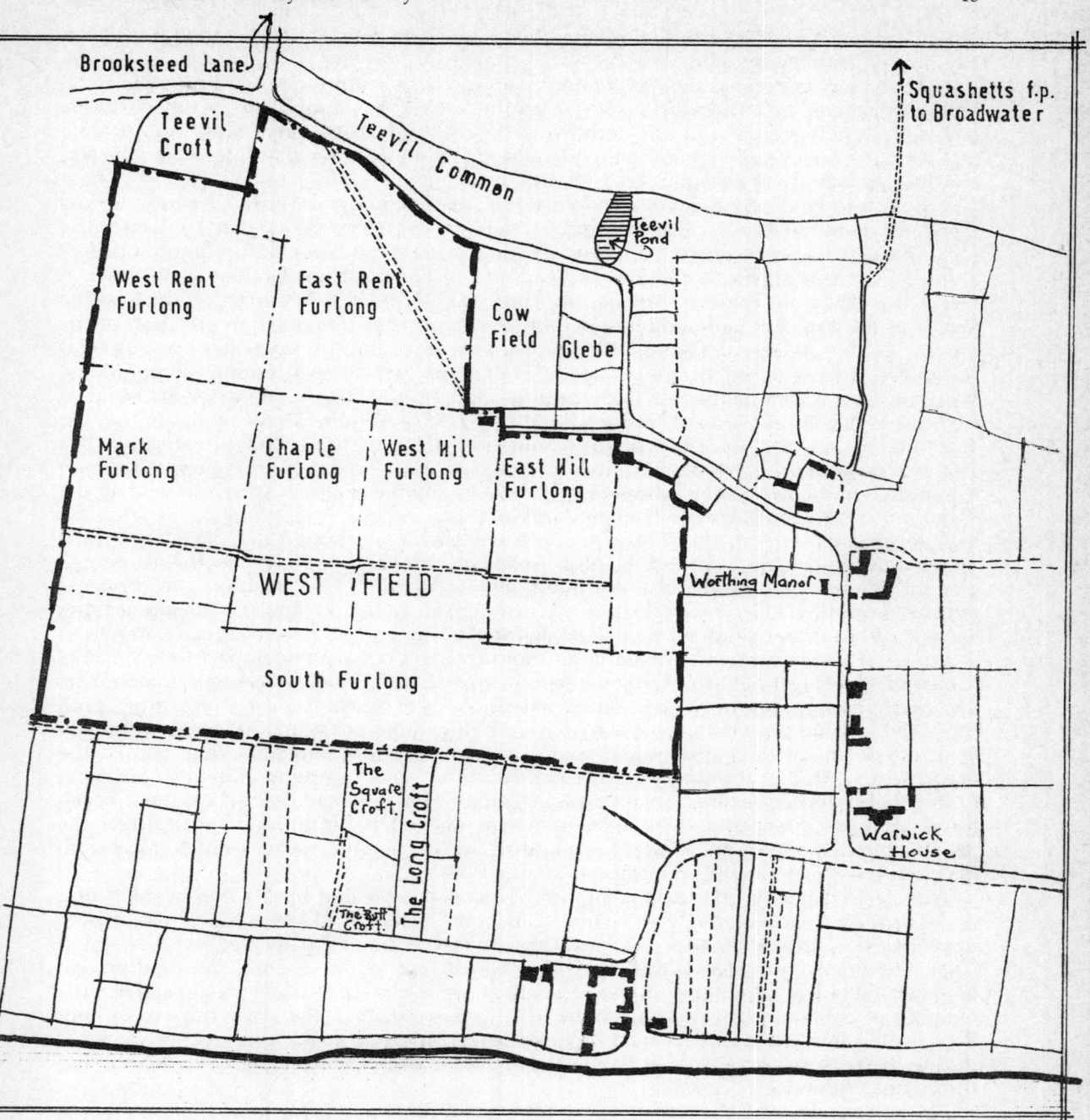

*Fig. 10. Map of Worthing, pre 1800.*

on the eastern side of Worthing Street to Ham Lane. The 'East Field' extended from Ham Lane to the Lancing boundary.[27]

The inhabitants derived their livelihood predominantly from agricultural pursuits and a limited mackerel fishery, which when plentiful would have supplied inland parishes, including Broadwater, in addition to those on the coast.[28] It is also very plausible to assume that certain families supplemented their livelihood by the occasional indulgence in the less law-abiding activity of smuggling.

It is therefore, clearly evident that Worthing was ill-equipped to cater for any visitors that were tempted to stay in the district. Even so, evidence shows that by 1760 those seeking the therapeutic powers of seawater sought accommodation at local farmhouses.[29] Some 38 years later, the popularity of Worthing received a considerable boost, when it received a visit from Princess Amelia, the youngest (15th) child of George III. In 1798 the health of the Princess had suddenly deteriorated after she contracted an affliction of the knee. On the advice of George III's physicians, a course of sea-water bathing was prescribed and in spite of the hamlet's limitations and almost primitive conditions, Worthing was recommended on account of its climate, easy beach and extensive sands.

Princess Amelia arrived at Worthing on 31 July 1798, and there can be no doubt that her visit directly affected the lives of the communities of Worthing and Broadwater. The 120-man party of the Derbyshire Militia, who arrived the following morning from Clapham Common, would have passed through Broadwater, and the sloop *Fly* which cruised off the shore must have cause both excitement and interest.

A week after arrival, on 7 August, Princess Amelia celebrated her birthday, which resulted in the ringing of church bells at Broadwater, royal salutes, and in the evening 'a general illumination throughout Worthing and its vicinity'. The health of the Princess improved, and by 7 December she was well enough to go home. However, before leaving she left £20 from her small income to be distributed among the poor of Broadwater.[30]

Princess Amelia's visit to Worthing did not provide a comparable impact to that of the Prince of Wales to Brighton. The anticipated expansion did not immediately materialize. This was possibly due to the continued inaccessibility of Broadwater and Worthing; both remained isolated from the principal roads and traffic routes of the area. The only approach from the north for pack horses and wagons was over an ancient track that crossed the South Downs (today the unclassified road that runs from Sompting church to Steyning Round Hill), and as a direct result neither community was serviced by a regular coach route. A more direct and substantial road was needed if Worthing was to attract the fashionable clientele of the adjacent spa and resort towns, who were essential if it was to develop into a fashionable watering-place.

This desired improvement in communications was provided by the construction of a new Turnpike Road, following an Act of Parliament passed on 24 May 1802. The Worthing to Ashington Turnpike Road was routed through the centre of Broadwater and the Findon Gap, and finally provided Worthing with a direct link to the existing turnpike system between Steyning and London. Since coaches were always routed via turnpikes, the opening of this road provided an immediate improvement in the coach service to both Broadwater and Worthing. Instead of there being only one coach every other weekday during the season, and a weekly wagon to London, there was now a daily service running throughout the year.[31]

As the western end of Broadwater Street formed part of this Turnpike Road, it was of occasional concern to the parish vestry, and a source of endless controversy. Being a Turnpike, the Trustees were empowered to erect toll gates, one of which was located on the Worthing/Broadwater boundary. It was situated across the northern end of Chapel

Road between the modern sites of the *Railway Hotel* and Messrs Bunce & Co.'s premises. [32]

The following tolls were authorized to be charged at each of the three gates (see Henfry Smail, *Worthing Road and its Coaches*): For every horse, mare, gelding, mule, ass, ox, bullock, or other beast of draught, drawing in any waggon, cart or carriage of the like nature, with wheels of less breadth than six inches, 6d at Dial Post and Ashington Gates and 2d at Worthing Gate. For every horse, mare, gelding, mule, ass, ox, bullock or other beast drawing in any other carriage, 4½d at Dial Post and Ashington Gates and 1½d at Worthing Gate. For every horse, mare, gelding, mule or other beast laden or unladen, and not drawing, 2d at Dial Post and Ashington Gates and 1d at Worthing Gate. For every drove of oxen, cows or meat cattle, 10d per score at Dial Post and Ashington Gates, 5d per score at Worthing Gate. For every drove of calves, pigs, sheep or lambs, 5d per score at Dial Post and Ashington Gates and 2½d per score at Worthing Gate.

Cattle passing from Worthing to or from Tevill Common to pasture or water were specially exempted from paying toll as were also beasts laden with material for repairing the road, manure, fodder, dung, lime or implements of husbandry; persons residing in the parish going to church on Sundays or any other Holy Day or attending a funeral; horses carrying the mail or packet; horses belonging to Officers or Soldiers on the march or on duty, conveying arms or baggage, sick or wounded; carriages conveying vagrants by legal passes; or carriages conveying electors.

Although the new Turnpike was welcomed by the Broadwater vestry, they objected most strongly to the siting of the turnpike gate within the parish, and in 1805 gave notice unsuccessfully to the Turnpike Trustees to have it removed on the grounds that it was an encroachment.

In accordance with the terms of the Act the tolls at each of the three gates on the Turnpike were auctioned annually, and their receipts rose from £550 for the first year to an average of £940 by 1822. It was, however, found that the toll receipts were insufficient to cover the maintenance cost or to pay the loan raised on the tolls, and therefore when the Act was due for renewal in 1822, the Trustees applied for it to be amended, so as to decrease the length of the road under their care, and provide for increased tolls. [33]

In consequence of this imminent renewal of the Turnpike Act, a vestry meeting was called on 12 September 1822 to discuss the merit in again seeking the removal of the Teville Toll Gate. Their resolve was 'that the inhabitants would use every means in their favour to prevent the gate being placed on any part of the road situated in the said parish', and the vestry clerk was instructed to advise the Clerk of the Trustees of this resolve.

A committee was appointed to pursue this plan, and its members agreed at their meeting on 1 November 1822 to attend the meeting of the Turnpike Trust at Ashington on 4 December. In the meantime the vestry clerk was instructed to ascertain both the width of Broadwater Road, and the sum annually expended for keeping it in repair. [34]

A further vestry meeting was held on 19 February 1823, when it was unanimously resolved that: 'A renewal of the Turnpike Act upon the terms intended by the Trustees of the Turnpike would be unjust and a serious burden upon the inhabitants of the Parish and the Public at large when travelling between Worthing and London'. The meeting considered that as the Trustees were accruing a surplus of £300 per annum, after having paid for the maintenance of the road, the continuation of the Toll Gate at Worthing was an unnecessary burden on the parish, and any deficiency in its maintenance costs, resultant upon its removal, would be collected from the increased number of tolls paid at the other two gates situated at Dial Post and Ashington. It was also thought inappropriate for tolls to be collected at the Worthing Gate for those travelling towards Shoreham and Arundel, or intermediate parishes, as the Act had established the road for the benefit of travel from

London to Worthing. The feeling of this meeting was sufficiently strong for them to resolve that they would petition Parliament for the removal of the Turnpike Gate.[35]

Although the parish vestry succeeded in getting the Teville Turnpike discontinued, the gate was not removed, for it was retained for the purpose of checking the post-horse duties, a further charge added to the already heavy expense of travelling in those days. There is to date, no direct evidence as to when the gate was finally removed, but contemporary maps indicate that it disappeared sometime between 1843 and 1848.

Once constructed, the new turnpike road established a new communication link with the surrounding area and London. Worthing immediately began to develop very rapidly. Although some houses were constructed in Broadwater, as will be described in Chapter Five, Worthing's development accounts for the majority of the threefold increase in properties that occurred in the overall parish of Broadwater which is revealed by the 1801 and 1811 census, and it had by about 1812 become larger than Broadwater.[36]

This initial development soon revealed that the narrow, dirty and unpaved lanes that had previously only had to serve a small hamlet were quite unsuitable for the quality of visitor Worthing now attracted. Far more damaging, however, were the totally inadequate sanitary facilities, for the hamlet at this time undoubtedly stank.[37] The majority of its effluent was still discharged onto the beach indiscriminately for the tides to clear away, utilising a network of open sewers or ditches which for centuries had only been required to drain and discharge surface water from the fields to the south of Richmond Road.

For Worthing to continue to develop some measure of independent authority was required to deal with the many problems it faced as an emerging fashionable watering place, for hitherto it had been governed as part of the ecclesiastical and civil parish of Broadwater. In theory its inhabitants in partnership with those of Broadwater were totally responsible for the conduct of parish affairs, and the state of Worthing was a poor reflection on the Broadwater Vestry.

Each year the Broadwater Vestry had appointed churchwardens, and those appointed are recorded intermittently from 1414 onwards. In the late 17th and 18th centuries there were usually separate churchwardens and separate overseers for Broadwater and Worthing.[38] In the late 18th and 19th centuries a constable or headborough was also elected in rotation from Broadwater, Durrington and Worthing.[39] In addition to the parochial administration there were the Courts Baron of both the Broadwater and Worthing Manors. The Worthing Court appears to have been held annually from the 16th century, and up to about 1750 dealt with land transactions, the regulations of agriculture, and other such matters as blocked ditches and the repair of houses. After 1750 its business was mainly confined to copyholds.[40] Broadwater Court had jurisdiction over similar matters, and throughout the 18th century the Lord of Broadwater Manor exercised his right of wrecks through his court baron. In 1749 arbitrators between the Lords of Worthing and Broadwater decided that the latter was entitled to all wrecks thrown onto the beach between Heene and Lancing.[41]

The decision to create new local government machinery capable of dealing with the urgent improvements so desirable and necessary for Worthing was taken in 1803. This was due to the efforts of a group of local men, who included both gentry and a cross section of the other inhabitants, all with the foresight and wisdom to look into the future. By an Act of Parliament [42] known as the Worthing Town Act, 72 commissioners were nominated to govern the town with power to replace themselves by co-option. Remarkably, only seven were needed to form a quorum, and in actual practice seldom more than a dozen took an active part in local affairs. The preamble to the Act stated that the hamlet of Worthing

*Fig. 11.   Baker's delivery man, 1805.*

should in future be known as the town of Worthing, even though the combined population of Broadwater and Worthing was still only just over one thousand.[43]

The Worthing Commissioners were empowered to raise a local rate of not more than 2s 6d (12½p.) in the pound. With this revenue they were required to drain the town adequately; to establish a police force; to improve lighting and to construct proper streets and to buy a fire engine. As the most active Commissioners were nearly all local businessmen or tradesmen, they usually started their meetings at 6 to 7 o'clock in the evening. The first meeting of the Commissioners was held on 13 June 1803, at the *Nelson Inn* in South Street.[44] For this use of his premises the landlord, Edward Blann, was paid half a guinea. The Commissioners continued to meet at the *Nelson* until 14 February 1812, when they changed to the *Royal George* in Market Street.

The town commissioners did not initially exercise their right to police the town for it was not until 1825 that a Beadle was appointed. His duties are listed in the minutes of the

Proceedings of the Broadwater Vestry.[45] His general duties were recorded as follows: 'That the duties of a Beadle may be properly discharged it is needful that he be a man of activity and sobriety, of strength of body and fullness of mind, undismayed by threats, uncorruptable by bribes. He is to rise early and to go to bed late, and always except when in bed to keep his eyes open. He is to patrol the Town three or four times every day between the hours of eight and five o'clock and twice between the hours of six and nine during the Summer half year, and between six and eight during the Winter half year'. Included in the detailed list of specific duties to be executed were the following:

1. To inspect all Public Houses and Taverns during his evening rounds.
2. Never to tipple [drink] himself.
3. Report to the Parish Vestry any paupers found drinking.
4. He is to inspect twice daily all public houses and on the Sabbath to ensure they closed at 10 o'clock.
5. He is to report to the clerk of the Commissioners the names of any person keeping their shops open on the Sabbath.
6. He is to prevent or suppress all affrays and riots.

Following the establishment of the Worthing Commissioners, the administrative powers of the Broadwater Vestry diminished, and its main responsibility became the care of the poor of both Worthing and Broadwater. Broadwater's Overseers' Accounts, together with the Vestry Minutes, all of which still survive, record both the decisions made by the inhabitants to regulate the affairs of their community, and the diverse ways they tackled the question of providing relief for the poor.

The Overseers' Accounts for 1662-3 show the parish administering a system of poor relief in the 17th century.[46] The form of relief used appears to have been both simple and direct, for the poor, aged and sick all received fuel and clothing, together with a weekly payment for their food and rent. In 1799 Broadwater joined with 18 other Sussex parishes to form the 'East Preston Union', which body was in future to administer poor relief for the whole area. The other parishes were Littlehampton, Tortington, Goring, Lancing, Ferring, West Tarring, East Preston, Durrington, Burpham, Wiggonholt, Leominster, Houghton, Amberley, Poling, Climping, Rustington, Ford and Angmering.

The East Preston Union was created under the authority given to rural parishes following the passing of Gilberts' Act (Geo. III c.38) by Parliament some 17 years earlier. The intention was to have a more united approach to the poor in each of the parishes represented. Their first joint venture was the construction of a common workhouse at East Preston, near Littlehampton, which was financed by a system of shares of which Broadwater held seven of the 70 created. A Board of Guardians was established for the poor, but its authority was limited exclusively to those resident in the workhouse.

Although a member of the Union, it was not the practice of the Broadwater Vestry to send any of the poor that were capable of work to the Workhouse or any of those who had previously been of respectable character. Only those who were either destitute or homeless or could no longer work due to age or infirmity were sent there. This possibly explains why the maximum number of poor from Broadwater in the Workhouse at any one time was only 11, and the recorded monthly average was approximately ten.[47] The Broadwater Vestry, therefore, retained almost total control of the poor in their parish, which required their forms of relief to be both wide in concept and capable of embracing, in a rudimentary way, most 20th-century social services.

As the Vestry administered poor relief not only for Broadwater, but also for the expanding town of Worthing, it is not surprising that poor relief expenditure rose from

£211 in 1776 to £835 in 1802-3, when 80 people received permanent outside relief. After reaching a peak of £3,384 in 1817/18, expenditure declined to £1,642 by 1822.[48]

Apparently in contravention of Gilberts' Act, from 1822 the Vestry appointed, annually, a committee of 17 people to assist the Parish Officers, which met every Friday to consider the various applications made for relief.

Help for the poor was provided in several ways. In the winter, when able-bodied poor had difficulty in obtaining employment, piece work in the form of collecting sand, stones, rocks and marl was offered, allowing them to earn what they could. In summer, if the applicant was accustomed to the sea, the committee sold, or gave them, a shrimp net. The Vestry Minutes record that the consensus opinion was that 'an industrious man' could thus earn sufficient money to maintain a family of five or six persons.[49] The market for the shrimps collected, however, appears to have been erratic. On 8 December 1820 Charles Tribe applied for work, and was advised to get his living by shrimping. In reply he stated he could get no sale for them. Again, on 23 November 1821, Edward Grevatt was instructed to go shrimping, and to take them to Lancing for sale, as the Brighton fishermen were in the habit of coming there for that purpose daily. On other occasions, the Vestry Overseers paid 2s 6d per gallon of shrimps, if the poor could not achieve a better price elsewhere.

Weekly allowances were also paid to certain applicants. Prior to 1830, there was no established scale of payment, either for individuals or families, as the committee considered each case on its merits and made their recompense accordingly. However, on Friday 17 December 1830 the Parish Vestry ordered that men employed by the Parish be

*Fig. 12.  Stonebreakers on the road, 1813.*

paid as follows: boy 6d and other 1s per day; single men 1s 3d per day; man and wife 1s 6d per day; and man and wife with one or two children or more being able men, 2s per day.[50] Casual relief was also paid during times of illness, or to assist in the burying of a relative. It was, however, ordered in February 1829 that no decorations would be allowed in future on coffins supplied by the parish.

Periodic help was given by the provision of both clothing and coal to those in need. Clothes were provided for children going into service, often on the provision that the child must remain in service for at least one month. Many different articles of clothing were requested ranging from calico shirts, pairs of stockings and trousers to new shoes. Not every application was fulfilled, for the committee did at times defer or refuse the requests, making observations and comments. A good example of this was an application for new shoes, where the applicant was instructed to get his old pair repaired!

Prior to Christmas, parish coals were purchased by the Parish Vestry from the revenue realised from the rents of the 'Poor Ten Acres'. Tenders were sought from local coal merchants, and once purchased the coal was redistributed to the poor, either at a reduced cost, or in exchange for a 'coal ticket' issued by the Vestry committee.

The Vestry minutes also include a vivid reminder of the operation of the settlement laws, which were the result of a series of Acts of Parliament. The Settlement Act of 1662 made each Vestry, through its Overseers, responsible for the removal of paupers or potential paupers to their place of settlement. This enabled the Overseers to ensure that the parish did not incur costs which others should bear. Whenever unknown applicants were interviewed for poor relief they were questioned to establish their eligibility. The Act defined the four qualifications for gaining a parish settlement, which were: birth; payment of rates on property assessed at or over £10 per annum; completing a full year as a hired servant; or serving the full term as an apprentice. If, after questioning, it was apparent another parish was liable for the relief sought, the Overseer would either send the applicant back to their parish of settlement, or let them remain if they had a settlement certificate, which indemnified the receiving parish of any financial liability.[51] When disputes occurred over who should incur the cost of poor relief, they were resolved by local justices of the peace, who also interviewed the applicants to establish their place of settlement, and then made an order that committed the 'parish of settlement' to pay.

Fathers who deserted their families and left them chargeable on the parish were always sought. Invariably it was the Beadle who was sent to apprehend them, but occasionally a reward was offered and others carried out this task. One such instance was on 12 December 1823, when a reward of one guinea was offered by advertisement in the *Lewes Journal* for the apprehension of either Harriet Hollands or William Etherington of Broadwater for deserting their children.[52] Included in the vestry minutes are also examples of such rewards being paid, and a picture of the burly village blacksmith taking his horse and cart to a neighbouring village and there apprehending the person in question readily appears in one's mind's eye!

Mothers of illegitimate children were asked for the names of the fathers, so that the Parish could order them to bear the cost of maintenance. On 23 June 1820 it was ordered by the Parish Committee that no bonds given for illegitimate children were to be accepted by the Guardians, or any other parish officer(s) unless the bond had been submitted to them for inspection. This action was taken to ensure that the bond clearly stated the names of the parties to become securities. At the meeting on the following week it was ordered 'that the Parish Officers be requested in future to apply to the Magistrates to commit women having illegitimate children to the House of Correction (at Petworth)'.[53] This was no idle threat, for on 7 February 1823 it was recorded that 'Harriet Lewis and Ann Baker, having been

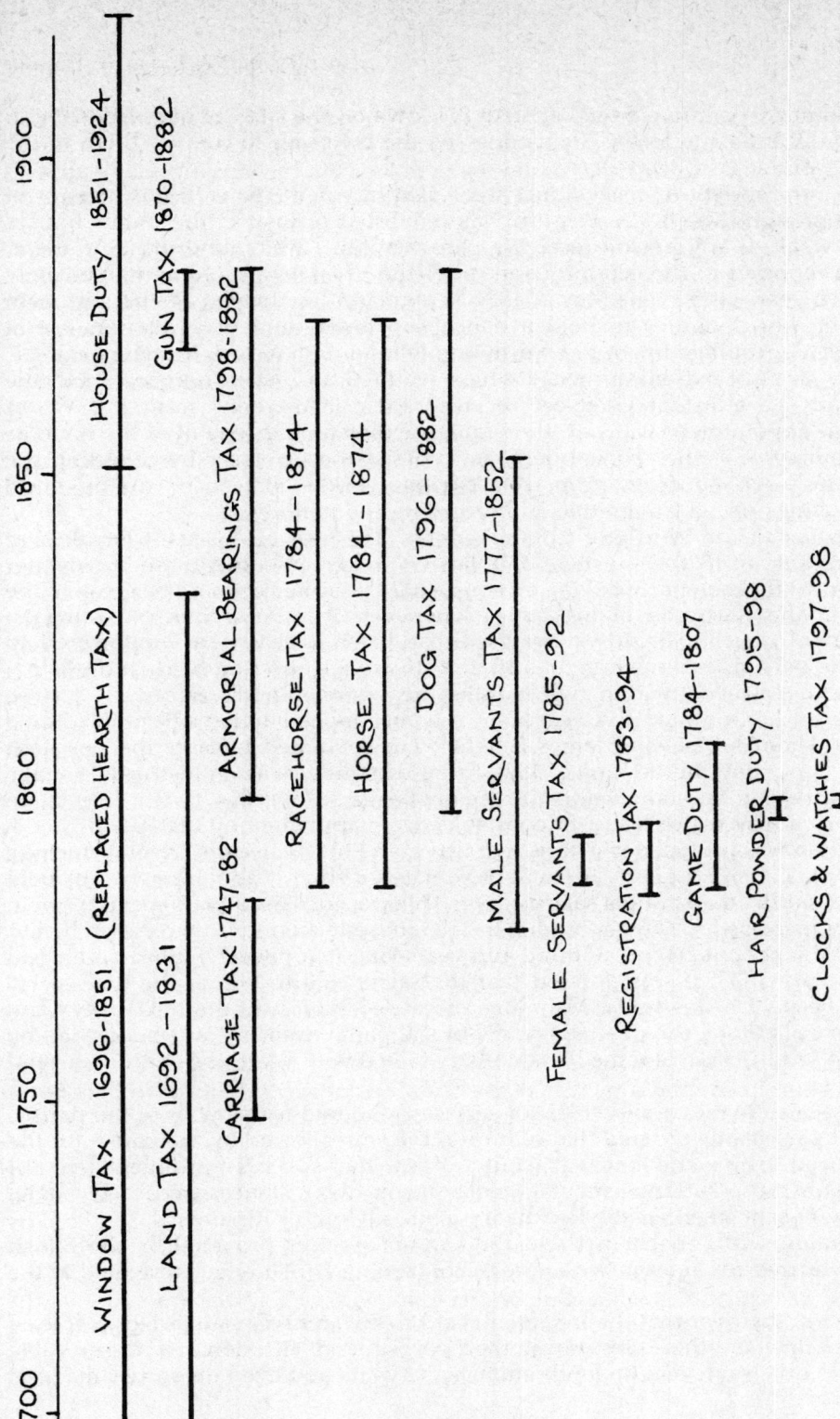

Table 1.

delivered of illegitimate children in the Parish of Broadwater, the latter of her second child, application [should] be made to the Magistrates by the Overseer to commit them to the House of Correction (at Petworth)'.[54]

Other acts of impropriety or misconduct were also frowned upon. In the January of 1822, the Headborough, Mr. James Bassett, was requested to inspect the public houses once or twice a week. If any person receiving parochial relief was found drinking there, they were to be reported to the committee in order that their pay could be immediately suspended.[55] Two years later in the May of 1824 a complaint was lodged against Elizabeth Hills for allowing her daughter to hold a dance and entertainment at their house at Broadwater, which encouraged men to be drinking there until 5 o'clock in the morning.[56]

Other than in cases of extreme urgency which required an instant decision, both the Vestry Clerk and the assistant Overseer received their instructions from the Vestry Committee. Their appointment was not, therefore, the direct management of the poor, as this was the Committee's role. Their brief was to assist the Overseer by collecting the annual poor rates (derived from property), paying weekly allowances to the poor, attending all meetings of the Committee and recording the minutes.[57]

At the suggestion of the Worthing Commissioners, the post of Assistant Beadle was created in the Summer of 1820. Its instigation followed an agreement with the Broadwater Vestry that in return for each party paying an equal share, assistance would be given to the 'Town Beadle' in the execution of his duties whenever necessary, thus providing an effective method of policing Broadwater. The Broadwater Vestry were empowered to appoint a suitable person, and the first to hold this office was John Rumbold, at the salary of 14s 4d a week. However, within two months the vestry minutes record his pay as Assistant Beadle be discontinued![58] A year later, the post appears to have been filled on a weekly basis, as Thomas Steel and James Knight were appointed to carry the Assistant Beadle's staff at 1s per day. In the June of 1824, James Knight was again instructed to take up the staff and act as an Assistant Beadle to keep out beggars.[59] By 1854, two overseers, an assistant overseer, a way warden and 10 constables were appointed by the Parish.[60]

Medical attention was provided in a variety of ways, and the overseer's accounts include an annual fee for a 'Parish Surgeon'. From approximately 1818 this appointment was held by Dr. John Shearsmith, at an annual salary of £45. This was increased to £50 per annum in 1821, and further increased to £70 per annum in 1825, despite an offer to the parish by Dr. Rogers to attend the poor at £40 per annum. Ten years later it appears Dr. Shearsmith had died; on 27 February 1835, it was ordered that the salary due to him at the time of his decease should be paid to his heirs. Mr. Gore succeeded him until the next Lady Day, when Mr. James Collet took the post at a salary of £70 per annum. He was succeeded by William Harrison until 1855, when the Parish Vestry joined with Worthing to employ a full time Parish Surgeon.[61]

Payments were also made to midwives for services rendered to the poor of the parish, and on 3 August 1821 it was ordered that in future, the sum allowed by the parish for the midwife be reduced to five shillings.[62] It would appear that specialist facilities were not available locally for those suffering mental illness, for in two instances (recorded c.1830) those afflicted were sent to either the Peckham lunatic asylum or Ringmer.[63]

The implementation of Parish relief and the various services provided by the Parish Vestry were scrutinized for at least two inquests concerning Parish relief were held at the *Maltsters*, c.1830.[65]

It is interesting to discover that the inhabitants at Broadwater were subjected to at least 16 different taxes, rates or other dues during the Georgian and Victorian period (see Table I). The taxes were diverse; levied on land, animals, servants and even on entries made in the Parish Vestry. Throughout the early entries in the church and Surveyor's Rate Books the letters H & C record those paying tax on horse and carts. It is also our opinion that the entry in the Vestry minutes dated 17 June 1831 when: 'Richard Best was to be desired by the overseers to destroy his dog', was the repercussion of a 'Dog Tax'.[64]

Returning to the development of the community at Broadwater, it is of particular interest to consider the reaction of the new activity of seaside tourism on local occupations. By the end of the 18th century, tourism had become well established and, as stated earlier in the chapter, the population of the coastal towns, and more particular Worthing had greatly increased. It would, however, appear that the initial influence of this rapid development was slight, for it served only to make agriculture more prosperous by providing a new and more easily accessible market.

An indication of both the size and relative importance of Worthing and Broadwater at the end of the 18th century is provided by the *Universal British Directory* for 1791, prepared by J. Wilkes and P. Barfoot. At Worthing 11 yeomen are recorded, with one being recorded as a bricklayer. Even though contemporary records clearly show that tourism had started, no record of any associated trade or profession is evident. In contrast, Broadwater had a higher proportion of urban occupations. It was the seat of the preventative service and its list of notables—two gentlemen, a parson, a riding officer, a surveyor of customs, four yeomen, two carpenters, a mason, a miller and a blacksmith—suggests it was typical of a large Sussex village community.[66]

It is therefore evident that the community at Broadwater must have been influential in the early years of Worthing's transition from a hamlet to a watering place, for Worthing's economy alone was totally inadequate to finance the scale of development so necessary for

*Fig. 13. Blacksmiths in round caps, 1840.*

it to expand and therefore succeed. Worthing's initial expenditure appears to have been aided by the investments made by certain landed gentry of Broadwater, a good example being the Newland family, who built houses in the expanding town, and also served as its Commissioners. Both the community at Broadwater and that at Worthing were, however, devoid of any industry other than agriculture, and therefore capital, albeit small, must have come from other sources.

Up until the late 18th century and during the early years of the 19th century, the village of Broadwater still retained its shabby appearance, but by 1811 it had apparently improved, as a result of Worthing's increasing prosperity.[67] In deference to the former pattern of decline, new houses were being constructed. Both the Manor House and the rectory had been rebuilt, and the *Maltster's Arms*, the earliest named inn, is recorded from 1796.[68]

Many of the established tradesmen, like the Paine family (who had been the village blacksmiths since *c.*1725) continued to provide the services that had been offered by their forefathers.[69] Some can be traced even earlier for their 17th-century tradesmen's tokens still survive. In the 17th century there had been an acute shortage of small change due to the government's reluctance to issue any coins in base metal, i.e., copper. The preference was for coinage minted in gold and silver, and they naturally became smaller as inflation escalated. Even pennies and half-pennies, the main coins used by the poorer classes, became scarce. During the Cromwellian period very few new coins were issued, with the result that by the middle of the century people took it upon themselves to issue a token coinage for their own needs. Shopkeepers, tradesmen and town officials all over the country issued farthings and half-penny tokens, mainly in brass and copper.

*Fig. 14.   17th-century Broadwater tokens.*

Two such tokens were issued by Broadwater tradesmen, William Robinson and Robert Turnagaine. The tokens issued by William Robinson were farthings made of brass. They were not dated, but it is thought they were issued during the 1650s and the pair of scissors depicted on them suggests that Robinson was a tailor by trade (see Fig. 14). The parish registers for Broadwater show that between 1558 and 1678 entries for members of the Robinson family were quite common. The name was variously spelt as Robinson, Robynson, Robisonn and Robison (as on the token). One entry records the burial of 'William Robison' in the churchyard at Broadwater on 8 March 1678, and it seems likely that this person was the issuer of the token. The initials of his name are represented by 'W R' on the reverse of the token whilst the 'M' is the initial of his wife's Christian name, which was common practice on these tokens. Although the sparse records do not show his wife's name, they do show the popularity of the name 'Mary' in the Robison family, and it is most likely that William's wife was also a Mary.

The other token was for a half-penny, and was issued by Robert Turnagaine. It was also made of brass and is dated 1669. Robert Turnagaine, son of William Turnagaine the elder, was baptised on 3 September 1626. His wife was called Susan. The parish registers record the baptisms of their three children: Mary on 19 December 1669, Elizabeth on 28 April 1673 and Thomas on 16 December 1675; the latter was buried on 3 September 1676. The initials on the token 'R S T' are, therefore, confirmed as those of Robert and Susan Turnagaine. There is no indication on the token of Robert's trade, but it is highly probable that it was either issued while he held an official position in the village or as an Inn token (see Chap. Five: The *Maltsters Arms*). On 2 October 1671 he appeared as a juror at a Court Leet when it was stated that for the past year he had been Headborough or Tithing man. In 1676 at a Court Baron, Robert's daughter Mary was admitted to a cottage next to the churchyard. Because she was a minor her father was appointed as guardian. This cottage was for Mary and her heirs, with remainder to Elizabeth Turnagaine her sister. It appears that Mary had no heirs, and that Elizabeth had married an Ambrose Martin, for on 16 October 1725 at a Court Baron, there was an admission of Thomas Moor of East Grinstead to the property on the surrender of Ambrose Martin and Elizabeth his wife. Robert was recorded as being buried on 21 May 1679.

The tokens of both William Robinson and Robert Turnagaine were probably only issued in small quantities, for in a village the size of Broadwater in the 17th century it is unlikely that more than about 50 of each would have been made. These tokens would have been redeemed by most of the shopkeepers, tradesmen or inn-keepers in the village. They were, however, discontinued in 1672 when Charles II issued a large amount of copper farthings. Today only a few of these tokens remain as museum or collectors' pieces, and the original tokens of the two illustrated are in the possession of one of the authors.[70]

Following the introduction of the decennial census the economic structure of Broadwater can be more fully analysed. The distribution of workers amongst the various occupations can be established, and significant patterns discerned. These census returns reveal the occupational distribution throughout the period 1712-1881. From the 19th century onwards many of the occupations which appear relate to the growing resort at Worthing. The middle and upper class visitors who were now attracted there provided employment for dressmakers, shoemakers, milliners and jewellers.[71] Catering for such visitors also provided employment for butchers, bakers and confectioners; possibly this explains the establishment of Knowles' Bakery in 1817.[72] The 1851 census, which records the parish of origin for each person, also reveals an apparent influx of people from the surrounding region.[73] Some may have moved to improve their standard of living; others to provide either a particular expertise, or the capital to start one of the luxury trades and businesses that were so necessary for the growing town of Worthing. The population disclosed by the 1821 census was 557, which by 1831 had only risen to 560. In 1841 the population of the village was 643, but the total may have included some holiday visitors.[74]

Possibly the greatest overall Victorian achievement was the building of railways, for their construction accelerated change, and allowed for the easier movement of population.[75] Not only did the railways provide employment during their construction; they also encouraged country labour to seek higher wages in the coastal towns, which in turn increased in popularity as the railway travellers poured in.[76] In 1844 the Brighton and Chichester Railway was constituted by an Act of Parliament, which provided authorisation for the construction of a line from Shoreham to Chichester. Prior to this, the London, Brighton and South Coast Railway terminated at Shoreham, and the final stage of any journey to either Broadwater or Worthing had to be completed by pony and trap. The first public train service from Shoreham to Worthing was implemented on 24 November 1845. The *Brighton Herald* for 29 November 1845 gives the following account of the start of the service to Worthing.

> Trains commenced running between Brighton and Worthing at seven o'clock in the morning and everything went well until one o'clock in the afternoon when an incident occurred.
>
> It would appear that the trains were working on a single track and men were still employed with horses and carts to increase the width of the embankment with a view to the laying of the other line. Ballast was being brought from a gravel pit near the old road from upper to lower Lancing, when one of the horses took fright at the unfamiliar spectacle of an approaching locomotive, and ran across the line.
>
> The train was travelling slowly at the time, but in spite of the efforts of the driver the horse was killed and the engine was partially derailed. The delay to the train service caused alarm at Brighton, with the result that the Brighton Terminus Superintendent and the Residential Engineer set out on a light engine to see what was wrong, but unfortunately this engine was also derailed near the same spot. Meanwhile, another train had left Brighton for Worthing, but on reaching the site of the mishap it was unable to proceed further since the tender of the original engine was lying in the ditch on top of the dead horse and the front wheels of the train itself were off the track. Some of the passengers in the 2nd train decided to get out and walk the remaining three miles into Worthing, but before they could reach their destination they were passed by the train which completed its journey drawn by 3 horses instead of a Locomotive.

The same account stated that the opening of the railway had 'set Worthing alive'. The streets of the town were crowded with people and hundreds lined the track to watch the trains arrive. Although drawn by horses, the first train was received with loud cheers.[77]

By 1871, Broadwater's population had doubled from the 600 revealed by the 1851 census to 1,228 persons, and building had at last started to fill its central gap. As a result of the northern extension of Worthing's boundary in 1875 the population in 1881 was only 841, but by 1901 it had increased to 1,187.[78] As will be clearly seen by reference to Chapter Five, by 1896 some terraced cottages and semi-detached houses had been constructed at the eastern end of the village, their style being typical of the late Victorian period.[79]

Although three Roman Catholic recusants were recorded in Broadwater in the late 16th century,[80] no further record has been found relating to nonconformity until 1820, when part of a house in the village was registered for Protestant worship. By 1874 there was a Primitive Methodist cottage meeting and between c.1875 and 1888 a stable was converted into a Primitive Methodist chapel.[81]

Throughout the Georgian and Victorian periods the expansion of Worthing placed excessive demands on the area's water and sewerage systems, which resulted in them continually failing to meet the demands placed upon them. The culmination of this situation was that in 1893 the area was subjected to the most disastrous outbreaks of

*Fig. 15.   Shepherd lad in smock, c.1870.*

typhoid (enteric fever) ever experienced in Sussex. It had, however, become apparent to central government as early as the middle of the 19th century that there was some connection between the inevitable overcrowding and lack of proper sanitation, and the outbreaks of cholera and fever that had become so prevalent.[82] Broadwater's vestry minutes reveal that a smallpox outbreak had occurred in the parish in 1830/31. On 20 May 1831 Mr. Tribe (the vestry's solicitor) was ordered to take measures for the prosecution of Thomas Coreswell for 'promoting and keeping up the smallpox in the Parish'. At the meeting a week later the parish surgeon, W. Shearsmith, was instructed 'to examine the Army of the poor having the smallpox with a view to ascertaining whether they were inoculated for the same'. The parish Guardians appear to have been concerned for at the next meeting it was further ordered that 'the houses of the poor who have had smallpox in them be whitewashed with quick lime at the expense of the Parish'.[83]

The early Victorian expansion of Worthing was not unique, for all over the country the population of towns had increased rapidly, with the result that there was a growing agitation for an improvement in the standard of urban sanitation. In consequence of this, the Health of Towns Act was passed by Parliament in 1848, and a General Board of Health was set up with powers to apply the Act upon a petition from the inhabitants of a town where the need was evident. The passing of the Act revived interest in Worthing's drainage problems, and it was urged by a number of the more far-sighted inhabitants that the Act should be applied to Worthing in order that the town's prosperity should continue. This feeling was strongly opposed by the Board of Commissioners who, in spite of the evidence before their eyes, saw no reason why the facilities provided during the early 1800s should not serve equally as well nearly 50 years later.[84]

After an almost farcical interlude of petitions, and counter petitions, charges and counter charges, and after one adjournment, Mr. Edward Cresy, the Government's Inspector, held an Inquiry into the 'Sewage Drainage and Supply of Water and the Sanitary Conditions of the Inhabitants of the Town of Worthing' on 9 April 1850. The Inquiry revealed an appalling state of affairs. Mr. Cressy records:

(i) that the whole of the streets in the town were totally undrained.
(ii) that certain of the houses were occupied by unhealthy families which were seldom free from fever.
(iii) open sewers and cesspools had been left standing for years.
(iv) in spite of the Commissioners' protestation as to the health of the town, and the village of Broadwater, a rapid increase in the number of cases of fever and infections had been reported to the Parish Surgeon.

The concluding words of the report came as a shock to the complacency of the Worthing Commissioners. 'The Town of Worthing having been improperly treated hitherto with regard to its drainage and water supply, and that as no sound principals have ever been applied to maintain the streets and houses in a healthy condition, it is most imperative that the Public Health Act should immediately be applied to it, and regard the annual outlay under the present Commissioners as excessive for the purpose to which it applied. I am of the opinion that all the improvements required can be realised and carried out with considerable saving to the rated inhabitants.'[85]

On the strength of this report, the old Board of Commissioners was abolished, the last meeting being held in 17 July 1852. The newly-appointed Board of Health held their first meeting on 9 August 1852, and with commendable promptitude they set about resolving the water supply and drainage problems, selecting a site in the High Street for both the new sewage well and waterworks. As will be seen this proved to be a most unfortunate decision.[86]

During the early summer of 1892 the town of Worthing experienced a prolonged period of drought, which, combined with its continuing growth, caused the town's water supply to fail again. Additional water supplies were therefore sought by the newly-formed Borough Council, and like their predecessors, the Local Board of Health, they resolved they would again explore the potential supply known to exist in the inherited water board enclosure located in the High Street. As can be seen on the enlarged plan of the enclosure (Fig. 16), three wells marked A, B and C had already been established. Following lengthy debate, the sinking of a further bore below Well 'C' was disregarded, as experience had shown that the flint beds and fissures that contained large quantities of water did not normally extend more than 80 to 100 feet below the surface. A new heading into the chalk from the bottom of Well 'C' was considered to be the most expedient, as this method had in

*Fig. 16.   Plan of waterworks Enclosure, 1893.*

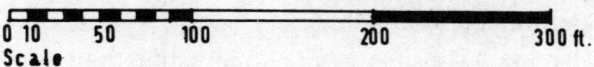

3-0" dia. Brick Barrel main
sewer laid about 1880

Sewer
abandoned 1880

Engine House

Pipe from Conductor

WELL 'B'
Iron cylinder well
6'-0" dia. 104'-0" deep
with 300'-0" bore hole
14" dia.

POND

Cooling Tank

Water Tower

Tunnel Bored 1885

WELL 'A'
Iron cylinder well
5'-0" dia. 60'-0" deep
with 300'-0" bore hole
14" dia.

Sewage
well

Engine House

Chain pump
well

WELL 'C'

To main sewer
in Lyndhurst Rd.

PLAN OF WORTHING WATERWORKS ENCLOSURE 1893
[Based on diagram in Dr. Theodore Thomson's
Report on the Typhoid Epidemic]

0  10      50        100              200              300 ft.
Scale

Standing

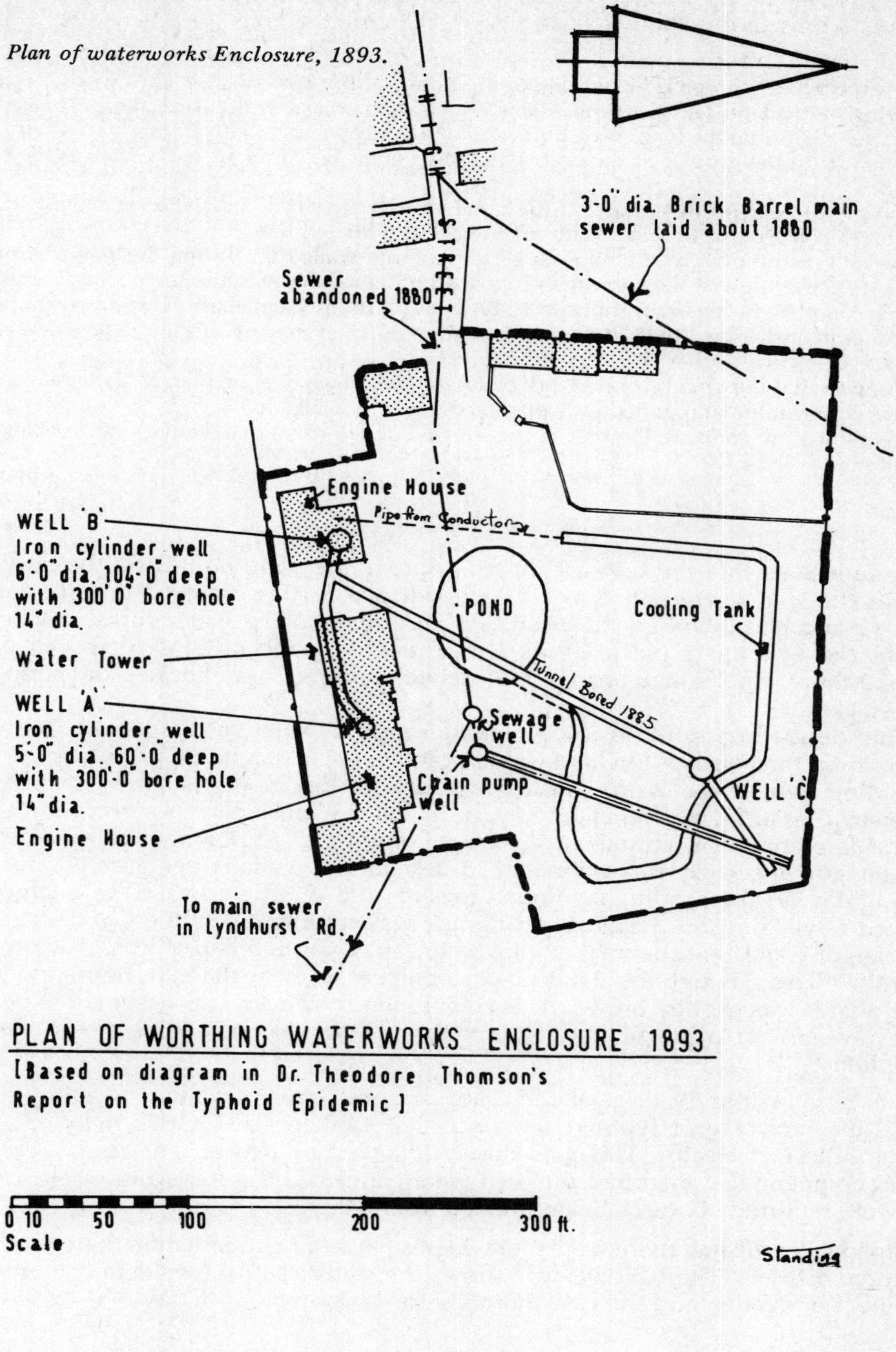

the past provided the largest yield. The Borough Surveyor submitted a plan and the following report to the Highways and Works Committee on 20 October 1892.

> With respect to the proposed extension of the tunnel at the Waterworks, I beg to give you the following particulars: The last tunnel constructed extends across the yard in a north-easterly direction to 83ft from the fence wall, and is 72ft 6in below ground, with a brick lined shaft 7 feet diameter up to the ground at the end. The tunnel is 6ft high and 4ft wide, brick walled and arched.
>
> I propose to extend this tunnel at the same level in the chalk, a distance of about 83ft, the size to be 7ft high and 4ft wide, with brick walls and arched roof.
>
> The end of the present tunnel is to be temporarily walled up during the progress of the works, to prevent the water from the proposed tunnel mixing with the town supply until the work is completed. The excavations to be brought up the present shaft, where a steam pump will be temporarily fixed to lift the water from the tunnel extension during the progress of the works.
>
> I suggest that the underground work be under the charge of a foreman accustomed to such works. The winding apparatus, etc., previously used is available.
>
> It is difficult to estimate the cost of this work, but I think under ordinary circumstances it would not exceed £300.
>
> M.ASPINALL
> Borough Surveyor

It was resolved that the Council should approve the plan, and direct the Surveyor to carry out the works referred to in his report. It was further resolved that the following articles should be purchased for extending the tunnel at the waterworks: 'Pair of 1 ton pulley blocks, 24 Colliers' picks, 3 suits 'Dreadnought', 3 suits oilskins, 6 caps, 6 pairs knee boots, 2,000ft of 7 inch rough boards, 140ft pitwood props, 3 well buckets and spring hook, 40,000 stock bricks'.[87]

Having decided upon the method of enhancing the water supply an experienced well engineer from the North of England was appointed. On 6 March 1893 work commenced on the heading, which was to run in a north-easterly direction. As the work proceeded, several small fissures were encountered, and isolated subsidence occurred, but this was not considered unusual. Tunnelling continued, and by 13 April when the heading was 68 feet in length, the yield was estimated to be about 60 gallons per minute. During the following day, as the heading continued towards the Worthing Infirmary, a large fissure estimated as yielding 2,623 gallons per minute was cut into. So sudden, and so great was the inrush of water that the men employed in the excavation had to leave their tools and run for their lives. Though there was no perceptible taste or smell to this new supply, it was noticed that it was slightly brown. This colouration, however, was assumed to be caused by the presence of oxide of iron. Regrettably, as will be seen, this was a disastrous assumption.[88]

On 3 May, within 19 days of the discovery and implementation of this new water supply, the first case of typhoid fever was reported to Dr. Charles Kelly, Worthing's Medical Officer of Health. This was closely followed by two further cases. Fears that a typhoid epidemic had engulfed the area were confirmed the following week, when 114 cases were reported, 42 cases being notified in one day.

In Broadwater village, there were more deaths per head of population than in any of the other three districts. The table below[89] shows the statistics of the epidemic, by recording the number of deaths, and the case mortality for each area.

|  | Cases | | | Deaths | | | Case Mortality % | | |
|---|---|---|---|---|---|---|---|---|---|
|  | M | F | Total | M | F | Total | M | F | Total |
| Worthing | 599 | 662 | 1226 | 65 | 90 | 155 | 10.85 | 13.60 | 12.29 |
| West Worthing | 20 | 38 | 58 | 5 | 10 | 15 | 25.00 | 26.31 | 25.86 |
| West Tarring | 29 | 26 | 55 | 5 | 4 | 9 | 17.24 | 15.40 | 16.36 |
| Broadwater | 17 | 25 | 42 | 2 | 7 | 9 | 11.76 | 28.00 | 21.43 |
|  | 665 | 751 | 1416 | 77 | 111 | 188 | 11.58 | 14.78 | 13.27 |

Between 28 April and 31 December 1893, 42 cases of fever were recorded as occurring in the 191 inhabited houses of Broadwater. This was revealed by an independent census undertaken by Dr. Thompson. He found a considerable proportion of these houses to be old, many being badly lit, damp, and inadequately ventilated. He also found the majority of Broadwater's 787 inhabitants to be in poor circumstances, being totally dependent on their fruit growing and agricultural pursuits.[90]

The village of Broadwater had no public sewerage system. Indoor water closets were rare and the drainage was chiefly into cesspits, while house water was often used to water the cottage garden. The only constant relationship between Worthing and Broadwater was the water supply. Even so, only 65 of the 191 houses were supplied from Worthing water works, the remaining 126 houses receiving their water from local wells.[91] The distribution of the disease was, however, general throughout the entire village. Subsequent investigation revealed why this was so. Of the 42 persons attacked, 34 confirmed that they had been in the habit of consuming 'Worthing' water, as they either worked in the town; resided in a house connected to the 'town water mains'; or were in service in the town. Some even confessed to ignoring the notices posted throughout the district.

On 25 and 26 August, 'sensational Articles' and illustrations were published by the *Daily Graphic*, under the headline 'Fever Stricken Worthing'.[92] The articles recorded that it was not only the visitors that had shunned the town; many of the wealthier residents had also left. To demonstrate the loss of trade which had resulted, it was noted that a local draper's takings for one day in the previous week was a mere 10½d.! The lady journalist also recorded how at Brighton Station, when she changed from a Pullman Car Express, guards and porters looked at her with curiosity when she asked to be directed to the Worthing train. The town itself was described as 'depressing as a city of the dead. It was possible to walk through the main streets of the Town, and probably only see two vehicles, one of those being a hearse. The blinds of houses were drawn, knockers on doors were wrapped in soft material to deaden the sound, gates were padlocked, and grass grew rank and coarse over what would usually have been well kept lawns'. In the hotel at which the correspondent lunched there had not been a single entry in the visitors book since 30 June. Down on the beach, bathing machines were drawn up high and dry, and boats laid by the score, dusty and unused under the sunshine. The only life to be seen was a solitary boatman and two children paddling.

As early as July, alternative sources of water were sought by the town council, and one Mullins, a water finder, was appointed. In his search for water he was often accompanied by several members of the council. The investigations into an alternative water supply in the Broadwater area were successful on land attached to Lyons Farm. A plentiful supply of water was obtained, and a second bore was made so as to increase the quantity.

Mains were rapidly laid down from this new source to a spot in High Street, close to the waterworks. Temporary engines were placed at the Broadwater end of these mains and a yield of 600,000 gallons a day was obtained. On 4 September, the work was so far advanced that a hydrant could be placed on the High Street end and from that date five out of the ten water vans were filled from this source.[93] At 1.45 p.m. on 22 September 1892, the engines of the waterworks in High Street were stopped for ever.

What then was the cause of this outbreak of Typhoid Fever, that finally resulted in 1411 cases being reported, 186 of which resulted in death? Two reports attempting to answer this question were published, one by the central Government's Inspector, Dr. Theodore Thompson; the other by Dr. Charles Kelly. Surprisingly, the reports differed in their conclusions. Dr. Thompson's premise was that the overlying soil above the new tunnel augmenting the town's water supply had been contaminated via a chalk fissure, that had linked the supply with the overflow pipe from the chain pump sewer well and the Park Road Sewer (see Fig. 6).[94]

Dr. Kelly did not, however, support this theory as it was his contention that even if soil pollution was occurring, the water in the new heading was derived from such a great depth, it would be impossible for it to be polluted by sewage. He records in his report that 'Two sets of men were employed in making the new heading. The day gang began to work on March 13th in excavating the chalk, while on March 16th the night gang began to line the tunnel with bricks. There is no doubt that the works became polluted by the conduct of one or two of the night gang, who were not regular labourers in the town. Some of the men who had been at work there gave distinct evidence of this, and some of the day gang complained at times of the foul air in the cutting when they went down to work in the morning. This information was given at the very beginning of the outbreak, although for obvious reasons no one cared to come forward and complain. I consider that this pollution was the main cause of the epidemic, and that it brought about a condition of the reservoir and service pipes which was potent for harm'.[95]

Even though the conclusions of Dr. Theodore Thompson cannot be fully substantiated, as certain of the sewers requiring scrutiny were removed prior to his detailed examination, it is probable that he was correct in his conclusions. Dr. Charles Kelly committed suicide not long after this outbreak.

This was the last major problem the community at Broadwater had to resolve as an independent body, for 10 years later in 1902, Broadwater became absorbed into the expanding Borough of Worthing.[96]

*Chapter Three*

# The Land

It is stated by J. R. Armstrong in his *History of Sussex* that any traveller in the county at the close of the 18th century would have noticed fundamental changes from the early or middle years. Some of these changes were the size of many of the fields; the increased amount of ploughland; and the almost complete disappearance of fallow land, the latter being made possible by the application of more scientific crop rotation. In Broadwater parish a considerable amount of land was enclosed from the 16th century onwards (part of Offington was enclosed *c.*1540) and by the time that the general Inclosure Act was implemented there were already in Broadwater a number of enclosed fields and crofts which are shown on the map of Area No. 1 (Fig. 18).

The area to be discussed in this chapter is shown in Fig. 17 and can be approximately defined as that area contained by the boundaries of the modern Upper Brighton Road on the north, the modern South Farm Road (earlier known as Brooksteed Lane) on the west, the Teville Stream on the south (now piped underground) and the parish of Sompting on the east. By using the tithe map, the total area of the land under discussion is calculated as being approximately 784 acres (384 acres of pasture, 378 acres of arable and 22 acres of buildings, gardens etc.). These areas exclude those small crofts and closes containing houses etc., either side of Broadwater Street. Four estates, Broadwater Farm, Decoy Farm, Lyons Farm and the Glebe lands account for approximately 512 acres (65 per cent) of the total area of 784 acres, while the remainder consists of a number of minor estates and land holdings.

The map shown as Fig. 17 is divided into areas which are separately depicted in order to discuss the various field names. Many fields with similar names often have a common meaning throughout the country and a specialist book on the subject *English Field Names, A Dictionary* by John Field (1972) has been consulted in order to unravel the meanings of the field names of Broadwater.

## Map of Area No. 1 (Fig. 18)
This area is depicted as it must have appeared prior to the enclosures of 1806/10. The full lines on the map show the early field enclosures, while the dotted lines show the subdivision of the great open North Field after enclosure.

### a) *Broadwater Green*
Although not specifically named, the earliest known outline of the Green appears on a map of *c.*1720,[1] and the shape is very similar to that of today. On the enclosure map of Broadwater, surveyed in 1806, it is clearly marked as Broadwater Green and was held as part of Broadwater Manor, either as common or waste land. A document of 19 April 1865[2] shows that the Green was conveyed to the Local Board of Health (established in 1852 to replace the Town Commissioners of Worthing) as a public pleasure ground by the ladies of

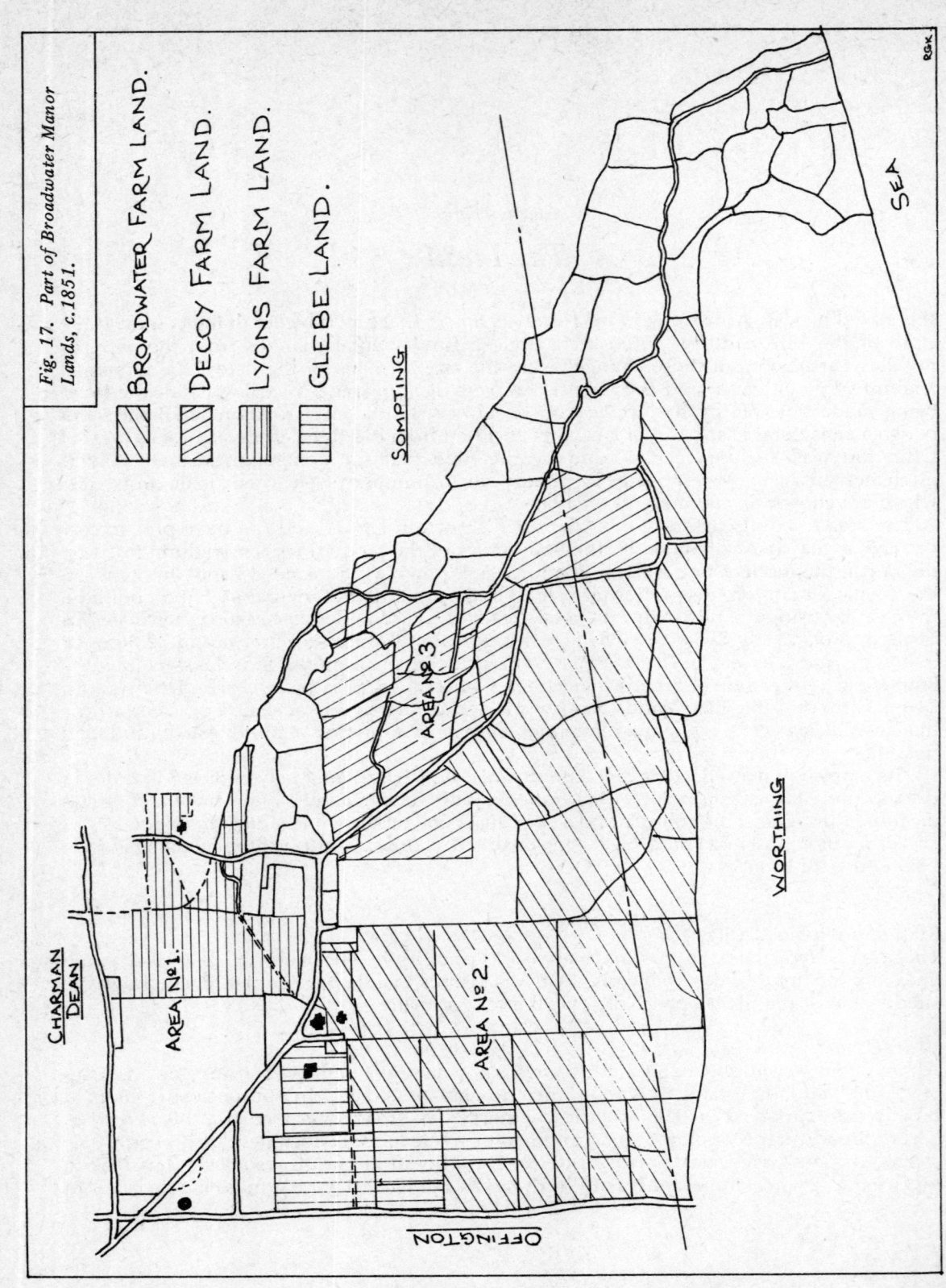

Fig. 17. Part of Broadwater Manor Lands, c.1851.

BROADWATER FARM LAND.

DECOY FARM LAND.

LYONS FARM LAND.

GLEBE LAND.

CHARMAN DEAN

AREA Nº 1.

AREA Nº 2.

AREA Nº 3.

SOMPTING

OFFINGTON

WORTHING

SEA

RGK.

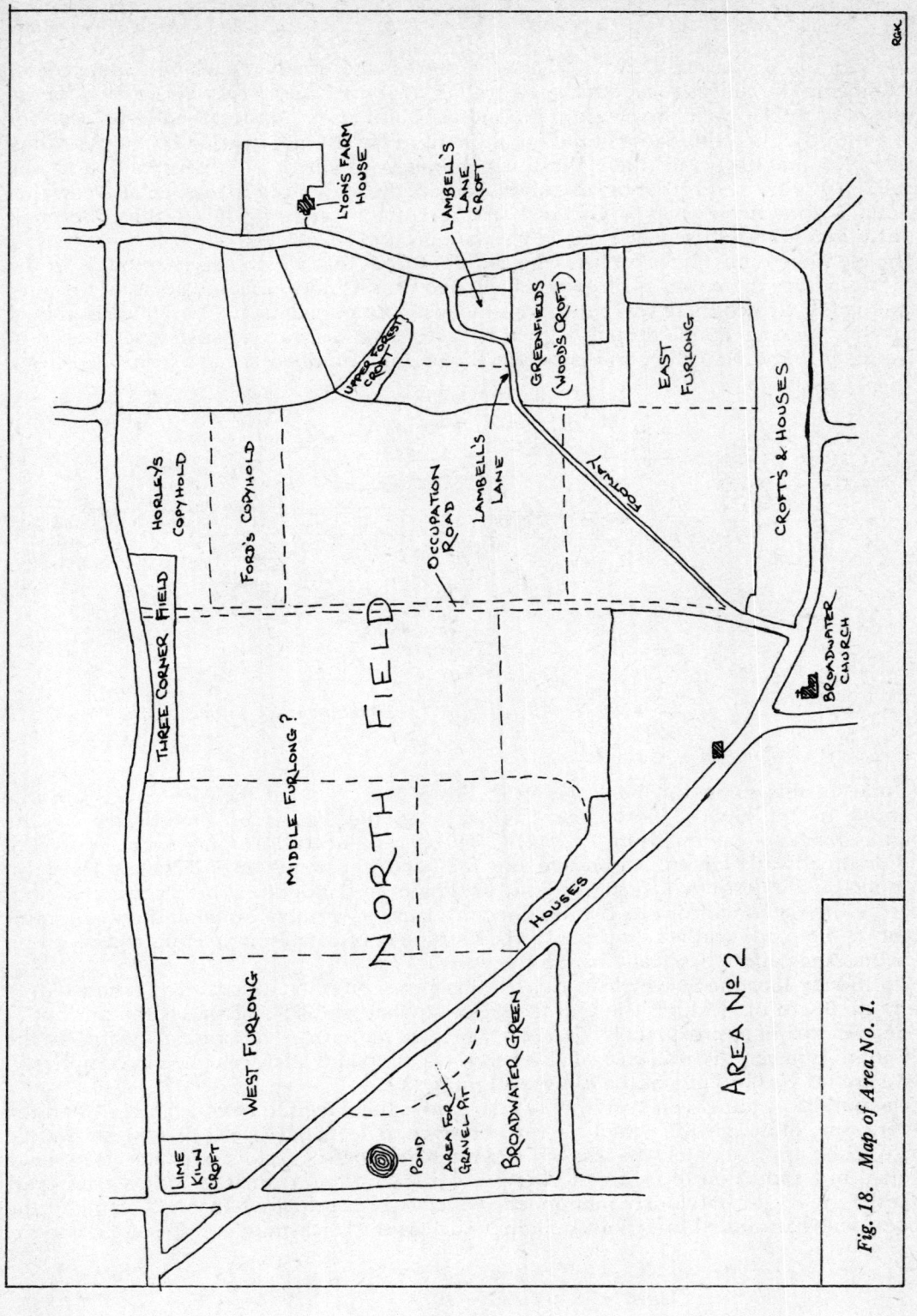

*Fig. 18. Map of Area No. 1.*

the Manor of Broadwater, Ann, Harriet, Frances and Emily Newland, spinsters of Cheltenham. The conveyance includes a covenant that the Green shall only be used for the purposes of public walks or pleasure grounds and if it at any time ceased to be used for such a purpose then the estate of the Local Board of Health (superseded by the Worthing Corporation in 1890 and then Worthing Borough Council) is determined and the hereditaments are to revert to the use of the Lady of the Manor of Broadwater as a parcel of the said Manor for ever. The Green is at present the property of Worthing Borough Council, and it is still used as a public pleasure ground.

The old Green must have looked very different from that which survives today. In the late 18th century there was a village pond situated near its northern end, adjacent to South Farm Road, by which there was a ducking stool used for punishments. Very little is known about this ducking stool although Fig. 19 is based on a drawing of such a stool used in Wiltshire at that time.[3] The pond is clearly shown on a number of maps from 1806-1898.

Fig. 19.  *Ducking stool on Broadwater Green.*

Opposite this pond on the Broadwater Street West side of the Green was an area awarded to the Surveyors of the Highways in the Parish of Broadwater by the Commissioners of the Inclosure Act (1810). The document records 'one piece or parcel of land on Broadwater Green, of one acre, one rood and 10 perches (approximately 1¼ acres) bounded on the north by a Turnpike Road leading from London to Worthing and on other sides by the remainder of Broadwater Green, for use as a public stone and gravel pit for repairing the roads and for Proprietors and Occupiers of Estates in erecting and repairing their buildings and fence walls within the parish'.

On 10 May 1865 the Surveyors conveyed this gravel pit, then described as exhausted, to the Local Board of Health.[4] The Ordnance Survey map of 1875 still shows the pit, but as having an area of approximately 2¼ acres, one acre more than the original award! By the end of the 19th century this pit had also become a pond and later was filled in completely. There are no visible signs of the old gravel pit today.

The outline of the Green on the 1720 map shows the Green to be much larger than the present one, although the actual area is not given. The Tithe Award of 1851 shows the Green to be approximately 10 acres in extent. A number of factors over the years have resulted in a reduction of its area to the present size of approximately nine acres. Apart from the gravel pit previously mentioned, which was eventually reinstated, some of the causes can be attributed to various buildings such as the blacksmith's shop situated on the south east corner of the Green in 1838[5] which was subsequently rebuilt in 1885. Its site can be identified as the road island in front of Paine Manwaring's shop. Mention should also be made of the school.

Another small structure worthy of mention was described as a 'wattle house' on Broadwater Green, between the years 1836-51 inclusive. It was probably the small rectangle shown on the south west corner of the Green on the tithe map. It was almost certainly constructed of wattle and daub, or actually made of wattle hurdles, and was owned by Harry Newland and occupied by William Blaker. The estimated rental for this structure was 10s and at the rate of 3d in the pound was charged at 1½d. No further details of this structure have been found. A drinking fountain was installed on the east side of the Green but, alas, was demolished when Broadwater Street West was widened.

The only structure now located on the Green is the modern pavilion, which is for the use of sports players.

A document dated 1929 and described as 'Broadwater Green Street improvement'[6] asked for advice and counsel concerning the widening of the Worthing to London Road for which a strip of some 22 feet of the Green was required. This presumably took place in 1937 when the School was demolished.[7] After 1959 another reduction of the Green took place at the north east edge under an Appropriation Order.[8]

Many events have taken place over the years on village greens throughout the country and Broadwater Green is no exception. Apparently cricket was played on the Green by the early 1720s and Broadwater Cricket Club, founded in 1771, still plays there. In 1837 a match between Sussex and an All England side took place there.[9] It is interesting to note that the public house opposite the Green was renamed the *Cricketer's Arms* about 1878. Markets and fairs have been held in Broadwater from the Middle Ages, the markets having virtually finished by the middle of the 17th century.[10] In the late 18th and early 19th centuries fairs were held for horned cattle.[11] These may have been held on the Green as was the Easter fair of 1891[12] and then the June fairs which were held annually there until 1922 and then revived in 1975.[13]

b) *The North Field*
This was one of the two great open common fields in Broadwater, the other being the South Field (see map of Area No. 2, Fig. 20). It would appear that Broadwater originally had a two-field system of agriculture as opposed to three which was common in a number of surrounding villages. These great open fields were usually divided into furlongs, which in turn were subdivided into one acre, and half-acre, strips in different parts of the manor in order that the tenants had their share of good and bad land. Over the centuries these strips were gradually exchanged by tenants until larger pieces of land evolved. A number of these areas were eventually enclosed, especially those around the edges of the open fields. This enclosing gradually reduced the area of common land.

The West and East furlongs are still referred to on the enclosure map of 1806 and although it is quite likely that the central area of the field was at one time the middle furlong, it is not shown on the map.

The effect of the Inclosure Act in Broadwater can be seen on the map. The total area of land held by each person prior to enclosure was ascertained and an equivalent area was awarded to him/her in the form of much larger parcels. The shape and size of most of the fields which still existed a few years ago were laid out as a result of the Inclosure Act. Modern farming practice has resulted in the removal of many of the hedges and fences, forming even larger field units.

## c) Lime Kiln Croft

This was an early enclosure which, prior to the general Inclosure Act, was owned by Thomas Richardson. To the north of this field, across the modern Upper Brighton Road, and adjacent to Hill Lane (now Hill Barn Lane) was another old enclosure called Lime Kiln Field. Both names suggest that there was an actual lime kiln. These kilns were used to burn chalk from which lime was produced, which was used to spread on the land as fertilizer. (Examples can be seen at the Chalk Pits Museum at Amberley, Sussex.) Sometimes chalk was used in its raw, lumpy, state. The soil from the Downs was often thin, leached and acidic and required lime and/or chalk in large quantities.[14] There are chalk pits all over the South Downs as a result of lime burning and the utilisation of chalk, and in Broadwater, further up Hill Lane, there was a chalk pit from which no doubt the chalk was obtained for those purposes.

## d) Three Cornered Field

Another old enclosure which before 1806 was owned by Richard Newland. The meaning of this name is 'a triangular piece of land'[15] and the map shows that the field could indeed be considered as roughly triangular in shape. This field lost its identity when the great North Field was divided during the enclosures.

## e) Upper Forest Croft

No special meaning can be found for the name of this old enclosure unless it was originally covered in trees. On the 1869 Ordnance Survey map a row of trees is shown along its northern edge, which coincided with the parish boundary at this point. Often derisory names were given to small pieces of land, e.g., 'Hundred Acre Field', and if this area was a small wood, then Upper Forest could have been used as a derisory term.

## f) Greenfields

This enclosure was formerly known as 'Wood's Croft' being part of the land of the Reverend Wood of Broadwater. In 1806 it was owned by 'Greenfield', presumably Mary Greenfield as it adjoined a small croft and house owned by her. Both this field and east furlong (to the south) lost their identities when they formed part of an area allotted to John Holmes in 1810.

## g) Occupation Road

In order for the owners to gain access to their various fields, which were located in the middle of the great North Field as a result of the Inclosure Act, a road (known as Occupation Road) was formed north to south from the modern Upper Brighton Road to the modern Broadwater Street East. This road later became known as Butcher's Lane and finally as Forest Road.

## h) Lambell's Lane

Across the North Field was a footpath leading in a north-easterly direction to meet a short lane recorded as 'Lambell's Lane' passing by 'Lambell's Lane Croft' (now both gone). The path continued in the same direction, from the end of this lane, across a footbridge over a stream in the brooks towards Upton Farm. At the farm it turned northwards to what is today Lambley's Barn. All efforts have failed to find anyone known as Lambell or Lambley in the Broadwater Parish Registers but a Richard Lambale is shown in the Subsidy List of 1524/5 (see Chapter Four) and it may well be this person or a relative who was connected with the Lane and Croft. It would seem that the modern spelling is therefore a corruption of the name.

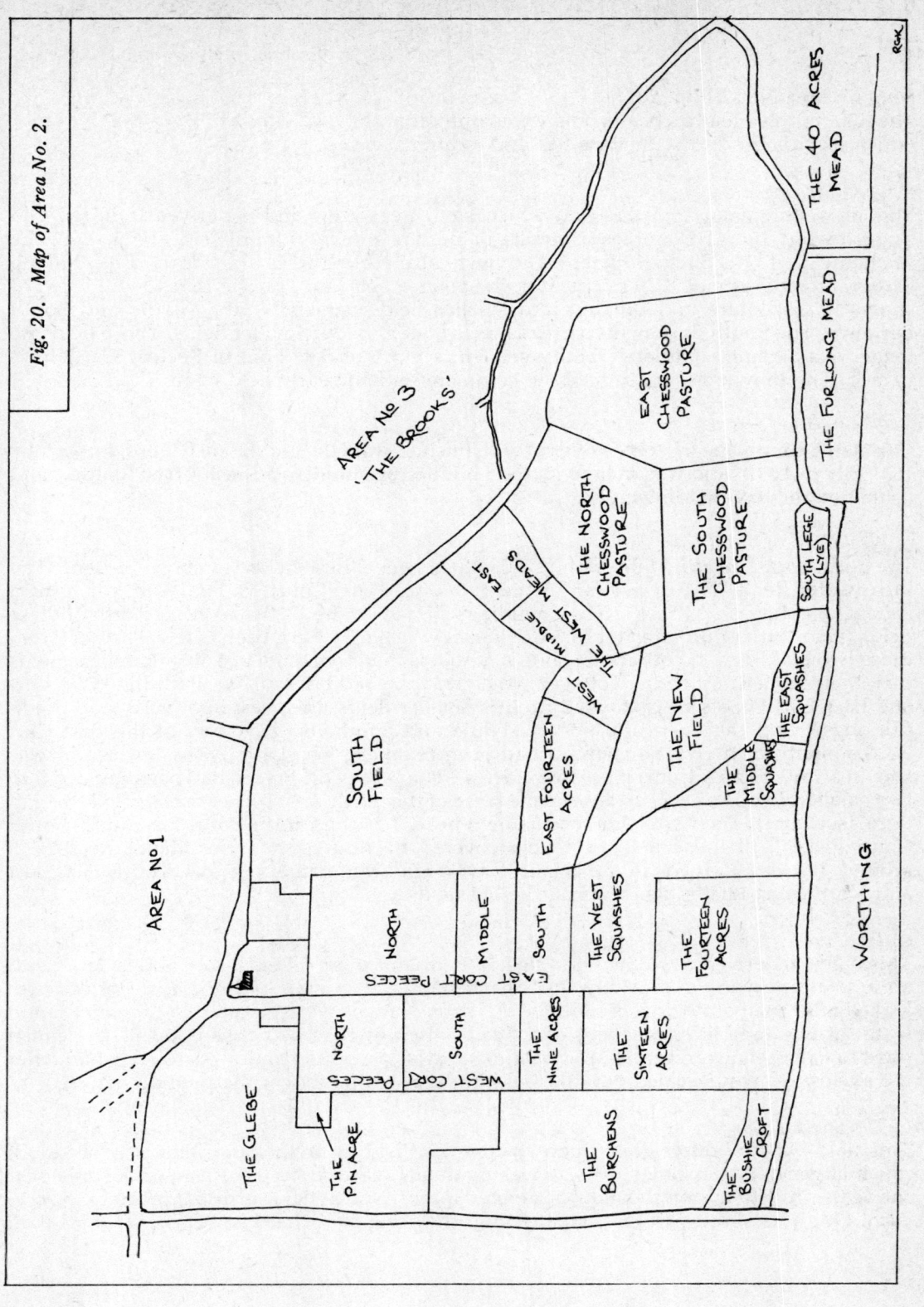

Fig. 20. Map of Area No. 2.

AREA No 1

AREA No 3
'THE BROOKS'

WORTHING

SOUTH FIELD

THE NORTH CHESSWOOD PASTURE

THE SOUTH CHESSWOOD PASTURE

EAST CHESSWOOD PASTURE

THE 40 ACRES MEAD

THE FURLONG MEAD

SOUTH LEGE (LYE)

THE EAST SQUASHES

THE MIDDLE SQUASHES

THE NEW FIELD

EAST FOURTEEN ACRES

WEST

THE WEST MEADS

THE MIDDLE

EAST

NORTH

MIDDLE

SOUTH

EAST CORT PEECES

THE WEST SQUASHES

THE FOURTEEN ACRES

NORTH

SOUTH

WEST CORT PEECES

THE NINE ACRES

THE SIXTEEN ACRES

THE GLEBE

THE PIN ACRE

THE BURCHENS

THE BUSHIE CROFT

R.O.K.

**Map of Area No. 2 (Fig. 20)**
The map of this area has been compiled mainly from the *c.*1720 map of Broadwater Manor which records the fields, their names and locations.

a) *The Burchens*
This name originates from land on which birch trees grew and is derived from the Old English word 'birce'. Examples of similar names are shown in John Field's book, e.g., 'Le Birchenfeld', 1334; 'Birchen Flatt'.[16] The twigs of the birch trees are still used for making garden brooms. About 1720 this field is shown as arable land, but by 1851 the tithe award shows it as pasture and divided into smaller fields named North, Middle and South Furlongs. The South Furlong in particular was split into four smaller fields. These fields no longer exist, being completely built over, but a block of flats built in Rectory Gardens is named 'The Burchens', presumably to commemorate the early field name.

b) *The Bushie Croft*
This name simply means 'land covered with bushes' from the Old English word 'busc'.[17] By 1851 this piece of land was owned by the London, Brighton and South Coast Railway and contained railway buildings, etc.

c) *West Cort and East Cort Peeces*
The north-south dividing line on the 1720 map between these fields is today represented by Broadwater Road. The derivation of the name 'Cort' or 'Court' is 'land with, or near, a cottage or cottages'.[18] There are two buildings shown on the 1720 map at the north of these fields (just south of Broadwater Manor House) which may have been cottages. Apart from these two buildings, no others are shown, and it is therefore quite possible that these fields took their name from earlier cottages which disappeared before 1720. Both the West Cort and East Cort Peeces were divided up into smaller fields, the West into North and South (furlongs?) and the East into North, Middle and South. By 1851 part of the East Cort Peeces, south of the Manor House, had been renamed 'The Lawn'. The lower part was shown as the 'Stoney Court piece and 8 acres'. The West Cort Peeces had been divided into two smaller fields by 1806, and the small piece at the north west corner was named the 'Pin Acre' (see later). The two fields were shown in 1851 as the 'North Court Piece' and 'South Court Piece'. All these fields are now covered by houses, and the Manor Recreation ground, but certain roads in the vicinity have been given names e.g. Westcourt, Eastcourt and Northcourt Roads, which recall the old fields.

d) *Pin Acre*
This name is derived from the Old English 'Penn' meaning an enclosure and is 'land with an animal enclosure'[19] probably the village pound. The manorial or parish officer who looked after the pound was the Pinder. All stray animals were placed into the pound, and were set free only after payment of a fine by their owners. A house opposite the Green (next to Paine Manwaring's shop) was known to be the pound and was probably built after the enclosures were carried out and the Pin Acre was no longer the pound.

e) *The South Field*
This field was the other great open or common field in Broadwater, and was no doubt much larger in earlier times. Its size was gradually reduced by piecemeal enclosures over the years. In 1810 the south field was divided into two great fields of approximately 15 acres each. One was allotted to John Holmes and the other to Richard Newland. In 1851, each

field still retained the name of South Field, but had encompassed other adjacent fields and expanded. Neither of these fields now exists, being covered by houses and roads such as Fletcher, Sheridan, Goldsmith, Congreve and Marlow Roads.

f) *The Sixteen Acres, the Fourteen Acres, the Nine Acres and East Fourteen Acres*
The meaning of these names are 'a piece of land having an area as shown or adjoining such a piece of land'.[20] All the fields shown have an area not much different from their title, and thus no doubt contained more or less the areage shown when first enclosed. Slight alterations in the field boundaries over the years could account for the discrepancies in the areas.

g) *The West, Middle and East Squashes*
The 'Squashes' lie along the north side of the Teville Stream and the name most probably signifies boggy or marshy land[21] especially as they are shown flooded on a map of 1826 (see 'The Brooks'). In a vestry meeting of 1818 it was ordered that a new bridge be built at the bottom of 'the Squashetts' over the stream[22] and by 1851 the initial 'S' was dropped and these were known as the Quashetts, a name which is now retained for the passage or 'twitten' running northwards under the railway in a tunnel, and through these old fields towards Broadwater village.

h) *The South Lege (or Ley) Meadow*
The word Ley means 'untilled land' from the Old English word 'loege'[23] (hence Lege in the name) and would therefore account for the fact that it was a meadow.

i) *The West Meads, Furlong Mead*
The word 'meads' means 'grassland mown for hay' from the Old English word 'moed'.[24] The West Meads were originally part of the marshes and were separated from the main area when Decoy Lane (Dominion Road) joined up to the Chesswood Pastures. The modern Dominion Road open space was, not many years ago, still a piece of marshland and had a horse tethered on it known as Kitty. This ground is still known locally by some inhabitants as 'Kitty's Field'. Dominion Road Allotments, which are administered by the local authority, lie on the remainder of the west meads.

j) *The North, South and East Chesswood Pastures*
The origin of the word 'Chesswood' is obscure and may be connected with the wood of the sweet chestnut tree which is used for fencing hurdles, gate posts, poles etc.[25] The fields may have had sweet chestnut trees growing there or around their periphery.

k) *The New Field*
This name implies land newly taken into cultivation or newly enclosed.[26] An example of the name of 'New Field' occurs in Lancing as an enclosure of the Tudor Period.[27]

**Map of Area No. 3** (Fig. 21)
The brooks form a very important part of this area, as it is suggested that from these the village obtained its name. At one time there was a large tidal inlet, which reached almost up to the modern Sompting Road and separated the parishes of Broadwater and Sompting (see Fig. 2). This inlet was known as the Broad-water (Bradenwatre, Brodewater, etc.) and it has been suggested that ships once anchored there. A recent borehole sunk in the area shows that seaweed exists at approximately seven meters deep (22 feet), underlying a

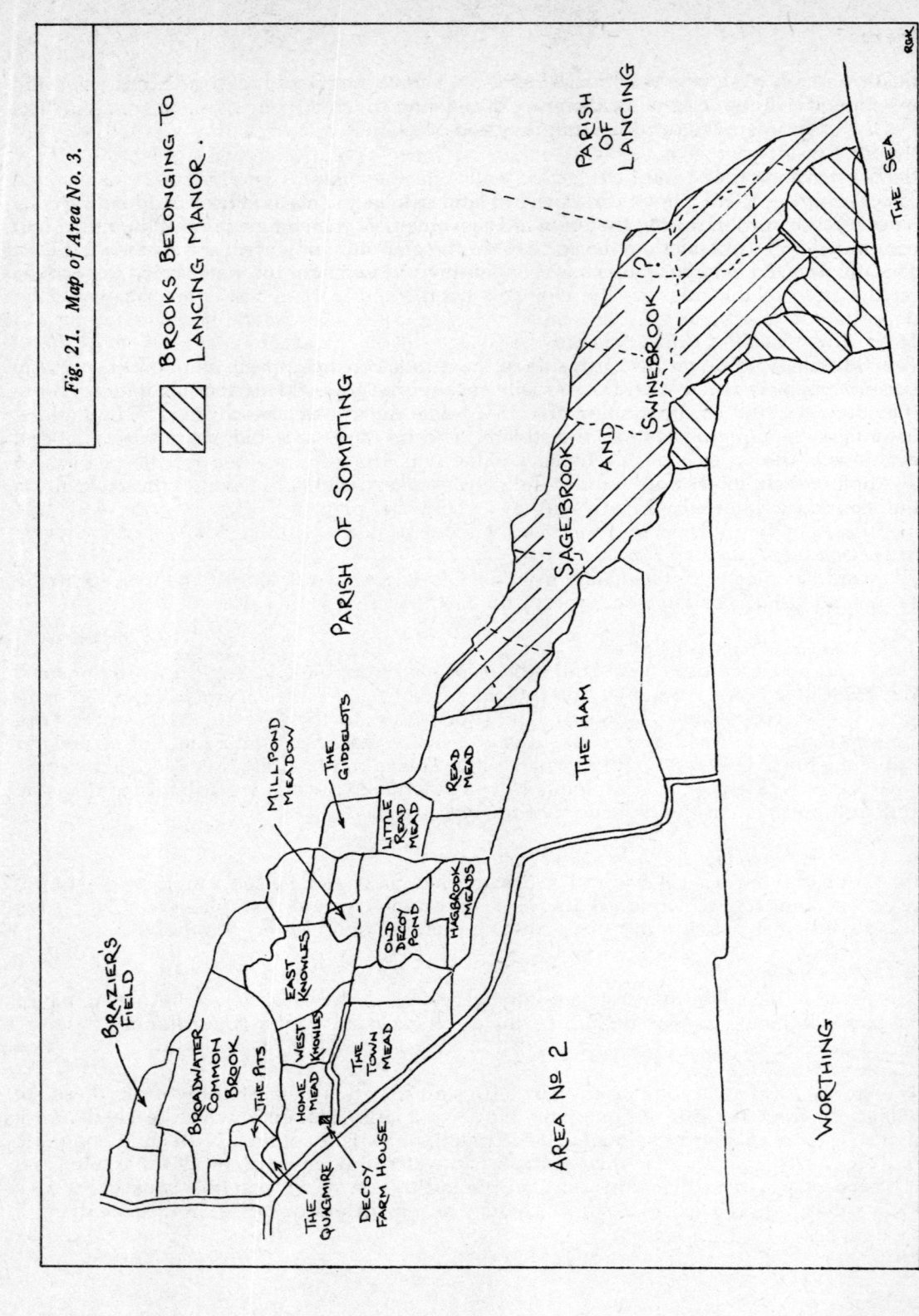

Fig. 21. Map of Area No. 3.

BROOKS BELONGING TO
LANCING MANOR.

PARISH OF SOMPTING

PARISH
OF
LANCING

SAGEBROOK
AND
SWINEBROOK

THE SEA

BRAZIER'S
FIELD

BROADWATER
COMMON
BROOK

THE PITS

MILLPOND MEADOW

THE GIBBELOTS

EAST
KNOWLES

WEST
KNOWLES

HOME
MEAD

THE QUAGMIRE

DECOY
FARM HOUSE

THE
TOWN
MEAD

OLD
DECOY
POND

LITTLE
READ
MEAD

READ
MEAD

HAGBROOK
MEADS

THE HAM

AREA No 2

WORTHING

RGK

mixture of silt, clay and recent marine shells. This silting up of the area was no doubt
instrumental in the gradual reclamation of the land from the sea.

One of the methods of reclaiming or inning the land was by building a dam to prevent
the tidal water coming in, which contained a sluice to drain the land at low tide. These
dams often took the form of long, high walls which eventually became roads, as was the
case at Lancing.[28] This, however, does not appear to be the method used at Broadwater as
it seems most probable that the eastward movement of the shingle beach had, by c.1250,
cut off the direct access of the sea and caused the gradual silting up of the area (see Fig. 22).
This possibly led to large water channels forming, the height of the water being dependent
on the state of the tide. As the channels overflowed at high tide more silt would be
deposited. Similar areas exist elsewhere in Sussex, e.g. Lancing and Shoreham (at the end
of the Adur), Lewes Levels, Pevensey Levels, etc. all of which had initial reclamation in the
early Middle Ages by means of sluice gates and dams etc., only to be flooded again in the
later Middle Ages. Most were not reclaimed again until Tudor or Elizabethan times.[29] There
is evidence of land reclamation in the early Middle Ages in the Broadwater, for marshland
used as pasture or arable land worth 10d in the early part of the 15th century was flooded
again by 1493.[30]

Apparently in the Middle Ages there was a small settlement called Little Broadwater on
the boundary between Broadwater and Sompting parishes.[31] This manor was first
mentioned in the 13th century, and it is not unreasonable to assume that the first area to be

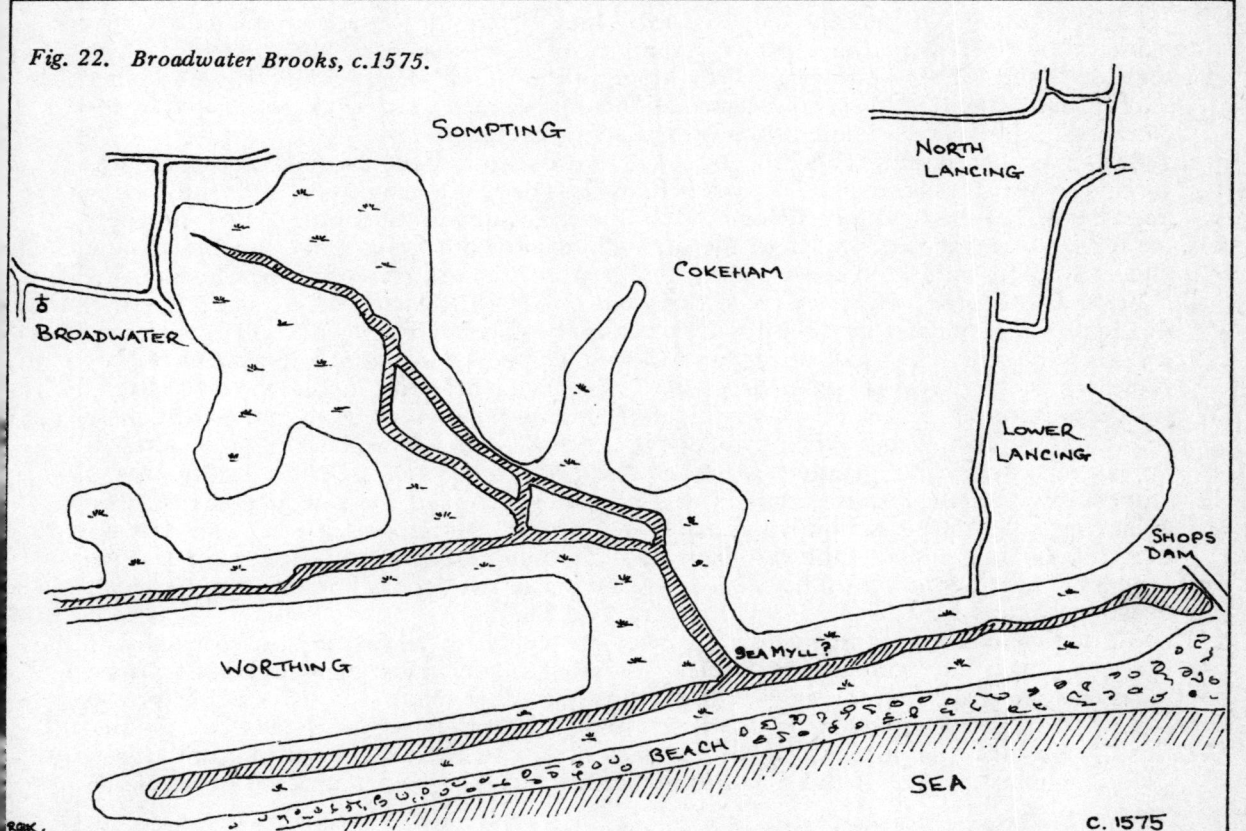

Fig. 22.   Broadwater Brooks, c.1575.

silted up in the Broadwater would be its upper reaches. The area shown as the *Broadwater Common Brook* could well represent the old manor of Little Broadwater. By the beginning of the 13th century it is the authors' opinion that quite a substantial area of the Broadwater was silted up, and that it was drained by the methods previously described. The term 'Little Broadwater' could well have described the water channels thus remaining, especially when compared with the size of the original inlet. The field of Little Broadwater was recorded in the late 13th century.[32]

Documents of Wiston Manor show some Broadwater land being held by tenants of Wiston from *c.*1254-1490, and later in 1526 there is a specific mention of tenants of Wiston holding land in Little Broadwater.[33] If indeed Broadwater Common Brook is identified as the manor of Little Broadwater, then perhaps it is not a coincidence that there are no mentions of it between 1490 and 1526, especially as this would seem to fall in line with the date of flooding in 1493 mentioned earlier. Another fact which tends to substantiate the above is that open fields were recorded for Little Broadwater and the title 'Broadwater Common Brooks' indicates open or common land.

*Braziers Field* is not shown as such on the 1720 map, and it seems most likely that this field was originally part of the Broadwater Common Brooks.

For many years Little Broadwater descended with Lyons Farm, and as the area under discussion lies immediately to the south of and adjacent to Lyons Farm land, it would seem to add further weight to the possibility that Broadwater Common Brook is the same place, or part of, Little Broadwater.

*The Quagmire* is an old enclosure near the above area which signifies an exceptionally boggy place. John Field in his book shows examples of names such as 'Quag Field', 'Quag Meadow[34] and 'Mirey Spinney', 'Mirey Moor', all meaning 'boggy land'. The Ordnance Survey map (6 inch) of 1869 shows a small pond on the site (this area is now covered by the entrance of the modern Penfold Road from Dominion Road).

*The Pits* was shown under this title on the enclosure map of 1806. Recently a borehole was sunk very near to this small field, and at 1.2 metres deep gravel was found. It is therefore most likely that the field took its name from pits excavated for obtaining gravel, probably for repair to the roads, similar to the area allotted for obtaining gravel on Broadwater Green. Another indication of reclaiming land from the sea can be seen if one considers the *West and East Knowles*. The name 'Knowles', 'Knowle Field', 'Knole' etc. are all examples of the name which means 'land with hillocks' from the Old English word 'cnoll'.[35] It is most probable that these hillocks were the residue obtained from the salt pans which were prevalent in this area in Saxon times and after. Peter Brandon in his book *The Sussex Landscape* mentions that salt-making has left its impression on the Sussex marshes by these low mounds. Salt water was retained by trenches or dykes and let off into shallow impressions dug in the marshes; the brine was leached out and boiled in 'salt-houses'.[36] After many years the residue formed small mounds which would lead to an area described as having hillocks, hence the name 'Knowles'. Apparently these salt-works marked the rapidly-retreating edges of the marshlands, and although the date of these two particular brooks are not known it must have been before 1300 for two brooks known as *Sagebrook and Swinebrook*, lying further south, were recorded *c.*1300.[37]

These two areas of approximately 100 acres of valuable meadow can be associated with the area which later contained a number of brooks lying adjacent to Cokeham. These measured approximately 76 acres in the 19th century (see map). The two original brooks were part of Broadwater Manor's demesne and in 1604 the Lord of Broadwater granted them to Sir John Caryll of Warnham and they descended with Lyons Farm until at least 1680.[38] A map of 1622 of the marshes at Lancing actually shows an area of brooks as belonging to Sir John Caryll.[39] Correlation of this map, later maps, and other data is sufficient to show that these areas coincide.

Another interesting piece of marshland is the *Hagbrook Meads*, which may have had ancient origins. John Field in his book gives an example of 'Hagg Meadow' and states that it is a 'place cleared of trees' from the old Norman word 'hogg'.[40] Although this origin seems unlikely for a place known to have been underwater, there is ample evidence of land in the Sussex marshes containing trees from a much earlier period.

It is recorded in 1799 that at Felpham near Bognor a north-east hurricane exposed a portion of submarine forest about five feet below the surface.[41] Large portions of the trunks of trees matted together with reeds, oak-leaves etc. were found. The same storm also exposed on the Strand, at low water, a large number of oak trees (over 40) all lying the same way, the largest diameter recorded being 4 feet. Similar trees have been observed after a north-east storm on Bognor beach. At Pevensey Levels the trunks of large trees have been found embedded in a mass of decayed vegetables. At Hoo Levels a submarine forest of over 200 trees was found, of oak and birch, the same species as found in the Sussex Woods. These trees are under 10 feet of water at high tide.[42] It is quite possible, therefore, that similar tree stumps may have been found when the Hagbrook Meads were first drained.

There are references to watermills in Broadwater in 1086[43] and 1300,[44] and it is known that Broadwater church received 14 shillings from mill-tithes in 1341.[45] A Cutmill Watermill was destroyed before 1493;[46] a Cutmill Lane is recorded in 1616 and 1635;[47] a *Millpond Meadow* in the same area in the early 18th century probably indicates the site of this watermill. The seamill was mentioned in 1576,[48] while 'Sea Myll' is shown on the previously mentioned map of 1622 at a site near the sea, later known as Semells or Semills Bridge (built *c.*1752[49]). These watermills were often established by tidal rivers, so that the ebb and flow of the tide produced the power for the mill.

It is known that by about 1250 the shingle beach had reached at least to the south-east of Lancing to form the Port of Pende.[50] This port was in the mouth of the channel to the south east of Lancing which eventually flowed up into the Broadwater and was mentioned between 1250 and 1420. It appears that further movement eastward of the shingle beach caused the disappearance of the port. In 1571 a dam was built across the channel at a place now known as Shopsdam Road at South Lancing (near the junction of Old Salts Farm Road and the Brighton Road). This dam contained a sluice which drained the land at low tide and consequently prevented the tidal water from returning to the Broadwater at high tide. This inning was carried out by the Lord of the Manor of Lancing, Sir Henry Goring, who was then able to reclaim more valuable land to add to his manor. It would also appear that he managed to reclaim some of the marshland lying in the Manor of Broadwater (see map) which adjoined his Lancing marshland at the south. These marshes are still shown belonging to the Goring family on the 1720 map, and they followed the same descent as Lancing Manor. It would seem that by the end of the 16th century most of the brooks have been reclaimed. The work 'brooks', as used in Sussex, does not mean a stream but the whole area of marshy ground.[51]

*The Town Mead and the Ham* were two common meadows or pastures recorded in the early 17th century.[52] Richard Newland was allotted the Town Mead of approximately 9¼ acres in 1810. The word 'ham' originates from Old English and means 'enclosure land beside a river'.[53] As the brooks were drained the 'ham' would have been adjacent to the main river or stream on the east and south. On the 1720 map is a road shown leading to the Ham and Chesswood Pastures (modern Dominion Road).

The same map shows the *Read Meads*, two fields known as the West and East Pastures. The spelling of 'Read' has caused some confusion as to its origin. If pronounced 'reed' then

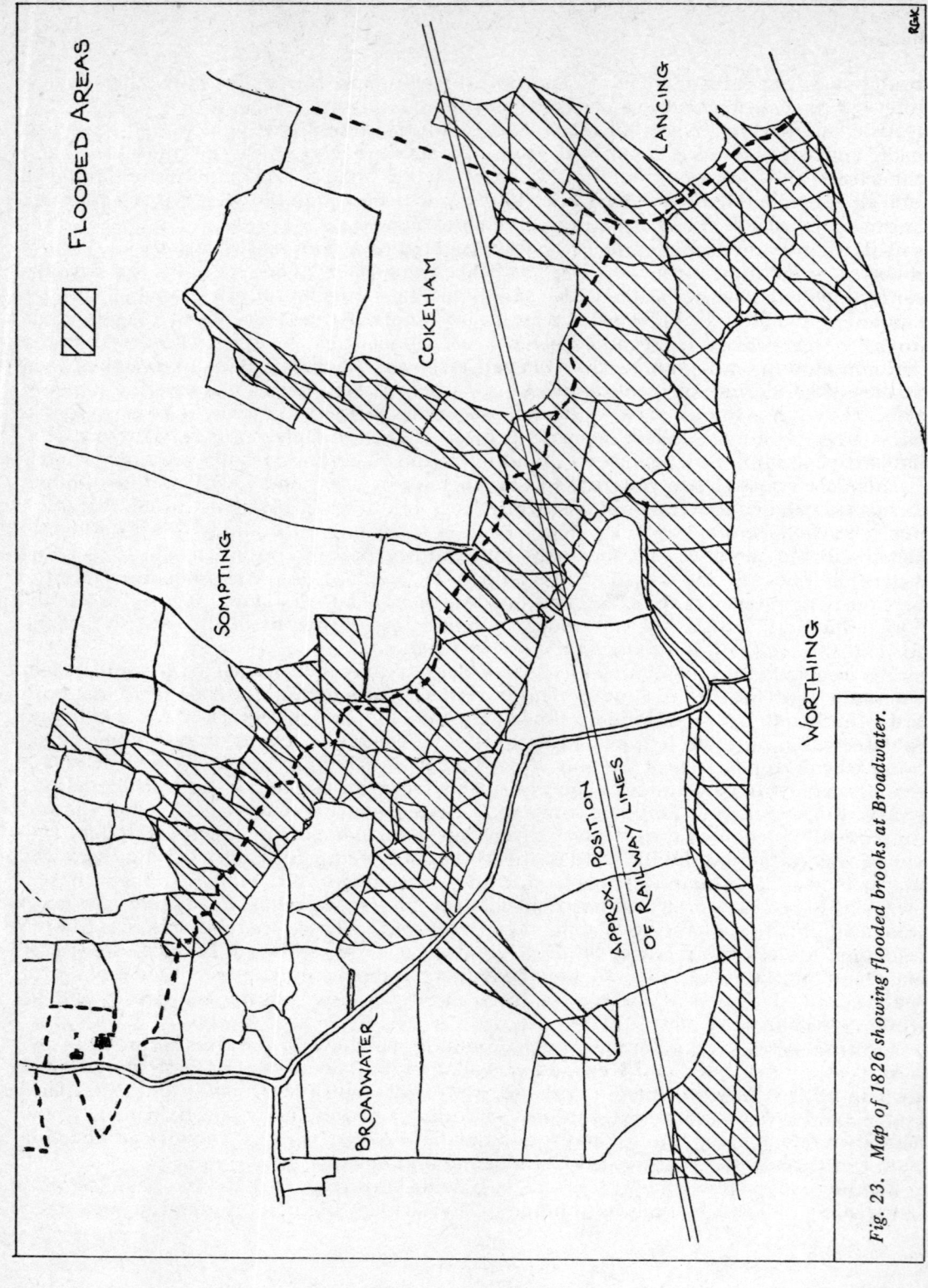

FLOODED AREAS

Fig. 23. *Map of 1826 showing flooded brooks at Broadwater.*

its origin was undoubtedly from the Old English 'hreod' and refers to 'land on which reeds grow'.[54] If the word was pronounced 'red' as shown on the 1806 Enclosure Map (Little Red Meads) then its origin could have originated from 'land with red soil' from Old English 'read'. However, given its marshy beginnings, it is most likely that the origin is one connected with reeds.

In 1820 a remarkable incident occurred when the sea breached the lower road to Lancing, presumably during a storm, and flooded the brooks, probably reverting almost to its medieval situation for a brief period.[55] The authors were fortunate in discovering a map drawn in 1826 bearing the title "A map made in pursuance of an Act passed in the seventh year of the Reign of His Majesty King George the Fourth entitled 'An Act for making and maintaining a Turnpike Road from Worthing to Lancing in the Country of Sussex and Groynes, Embankments and other Sea Defences for protecting such Road and the lands adjoining from the future encroachments of the sea' of lands in the Town of Worthing and Parishes of Broadwater, Lancing and Sompting and Hamlet of Cokeham in the said Act subject to an Annual Assessment". It was surveyed by Ralph Joanes.[56] A copy of this map has been reproduced showing the flooded area as diagonal hatching. Apparently from 1826 land alongside the streams paid a special protection rate against being flooded by the sea.[57] It is interesting to note that the Ordnance Survey map (6 inches to the mile) of 1869 shows the brooks area as still liable to flooding.

With the coming of the railway, the town's potential market was enlarged, and the area of the brooks became one of the parish's most valuable assets as land suitable for market gardeners. In recent years much of this land has been redeveloped for light industrial purposes, and is now known as the East Worthing Trading Estate.

## Broadwater Manor Farm

During the medieval period Broadwater appears to have been an important manor with owners such as Robert le Savage, Sir John de Gatesden and Sir John de Camoys. However, during the middle part of its history, most of its manorial lords lived elsewhere, and from the 15th century onwards it diminished in importance to become a farm.[58] During the early part of the Georgian period, the manor changed hands several times until it was sold to John Newland, the tenant of Broadwater Farm[59] in 1793, by Patty Clough. (In 1752 George Penfold was tenant, by 1780 Messrs Penfold & Newland and in 1790, John Newland.) The farm included 834 acres in the 1780s and until 1783 it was the largest estate in the parish. John Newland then sold some 471 acres, the northern part of the farm including Cissbury Ring, to William Margesson of Offington.[60]

John Newland (who died in 1806) devised his farm to his eldest son, John Newland Junior who, like his father, held a number of parochial offices.[61] In 1848 John Newland Junior died and the farm passed to Harry Newland, his youngest brother. (John Newland Senior's other sons had all previously died–William in 1790, George in 1815 and Richard in 1839.) Harry Newland took a part in local affairs and acquired a large amount of property in Worthing. He died in 1857 and the property reverted to his widow Ann. From 1836 onwards the Surveyors books of Broadwater show part of John Newland's estate being sold off in pieces. After 1870, when Harry's widow Ann died, the farm then passed to John Newland Junior's daughters Emily, Frances and Harriet. In 1880 the daughters, the ladies of the manor, settled it on William Foard Tribe, a local solicitor and steward of the manor. The three ladies had gone to Cheltenham after their parents had died, and Tribe was the tenant of the Broadwater Manor House. His daughter Fanny owned the manor by 1895. During the period 1870-1929 there were several private occupiers of the Manor House, the last two being the Misses Annie and Edith Nicholls who purchased it from the Trustees of

W. F. Tribe. After Edith died in 1928, Annie Nicholls sold the house, together with approximately 11 acres of land, to the Seaview Estates Development Company. Early in 1930 the property was purchased by the Rev. J. D. Burton and Mr. M. D. Neligan, who turned it into the boys' preparatory school, known as Broadwater Manor House School, which still survives today.[62]

The manor house iself never attained the grandeur and size of Offington, but was mentioned in 1256 together with a private chapel.[63] The present building appears to be a mixture of several dates, the oldest part being the north wing with rubble walls and a late medieval roof. The main house is apparently part of a longer 17th-century timber-framed house extending east and west. A south wing was added by 1720[64] and a new block added in the early 19th century. Other recent alterations include new building to the north of the house and the rebuilding of parts of the old 17th-century building.

## Decoy Farm

This farm, originally part of Broadwater Manor, lay to the south-east of the village in the area of the brooks, and may well have been on the site of Pechwick, a dairy farm recorded from the late 13th century.[66] Decoy Farm is depicted on the map of c.1720 when it consisted of approximately 23 acres. It undoubtedly took its name from the decoy pond, which was roughly rectangular in shape with an arm at each corner, and was designed to snare wild fowl and ducks.[67] The pond is shown as 'The Coy' on the 1720 map and had probably been in existence for many years. However, John Evans in his *Picture of Worthing* in 1805 stated that the pond was no longer there and that the farm was a dairy farm. It appears that it remained as such during the 1820s when it supplied much of Worthing's milk.[68]

By 1792 the farm had been enlarged to approximately 83 acres, and when John Newland died in 1806 the farm was devised to his son Richard, who was allotted 71 acres at the enclosure of Broadwater.[69] William Newland owned the farm by the middle of the 19th century and over the latter part of the century parts of the farmland were sold off. The farmhouse was situated near the junction of the modern Dominion and Harrison Roads and is shown on the 1720 map. However, it was demolished by 1909[70] and all that now remains to commemorate the farm is Decoy Villas in Dominion Road, although the name on the block of houses is almost obliterated.

## Lyons Farm

This farm, originally the Manor of Lyons, straddled the boundary between Broadwater and Sompting parishes. It is thought to be associated with the Lyons family of Broadwater and Sompting, of which there are records between 1288 and 1366.[71] One of the more important members of this family was Henry de Lyons, a knight, who held land in Broadwater in 1296[72] and attained several offices during his lifetime. He was elected as a magistrate for the county of Sussex in September 1279, a Guildford Gaol Delivery Justice in 1292, and he was summoned for military service in 1297. It was recorded that he held land in Chichester, Arundel, Bramber and Pevensey rapes.[73] There do not appear to be any more mentions of the Lyons family name after 1349; it has been suggested that the family was wiped out by the Black Death and thus the holding reverted to the overlord of Broadwater.

However by the late 15th century the manor was held by Richard Grandford whose grand-daughter, Parnel, wife of John Shirley of Isfield, held it in 1501.[74] In 1544 it was held by John's son Edward who sold the reversion to Sir William Goring of Burton (nephew of John's second wife Margery)[75] and it appears that he held the manor five years later.[76] As Sir William Goring held the Manor of Lancing at that time, he incorporated Lyons' title in with his Lancing estates to form 'The Manor of North Lancing and Monks, South Lancing, and Lyons'. Although this combined title remained for the Lancing Manors until its dispersion in the 1920s, Lyons did not actually descend with it, for in 1587 Edward Jenny granted Lyons to Edward Apsley, who was possibly his brother-in-law.[77] Sir John Caryll of Warnham is recorded as holding the manor in 1595[78] and after his death it apparently descended with the West Harting manor until at least 1680[79] when it seems that Richard Penfold was tenant.[80] John Penfold had the freehold before his death in 1738, his son John being his heir.[81]

A list showing land tax in 1752,[82] suggests that 'Lyons Farm and Taylors' were owned by Mrs. Penfold, possibly the wife of John who died in 1738. 'Taylors' is undoubtedly Taylors Mead, parts of which fall in both parishes totalling 8½ acres (see Fig. 24). There is an Allen Taylor recorded in the Vestry accounts of Broadwater for 1663, 1678 and 1694[83] who may be associated with these old enclosures.

An advertisement which appeared in the *Sussex Advertiser* on Monday 11 June 1770 shows that a John Penfold occupied (and almost certainly owned) Lyons Farm. This is probably the son John mentioned previously, whose father died in 1738. The advertisement also shows that the farm contained 240 acres. During the Georgian and Victorian periods, and probably for many years before, the boundary between the parishes of Broadwater and Sompting traced out a most peculiar path through the southern part of the farm, passing through the farmhouse west to east (see map). This put the outbuildings and farm cottages in Broadwater parish, and the major portion of the house in Sompting Parish!

A study of the Broadwater Land Tax records which are deposited at West Sussex Record Office, Chichester, shows that a Reverend John Penfold owned the farm in 1780 with Mr. John Baker as occupier. Over the next 35 years the farm was owned by various members of the Penfold family as follows: 1782-4, owner William Penfold, occupier Mr. Henry Duke; 1785-89, owners Messrs. Penfold and Newland, occupier Mr. Henry Duke; 1790-95, owner Hugh Penfold, occupier Mr. Henry Duke/John Penfold; 1796-1815, owner John Penfold. In 1806 the farm consisted of approximately 221 acres (212 acres in Sompting parish and nine in Broadwater). In 1813 Charles Groome acquired the property as owner/occupier and was succeeded by Thomas Groome in 1829.

The shaded areas shown on the map of the farm in 1834 (Fig. 24) were those fields which were not part of the farm at the time of the enclosure in 1806. The north field was allotted to Mr. John Ford in 1806 and in 1818 was owned by James Stubbs, from whom it was acquired in about 1833 to form part of Lyons Farm. The 'Old Orchard' and 'The Braziers' were part of the estate of Samuel Heather in 1806 and Edward Penfold in 1813. It appears that these two enclosures were also acquired as part of Lyons Farm in about 1833. The addition of this land brought the total acreage of the farm to 257 acres by 1834. The map shown has been produced from two separate maps, both drawn in 1834. The first map was surveyed and drawn by William Figg of Lewes, and only depicts the southern part of the farm, namely, the fields surrounding the farmhouse. The second map is the tithe map of Sompting parish drawn by John Adams of Hawkhurst, Kent, which shows all the land belonging to Lyons Farm lying in Sompting. By 1857 Thomas Groome's son Charles was the new owner when the farm contained approximately 300 acres.[84]

By 1857 H. P. Crofts had acquired Lyons Farm and it was later recorded as 313 acres, most of the additional acreage being the brooklands in Broadwater which were obtained from Edward Barker sometime between 1836 and 1846. Later, in 1879, a settlement was made, in contemplation of a marriage between Blanche Ellen Crofts (H. P. Crofts' daughter) and Samuel Barrington Tristam.[85] By the 1920s a development had begun round the house and in 1923 Blanche Ellen Tristam and others sold the farm. There were a number of transactions in the 1930s when the farm changed hands several times. In the

1940s most of the northern part of the farm above the Upper Brighton Road was occupied by Lyons Farm nurseries.[86] In 1956 Worthing Corporation (now Worthing Borough Council) purchased the farmhouse and a small area of ground. The farmhouse was demolished and the land became 'Lyons Farm Recreation Ground', and it is now maintained by Worthing Borough Council (1982).

In 1902 the boundary was changed and approximately nine acres of Lyons Farm in Broadwater were placed in Sompting parish. (Points A and B were joined up on the map thus losing the peculiar area as shown previously.) In 1933, however, the whole of Lyons Farm and Upton Farm were placed under Worthing Borough Council.

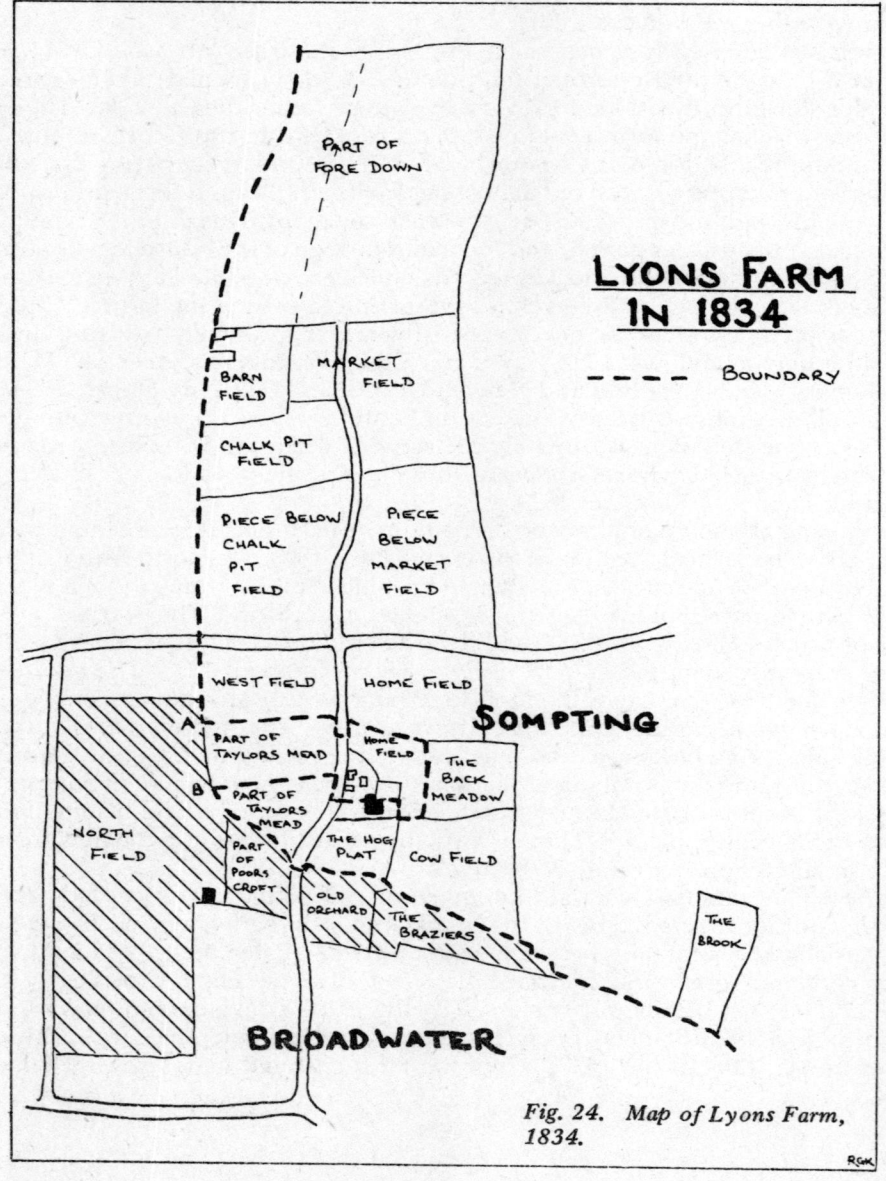

Fig. 24.  Map of Lyons Farm, 1834.

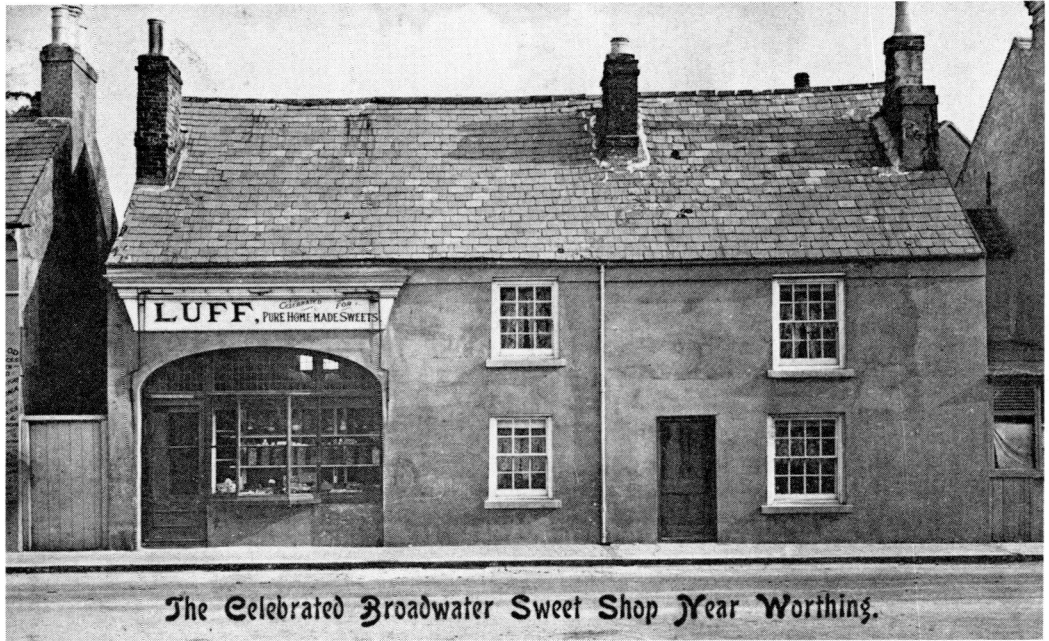

This early 20th-century photograph shows the old cottages north of *The Cricketers*, the latter being the tallest of the ee buildings. The old buildings on the right stand on the site now covered by a property once used as 'Boorer's Garage showrooms'.

2.  Luff's sweet shop in Broadwater Street West, now converted into two modern shops (see Section 1, no. 7).

The Celebrated Broadwater Sweet Shop Near Worthing.

3.  A view of Broadwater Street West at the turn of the century, looking north, showing *The Cricketers* on the right and the Old Forge on the left (see Section 1, no. 8).

4.  Pear Tree Cottage in May 1860, just prior to its demolition. The cottage stood at the site at the northern end of the modern 'Cricketers' Parade' (see Section 2, no. 12).

. Broadwater Street West, looking south, c.1912. Wheatland's shop and 'Rose Villa' are on the left (see Section 3, nos. 16 and 17) and 'Gower Cottage' and 'Broadwater House' are on the right (see Section 13, nos. 62 and 63).

6. 'Rose Villa', early this century. The large tree is in the entrance of a small field to the north of the old *Maltster's* public house.

The buildings which replaced Rose Villa, built in the late 1920s and seen here about 1930 (see Section 3, no. 17).

8. The school children on their way home from the old school on the green c.1904.

*51 WORTHING - Broadwater Village Children going home from School. — LL.*

9. Broadwater Street East, c.1916, showing 'Northgate Cottages' on the left (see Section 4, no. 21) and old cottages converted into shops on the right (see Section 12, no. 60).

10. The flint building is 'Ivy Cottage' and 'St Mary's', in Broadwater Street East (see Section 4, no. 24).

1. Broadwater's oldest dated house (1701). This photograph was taken in July 1960, just prior to its demolition (see Section 5, no. 28).

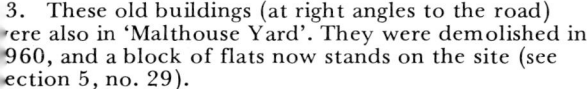

12. Old cottages in the area known as 'Malthouse Yard' (see Section 5, no. 29).

3. These old buildings (at right angles to the road) were also in 'Malthouse Yard'. They were demolished in 1960, and a block of flats now stands on the site (see Section 5, no. 29).

14. The demolition of some of the 'Malthouse Yard' cottages in July 1960.

15. A view looking west along Broadwater Street East in 1959. On the left is 'Alma Cottages', with an antique shop. All these were demolished in 1960 (see Section 5, no. 30).

16. Another view of 'Alma Cottages' in 1959.

17.   Broadwater Street East, *c.*1912. The shop at left is the Post Office (see Section 5, no. 30).

18.   Broadwater Street looking east, *c.*1915. On the extreme left is the old Broadwater Fire Station, next door to the *Old House at Home* public house (see Section 6, nos. 31-33).

19.   Old South Terrace in Broadwater Street East. The buildings have been demolished and replaced by 'Knowles' Bakery' buildings (see Section 6, no. 33).


20.   The shop shown here is now 'Jex the Newsagent'. At the side can be seen evidence of the former adjoining buildings, which were known as 'Cooks Cottages' (see Section 8, no. 37).

1. The fine old flint built house shows a date of 1887 (see Section 7, no. 36). The shop is that now occupied by 'Jex the Newsagent', whose former premises were in 'Eastern Terrace' in Sompting Road.

2. (above) 'Jex's' shop in its former premises on the corner of Southfield Road and Sompting Road. This block—Eastern Terrace—was demolished when the Sompting Road was widened (see Section 8, no. 9).

3. (right) Sompting Road looking north, before widening. In the centre is 'Clifton Cottages', and further down the road is 'Carter's Bakery'. All the buildings on the left have been demolished (see Section 8).

24.   Two late Victorian terraces on the corner of Sompting Road and Dominion Road. On the left is Oxford Terrace, and Cambridge Terrace is on the right (see Section 9, nos. 50 and 51).

25.   On the right is the side of the old 'Elm Cottages' which were demolished in the late 1960s. On their site is the present 'B & Q' do-it-yourself store (see Section 8, no. 38). In the centre is the *Elms* public house (see Section 10, no. 53).

5. The house on the end of this parade of shops at the corner of Broadwater Street East and Beaumont Road is now bakery and a wool shop.

27. 'Acorn Cottage' in Broadwater Street East (see Section 11, no. 57).

28.  Broadwater Church from a pre-1826 engraving, before its spire was removed (see Section 12, no. 59).

29.  The cottages near the church are now shops, and the cottage at right was demolished many years ago (see Section 12, no. 60).

30. (*right*) The old Rectory 'Muir House' in June 1959; it was demolished in August of that year (see Section 13, no. 61).

31. (*below*) Old 'Broadwater House' with a workman on a ladder and 'Gower Cottage' in 1930, a few years before their demolition for road widening (see Section 13, nos. 62 and 63).

32. Broadwater Street West looking north, showing 'Broadwater House', 'Gower Cottage' and 'Bath House' on the left (see Section 13, nos. 62-65).

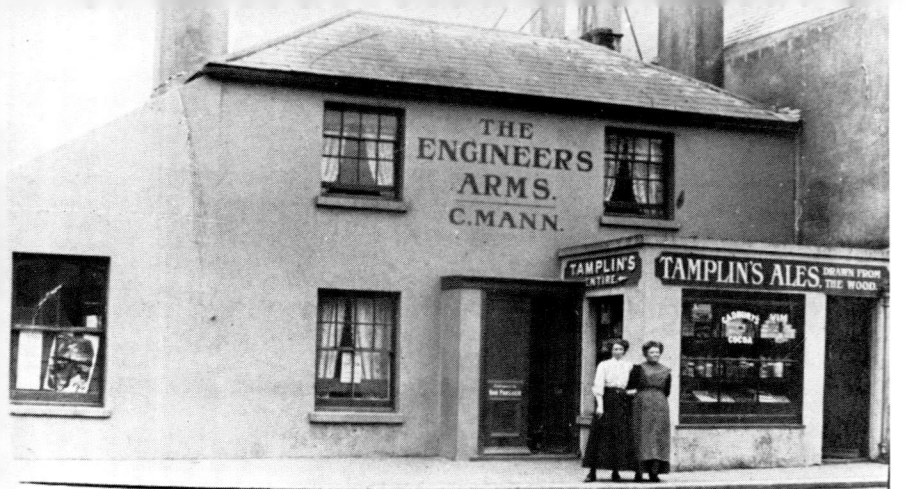

33. *The Engineer's Arms,* on a site now occupied by the eastern end of Paine & Manwaring's showrooms (see Section 13, no. 69).

34. (*right*) Paine, Manwaring & Lephard's shop window in the late 1920s (see Section 13, no. 70).

35. (*below*) A steam engine belonging to Paine, Manwaring & Lephard Ltd., hauling three vehicles belonging to Jordan & Co.

36. (*above*) Paine, Manwaring & Lephard's premises in 1938, when the old forge on the corner of the green was being demolished (see Section 13, no. 70).

37. (*right*) This 18th-century cottage to the west of Paine & Manwaring's shop still stands today (this photograph was taken in 1960) (see Section 14, no. 71).

38. Children at play by the old school on the green (see Section 14, no. 72).

PAINE, MANWARING & LEPHARD, LTD.

**1725.**

**1925.**

BI - CENTENARY COMMEMORATION

# DINNER

AT THE

PARISH ROOM, BROADWATER,

## On Friday, December 4th, 1925,

At 7 o'clock.

39. This is the cover of the menu for the firm's Bicentenary Commemoration Dinner. The small picture shows the original forge on the green, c.1880, with the old school behind (see Section 14, nos. 72 and 73).

40. The old forge of Paine, Manwaring & Lephard, with the school just visible behind. Further to the rear is the drinking fountain presented to the villagers by the Ladies of the Manor, the Misses Newland.

*Chapter Four*

# *A Pictorial Survey*

To set the atmosphere of bygone Broadwater, a Pictorial Survey has been prepared. To assist in the location of the properties shown on the plates a plan has been prepared (see Chapter Five) based on the Ordnance Survey map of 1898, on which each building, or group of buildings has been given a number. This number, when appropriate, is shown below the plate and refers to the historical notes of the relevant property in Chapter Five.

*Chapter Five*

# Broadwater Street

W. G. Hoskins states in the introduction to his book of 12 essays on England, *One Man's England*, that 'Every few square miles of England has its marked character'. Broadwater is no exception, for its character at any given time in history is totally reflective of the people, their occupations, and the various properties that comprise the village. In this chapter, a detailed history of Broadwater Street, all these ingredients have been used to capture the character of Georgian and Victorian Broadwater.

When considering the architectural styles of the properties known to have been constructed either before or during the Georgian period, the immediate reaction is to anticipate the discovery of some half-timbered medieval buildings, interspersed with the typical Georgian or Regency houses, whether in a terrace or as a detached villa. As can be seen, such anticipation when applied to the properties of Broadwater Street is, however, possibly incorrect, for village architecture of this period appears different in concept. Most of the buildings of this period that survive were constructed in the most readily-available local material–flint. This was usually knapped, laid in either random or regular courses. Some have unfortunately been subsequently faced with render, disguising their former charm. Without a doubt, the roofs of those properties that date from the beginning of the 18th century were originally covered with thatch, having possibly been laid by John Hide, the local thatcher. Thatch was as practical as it was beautiful, being warm in winter and cool in summer, and was also easily adaptable and therefore able to fit almost any shape of roof. Hence the interesting shapes of the earlier cottages that survive adjacent to the northern side of the churchyard. By the end of the Georgian period, however, slates, which easily split into thin sheets, became a substitute for thatch.

Our research has shown that from *c.*1800 some farm labourers' cottages had been built by small speculative builders, either in rows or in ones or twos wherever small parcels of land had become available. From the probate returns it appears they rarely contained more than two or three rooms, and were often cramped and insanitary. Some of the older houses, owned by the established tradesmen, became sub-divided into labourers' cottages, when they built their own new houses.

Most of the Victorian additions to Broadwater were terraced buildings, many of which were built by the wealthy tradesmen for their workers. Most were constructed of brick, and nearly all were two storeys high, their dimensions being controlled by by-laws imposed by the new, socially-minded, local authorities. The initial expansion of Victorian Broadwater was restrained by both topographical and man-made restrictions. The shape of the old open field system, now owned by individuals; the established road patterns; and the numerous ditches all hindered development, which in turn resulted in some of the older houses being either redeveloped or reconstructed in Victorian style.

### Historical notes on the properties
In the historical notes which follow there are continual references to certain records. As they have probably never been used before for a history of the Broadwater area, a small list

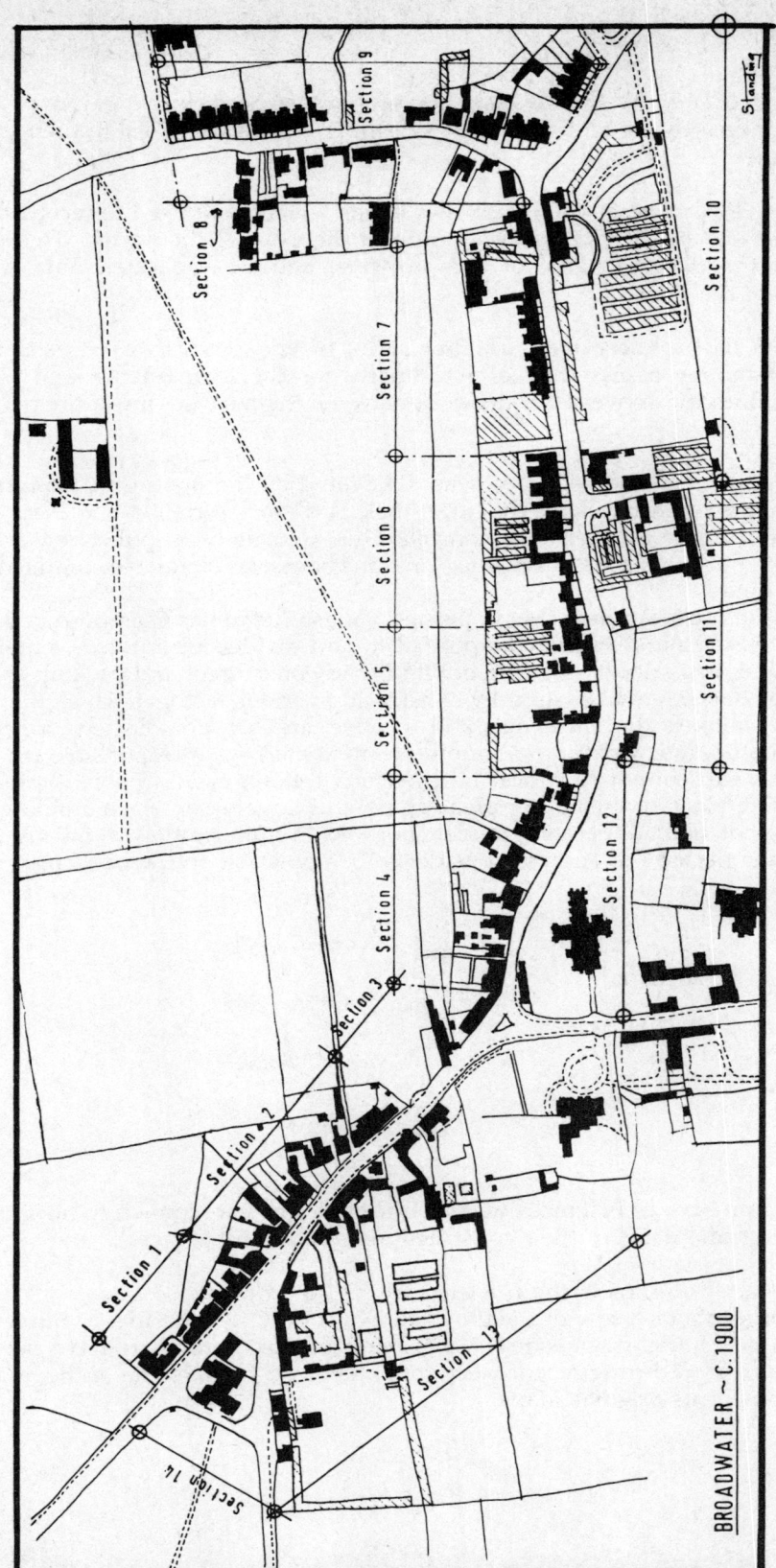

*Fig. 25. Master plan of Broadwater.*

BROADWATER ~ C.1900

Section 1
Section 2
Section 3
Section 4
Section 5
Section 6
Section 7
Section 8
Section 9
Section 10
Section 11
Section 12
Section 13
Section 14

of them, together with a brief explanation of their use has been prepared for the interested reader. The records are all held by the Worthing Borough Council in their archives. They are as follows:

a) *Poor Rate Books*. These were a series of books which were used to record the amount of money assessed of each property to support the poor of the parish. This was 4s in the pound on the rateable value of the property, and was collected once a year by the Overseers of the Poor.

b) *Surveyors Books*. These were another series of books which were used to record the amount of money assessed of each property for the maintenance and upkeep of the highways. Both the above series of books between them cover  the entire period of 1818 to 1894.

c) A very important undated book was discovered by the Borough's Honorary Archivist; subsequent research revealed that the book is almost certainly the local enumerator's hand-written copy of the 1821 census. This Census was published by the central government purely as a list of statistics, and this book was obviously compiled to obtain the necessary details.

To assist in the location of the properties, a master plan has been prepared (Fig. 25). It is based on the Ordnance Survey map of 1898, and divided up into convenient sections in chronological order down one side of Old Broadwater Street and back up the other. Each section was determined by carefully considering various factors such as the geography of the area, whether the buildings still survive and, if demolished, whether modern developments (road widening, shopping centres etc.) were responsible for their demolition. In the subsequent historical notes which follow, each section is preceded by the appropriate portion of the master plan, drawn to a larger scale. Each building is numbered and shown hatched on these larger scale portions in conformity with the key below, which identifies the period the authors consider to be applicable to the building.

Georgian

Victorian

Out buildings

Glasshouses

There are a number of instances when earlier buildings are known to have existed on the site, although the dates of their construction are unknown.

**Section 1–Parish Rooms to the** *Cricketers* (Nos. 1-8 on plan)
This section contains a row of buildings shown on the 1898 Ordnance Survey map which still exist (No. 3 was demolished). A number of these buildings have been renovated, modified or rebuilt during recent years, but still either retain some of the original fabric of the buildings or its original shape.

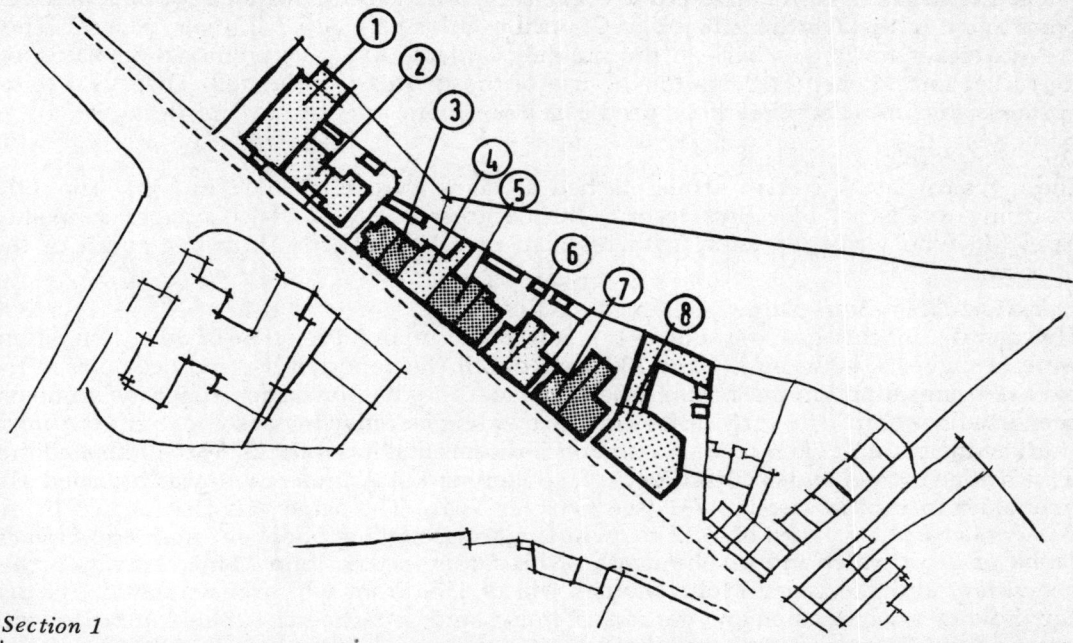

*Section 1*

| Nº | DESCRIPTION | MODERN ADDRESS | CURRENT USE |
|---|---|---|---|
| 1 | Parish Rooms | Broadwater St. [West] | Hired Room |
| 2 | Oak Cottages | 86/88 " " " | Residential |
| 3 | Ruby House | 82/84 " " " | Modern Shop |
| 4 | House | 80 " " " | Shop |
| 5 | Houses | 76/76A/78 " " " | Shops/Commercial |
| 6 | Houses | 72/74 " " " | Commercial |
| 7 | Houses | 68/70 " " " | Converted to shop |
| 8 | House | 66 " " " | Cricketers P.H. |

*The Parish Room* (No. 1 on plan)
This building, erected in 1889 as a Reading Room, was paid for by public subscription. It was originally administered by a management committee but by 1898 was apparently used very little. In 1900 it was run by the Parish Council continuing as a Parish Room and Reading Room.[1] During the typhoid epidemic of 1893 the room was used for the reception of cases when 22 patients were accommodated.

It is constructed of bricks and originally consisted of a large room or hall with living accommodation at the east end for a caretaker and his family. Over the years the Parish Room has been used by many organisations, including the Broadwater kindergarten for children over four years old, and, from the late 1920s as a headquarters for the 4th Worthing Girl Guides[2] and the 3rd Worthing Scouts.

The Parish Room is still hired out to organisations and is administered by the Amenities Department of the Worthing Borough Council.

A caretaker no longer lives in the building and the living accommodation has been converted into kitchen facilities for the use of those who hire the hall. There is a room upstairs which now appears to be used as a store-room.

### Oak Cottages (No. 2 on plan)

These typical late Victorian semi-detached cottages were brick built in 1884. The 1912 Worthing & District *Blue Book* records the occupier of No. 2 Oak Cottages as Walter Appleton who was proprietor, with his son, of a bootmaker's shop just south of the *Cricketers*.

### Ruby House (No. 3 on plan)

This pair of flint cottages, the subject of a newspaper report at the time of their demolition, were, it suggests, between 150 and 200 years old. It was reported that mortice holes in the old oak beams found in the building were unusual and that the beams may have originally been used in a ship. The early history of this building is somewhat obscure, but a thorough study of the Land Tax and other documents indicates that it is most likely that this building was the one owned and occupied by Ayling Shepherd of Arundel, who was recorded as a freeholder in Broadwater in 1731 (see Chapter Two). The same was also shown in the Broadwater Land Tax List of 1752 as owning a house. Ayling Shepherd married Margaret Monk of Broadwater and on the death of his father-in-law, John Monk, he was both a beneficiary and executor to John Monk's will of 1756 from which he inherited 'All that copyhold messuage, tenement, garden, premises and appartments situated in Broadwater occupied by Thomas Giles, and holden of the manor of Broadwater.' (Research has suggested that this building was on the site of the present *Cricketer's* public house). Ayling Shepherd died in 1757 but the Land Tax records show that his son, also Ayling, took over the property until 1820 when it was split and Edward Hards and family were occupiers of one part with Shepherd and his family apparently in the other. However, the census of 1821 shows that Shepherd and his family had by then removed to the previously mentioned inherited property of John Monk, leaving Edward Hard, his family and others to occupy the flint cottages, although Shepherd was still shown as the owner. In 1829 the property was acquired by Edward Briggs (whether from Shepherd or Hard it is not certain) and it remained in his possession until *c.*1851 when the Surveyors' Books show that a John Sayers became the owner for about the next 10 years. John Bright was the new owner for approximately a year in 1862, after which it was finally acquired by Robert Stather, who retained it for virtually the remainder of the Victorian period. During this time there were a number of different tenants, the longest occupancies being those of the Tupper family, who are shown there in the census returns for 1841 and 1851, and David Harrison from 1871 to the late 1890s.

For the majority of the time a single family resided in the house but in the early 1820s and again later in the 1860s two families were in occupancy. By 1907, the building was numbered 84 and 82 Broadwater Street (later Broadwater Street West) and named Ruby House.[4] Later in 1912 it was shown as Ruby Cottage.[2] Although two families again occupied the building at the turn of this century only one central door in the front is shown in all the known photographs.

In January 1955, the building was demolished and the newspaper report previously mentioned also informed the readers that there was an old oak beam found above an inglenook fireplace. The existing modern commercial shop was built by B.I.C. Ltd. on its site and it was for many years 'Meredith's' the toy shop.

*House* (No. 4 on plan)

According to the Surveyors' Books and the Ordnance Survey map of 1875 this two-storey house was built between 1868 and 1873 but very little else of its original history has emerged. In 1907 the Household Compendium for Worthing shows that the house was named 'Haslemere', a name which was used for several years. When the adjacent building to the north (Ruby Cottage) was demolished in 1955 a newspaper report [3] mentioned that the house was to be adapted for use as a shop together with living accommodation. Before such work was carried out dimensional sketches of the original house were made and are reproduced here.

At the present time (1982) the building is utilised as the 'Worthing Gun Shop'.

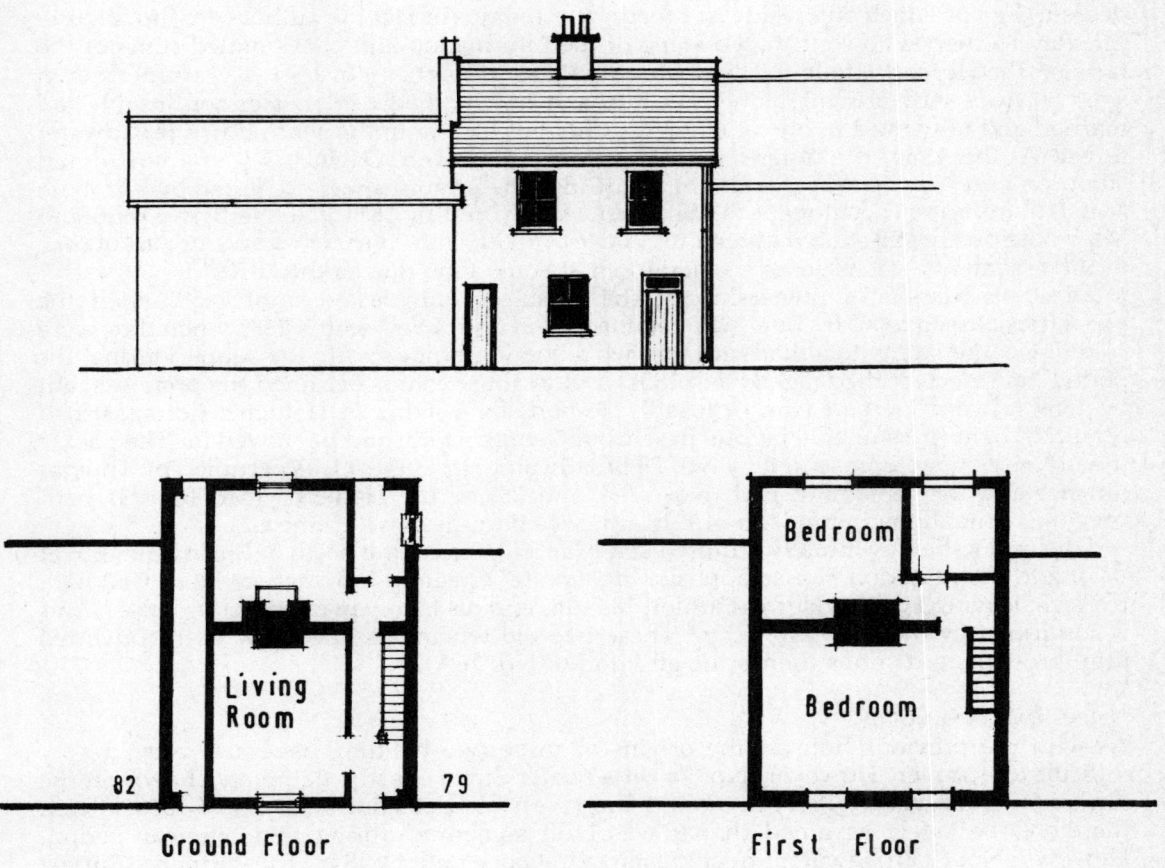

*Fig. 26.   Measured survey—80 Broadwater Street (West).*

*Houses* (No. 5 on plan)

The origin of these two houses is uncertain but all the available evidence indicates that they were originally copyhold premises and, as such, were not entered separately in the Land Tax records. The 1806 enclosure map shows tenements on this site and it seems quite evident from the style and condition of the present buildings that they are the same. It is also quite possible that they are much earlier than 1806, but as yet no positive evidence has been obtained to substantiate this. In 1821 the census shows the premises were owned by Mr. Ayling Shepherd, with various tenants who included Thomas Herbert of Broadwater (baptised 1779) and his wife Jane from Findon, a laundress. Thomas was one of the sons of William Herbert who was originally from Lancing. He married Mary Burchett of Broadwater and may well have lived in the same premises before his son. William and Mary Herbert were the ancestors of the old Broadwater family of Herbert, several descendants of which still reside in Broadwater today. (In fact the authors are indebted to Mr. Ray Herbert who contributed some of the information and corroborated some of the facts on the Herbert family for the history of these properties.) In 1841 Jane Herbert, then aged 60, was shown living alone, her husband having died earlier. Her son Joseph had married and now lived in one of Holden's Cottages further to the south down Broadwater Street. At this time, the other tenants in the building were David Baker, an agricultural labourer, and his wife Mary. Later in about 1848 the premises were acquired by Elizabeth Marshall from the executors of the Shepherd family and by 1851 Jane Herbert, David and Mary Baker were still shown as tenants. A deed of 1904[5] informs us that one, or part of one, of the tenements was used as a schoolroom at some time during the 1850s.

Elizabeth Marshall's ownership of the premises only lasted until 1850 when the properties passed to a Mr. Tate, who retained them until 4 September 1888 when they were sold to George Paine, together with the two adjoining properties to the south. During this period Jane Herbert died (aged 70 in 1851) and various tenants occupied the premises, but by 1889 Edward Herbert (son of Joseph Herbert, then living in Holden's Cottages) had acquired them (presumably by purchase from George Paine) and he moved in. The part of the premises now represented by No. 78 Broadwater Street West was occupied by Thomas Butcher and the remaining part (Nos. 76A and 76) by the Herberts. (Mr. Ray Herbert, previously-mentioned grandson of Edward, was born in these premises.)

Edward Herbert eventually acquired some land further to the north in Broadwater Street West and built Gordon House opposite Broadwater Green in 1904, where he moved with his wife, leaving Edward Herbert junior, his son, and his family in the other premises. This is confirmed by the 1907 Directory.[4] These two old tenements have now been converted into three modern shops (hence the addition of No. 76A).

*Houses* (No. 6 on plan)

As with the previous houses, the origins of these two building have also proved very difficult to uncover. However, No. 74 Broadwater Street West is definitely shown on the tithe map (surveyed in 1848) but is not shown on Charles Hide's survey of 1838. It can, therefore, be safely assumed that it was built sometime during that ten-year period. However, No. 72 Broadwater Street West had not been built by 1848. The Ordnance Survey map of 1875 (surveyed in 1873) shows a rear return added to No. 74 creating a space in the front where No. 72 was later built. A painting of Broadwater about 1870[6] shows the empty space apparently used as a garden, with trees and a flint boundary wall.

The ownership of No. 74 follows the same descent as the previous buildings, viz. Elizabeth Marshall and then Mr. Tate. In about 1886 during Mr. Tate's ownership it appears that No. 72 was built in the space formerly used as a garden. Mr. Tate sold the buildings to George Paine on 4 September 1888 along with those to the north (Nos. 78, 76A and 76 Broadwater Street West). William Manwaring, junior, occupied No. 74 for several years from 1889. A deed [5] records that the two buildings were known as 'Belle Vue' in 1904 and an old photograph, assumed to be of a later period, shows No. 72 as the Broadwater dairy. The building still exists, but has been converted into modern shops.

*Houses* (No. 7 on plan)
The first positive proof of the existence of these two houses is shown on the enclosure map of 1806, although their appearance suggests a much earlier date. By the 1821 census they belonged to Mr. Ayling Shepherd with various tenants occupying them and by 1848 Thomas Gibbard had acquired them from the executors of the Shepherd family.

By 1853 Thomas Luff, who lived next door in a house on the site of the present *Cricketers* public house, took over the premises and let them to various tenants. In 1876 he moved into the northern half of the premises, the other half being let to George Hook, son of William Hook, a former shoemaker of Broadwater. In 1887 Thomas is shown as owner/occupier to both premises and by 1907 he had died and Mrs. Luff still lived there. At some time the northern part of the premises was converted into a shop, and for many years during the first half of the 20th century it was known as 'Luff's sweet shop'. The Worthing *Blue Book* Directories show Mrs. H. Luff in 1927 and Miss S. Luff in 1939/40 still maintaining the premises as a confectioners. The premises still in existence have now been completely converted into modern shops and at the time of writing (1982) they are split between two shops, 'Shelagh Cavanagh' and 'Gerrards'.

*House/Cricketers Public House* (No. 8 on plan)
On the site of the present *Cricketers* public house was an earlier house which all the available evidence suggests was very old, and it was most probably the copyhold premises of John Monk, who left it in his will of 1756 to his son-in-law Ayling Shepherd. At the time of the will the property was in the occupation of Thomas Giles and by 1821 Ayling Shepherd owned and occupied the property. In 1848 the property, together with the adjacent premises to the north, was acquired by Thomas Gibbard who, in the 1851 census, was described as a carpenter by trade from Westerham in Kent. He lived there with his children (his wife being, presumably, dead). Earlier, in about 1830 Thomas lived in a house opposite the churchyard (tithe no. 149) and the Overseers Records show that in February 1832 a Thomas Gibbard was Headborough of Broadwater, when he reported to the vestry meeting on the state of the beer shops in Broadwater. (The Headborough was a Constable or Deputy Constable who helped to maintain law and order).

In 1851 Thomas Gibbard had a lodger, Thomas Luff, who was described as a visitor from Kirdford in Sussex, a coach wheeler by trade. It appears that by 1853 Thomas Luff was the new owner/occupier of the property, for on 31 August 1853 it was annual licence day at the Petty Session and Thomas Luff of Broadwater, brewer, applied for a spirit licence for the house now used by him as a beerhouse and was refused. Opposing him was Mr. Edward Goodyer of the *Maltster's Arms* on behalf of the rector, parish officers and principal members of the village.[7] To obtain the significance of this refusal a clear picture of the drinking habits during this period is required, and we must revert to the 1830 Beerhouse Act which allowed any householder, who was assessed to pay the poor rate, to sell beer from his own house on payment of two guineas.[8]

Many of the early 18th-century publicans started by selling beer from their houses which resulted in heavy drinking. The Victorians also liked to drink, and this was made easy by the liberal opening hours (some opened from 5 a.m. to 12.30 a.m. on weekdays and 1 to 3 p.m. and 6 to 11 p.m. on Sunday).[9] The lower classes drank heavily on beer, rum and gin, the latter leading to an abundance of gin shops[10] causing many social problems for nearly half of Victoria's reign. However, during the 1850s the heavy drinking of early Georgian times was being discouraged, especially of spirits and maybe Mr. Goodyer's opposition to Thomas Luff's application for a spirit licence in 1853 was for moral reasons. One cannot, however, rule out the possibility that it might have meant opposition to his own establishment just down the road!

Thomas Luff remained as owner of this property until 1876 when he removed to his adjacent property. During this period the property was named the *Brewer's Arms* and this might have been when the old house was converted into a Victorian public house. During the 1870s there was an improvement in the beer and public houses due to the marked change in the general drinking habits, there being a decided preference for less drinking and lighter wines by the better classes.[10] By 1879, after several changes of ownership during the past three years, John Dudney was the new owner with Benjamin Read as the landlord. Old photographs of the public house show Dudney's advertisement for his beer on the side of the building.

By 1878 it was known as the *Cricketers Arms*[11] and in 1885 it was owned by Robert Mews and remained so for the rest of the Victorian period. In 1888 Mrs. M. J. Medlock, grandmother of the present licensee Mr. Wilfred Page, obtained the licence, but she may well have been in occupancy some years before. From 1924 Mr. W. Page's father was licensee until 1946, when the present licensee and his wife Jean took over. During the early 1890s there was an increase in palatial restaurants and a rise in the number of tea shop restaurants.[12] This would no doubt have been the reason why such a tea room was situated in the *Cricketers* during Mrs. Medlock's period as licensee.[13]

**Section 2–Site of Cricketers' Parade** (Nos. 9 to 15 incl. on plan)
This section contains all the buildings which were originally on the site of the modern Cricketers' Parade constructed in the early 1960s.

*Houses and Shop* (No. 9 on plan)
The 1898 Ordnance Survey map shows two houses set back from the street with other buildings at the front of the property. In the 1821 census only one building was recorded, owned by a Mr. Blaker, described as a house and garden inhabited by a poor man, William Richardson and his wife Mary. By 1838 it appears that the property was a workshop of Mr. William Blaker and remained as such for many years until 1860 when Blaker died. It was then in the hands of his executors until 1866 when Edward William Blaker took over. The continuation of this property is not clear but it appears that Robert Stather acquired it in 1869, and by 1874 there were three buildings recorded in the Surveyors' Books for this site. In 1886 the house and workshop of Walter Appleton (bootmaker) was shown built at the front of the property. Later Directories of 1907 and 1912 record three families in the buildings at the rear and two in the front (one of which was still the bootmaker's shop). These buildings were eventually demolished and part of Cricketers' Parade now covers the site.

*Holden's Cottages* (No. 10 on plan)
A John Holden, formerly of Fittleworth, is first identified in the 1821 census which reveals his occupation as butcher, his residence being situated to the south east of Holden's Cottages (No. 63, section 13). By 1834 he had moved across the road into a house (No. 14,

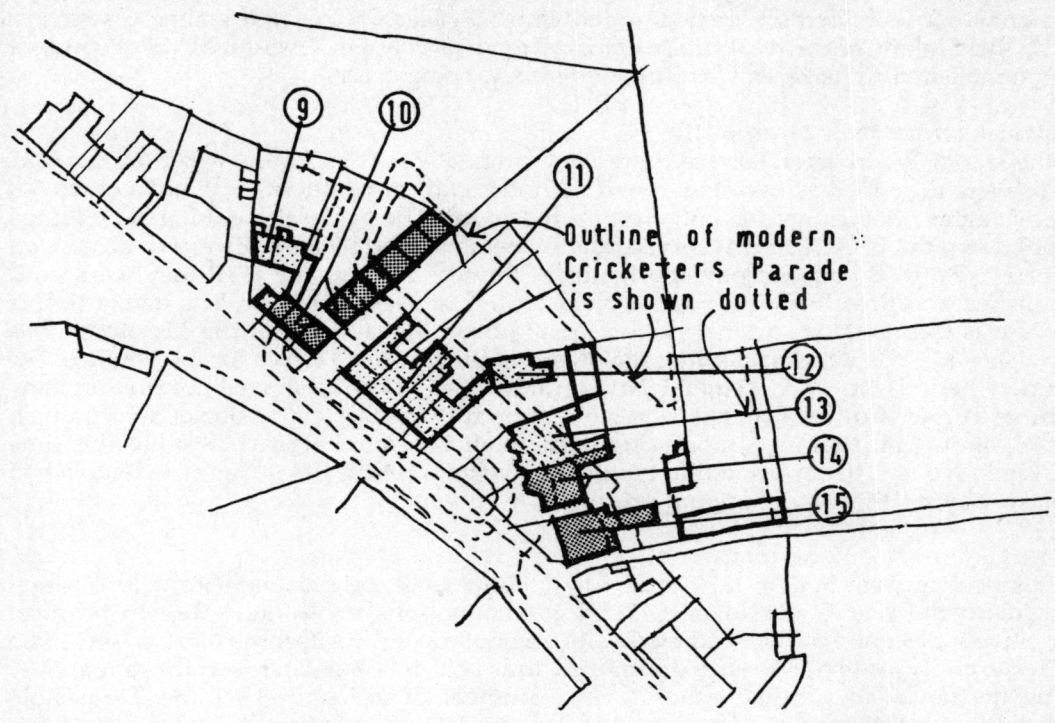

Outline of modern
Cricketers Parade
is shown dotted

*Section 2*

Standing

| N° | DESCRIPTION | MODERN ADDRESS | CURRENT USE |
|---|---|---|---|
| 9 | House and Shop | Cricketers Parade | Modern shops with |
| 10 | Holdens Cottages | " " | Commercial and |
| 11 | Broadwater Terrace | " " | Residential over. |
| 12 | Terrace Cottage / Pear Tree Cottage | " " | [all original houses demolished] |
| 13 | Police Cottage | " " | |
| 14 | House | " " | |
| 15 | House | " " | |

this section) and appears to have built the above cottages sometime between 1834 and 1838. From the evidence contained in later maps and directories the cottages contained two buildings facing the street and six others behind, set at right angles to the street.

John Holden died in 1838 and the property was in the hands of his executors for a number of years until 1846, when it is recorded as being owned by his wife Frances. The cottages were retained by her for many years until she died on 29 November 1868, aged 84 years. The property was then acquired by Thomas F. Wisden who retained it for the remainder of the Victorian period.

There were numerous occupants in the cottages over the years but one worthy of mention was Joseph Herbert, great grandfather of Ray Herbert (see notes on No. 5, Section 1) who lived in one of the two cottages facing Broadwater Street. Eventually these cottages were demolished to make way for the modern shopping centre.

*Broadwater Terrace* (No. 11 on plan)
On the site of Broadwater Terrace there were originally two buildings which in the 1821 census were described as two semi-detached houses (at the northern end) and a butcher's shop, slaughter-house, garden and croft (to the south) The age of these original buildings are unknown but in 1821 they were recorded as being owned by a Mr. Ewens of Brookham in Surrey. By 1868 both were in the hands of Frances Holden. By 1870 they were both demolished and Broadwater Terrace, a block of four houses, was built. The owner of this terrace was George Norton who previously had been the landlord of the *Maltster's Arms* from c.1864 to 1870. As well as being the owner of Broadwater Terrace for the whole of the Victorian period, he also occupied No. 1 until 1877 when he moved to another new building, Terrace Cottage (see notes on next property). The Surveyor's Books, which finish in 1894, show him again as an occupier from about 1884 until at least 1894 but this time residing in No. 4. The terrace did not quite survive for a century as it was also demolished to make way for the new shopping precinct.

*Terrace Cottage* (No. 12 on plan)
This flint cottage was built in 1877 and undoubtedly took its original name from its position adjacent to the rear of Broadwater Terrace. Photographs show the house to be most decoratively designed in flint and bricks. Its original owner was George Norton who lived in the property until 1884 when he moved into No. 1 Broadwater Terrace, apparently letting his house to various tenants over a number of years. In 1907 the 'Household Compendium of Worthing' shows Mr. Norton an occupier again and in 1912 the Worthing & District *Blue Book* directory shows the name of the property had been changed to 'Pear Tree Cottage', a name which it retained for the rest of its existence. The cottage was demolished in 1960 to make way for Cricketer's Parade.

*Police Cottage* (No. 13 on plan)
From about 1838 a barn and stable were shown on the site of this cottage, and at about the same time that Broadwater Terrace was built in 1870 it was recorded as 'Megg's house and stable' owned by T. F. Wisden. The Surveyor's Books reveal that by 1881 the building had been converted into a Reading Room, and initial research indicated that this could have been the Primitive Methodist preaching room (made from a stable) which is mentioned in the Victoria County History.[14] However, later information received from deeds show this to be incorrect (see Section 7, No. 38) . This room apparently closed in 1888. At about this time a house was built on the site and by 1907 it was known as 'Police Cottage' and used by the West Sussex Constabulary. The building was later known as 'Wrest Cottage' and eventually demolished when Cricketer's Parade was constructed.

*House* (No. 14 on plan)
The history of this building has been difficult to trace. It is known that a house was built on the site in about 1834 which was both owned and occupied by John Holden. Surprisingly, the Surveyor's Books do not appear to record the existence of the house between 1869 and 1885. It can, therefore, only be assumed that the house was either still in existence, or demolished and a new one built. In 1907 it was known as the 'Laurels' but from at least

1927 onwards it was 'Greenways'. This building was also demolished to make way for Cricketer's Parade.

*House* (No. 15 on plan)
This house was also built about 1834 and owned by J. Holden. The Surveyor's Books of 1839 record that William Paine had by then moved into this new house with his family, the house at that time being in the hands of the executors of John Holden. A few years later William Paine is shown as the owner of the building. The few views existing of this property reveal it to be brick built and positioned at an angle to the main street. William Paine, a blacksmith, was the youngest son of Richard and Sarah Paine of Broadwater, and the great grandson of William Paine senior, a blacksmith of Broadwater who was born in 1696. Over the years the Paine family lived in at least two other properties before finally settling in the premises now under discussion.

In the 1851 census William (aged 46) and his wife Elizabeth (aged 39) are shown with four daughters and three sons, the youngest of whom is George, a 'scholar' aged 6. William outlived his eldest son, also a William, but died in 1863. His wife had previously died in 1855 and the youngest son George took over the property (this being the custom in Broadwater) and lived there for the remainder of the Victorian period. An advertisement in the *Worthing Gazette* of 20 March 1883 showed that G. Paine, a machinist, of Broadwater was selling 'Paine's Counter-Balance Continuous Ventilator Stays' for conservatories and Greenhouses'. Apparently this apparatus could 'easily open and close 120 ventilators in one minute', and they were fitted to many greenhouses in the district.

Mr. George Paine was a renowned and well respected person in the district and eventually became an Alderman. At one time when he was ill, sand was spread across the street outside his house to lessen the noise of any passing vehicles, so as not to disturb him. George Paine died on 23 June 1903 and his wife continued in the house for several years. Eventually, the house known by then as 'Hadley House' was demolished and the site covered by part of Cricketer's Parade.

**Section 3–Gateway Building Society to National Westminster Bank** (Nos. 16-20 incl. on plan).
With the possible exception of the first building in this section (Gateway Building Society) all the buildings shown on the 1898 Ordnance Survey map have been since demolished and replaced by modern buildings.

*House* (No. 16 on plan)
Prior to 1873 only one building is recorded on this site which is described in the 1821 census as a house and garden owned by Edward Penfold and occupied by Samuel and Lucy Harwood and their three children. By 1839 the building was empty and remained so for several years. As far as can be determined from the limited information available, the house was divided in two. In the 1851 census, one half was shown as empty and the other was occupied by Harriett Puttock (a milliner and dressmaker) and her family. By the 1860s it had been acquired by Thomas Gibbard and was retained by him until the late 1870s. It then passed to Benjamin D. Marner, the son of Daniel Marner, a bricklayer from Findon, who retained it for the rest of the Victorian period. It is quite probable that Benjamin Marner was also a bricklayer and as the building was altered or rebuilt after 1873 he probably did the work himself.

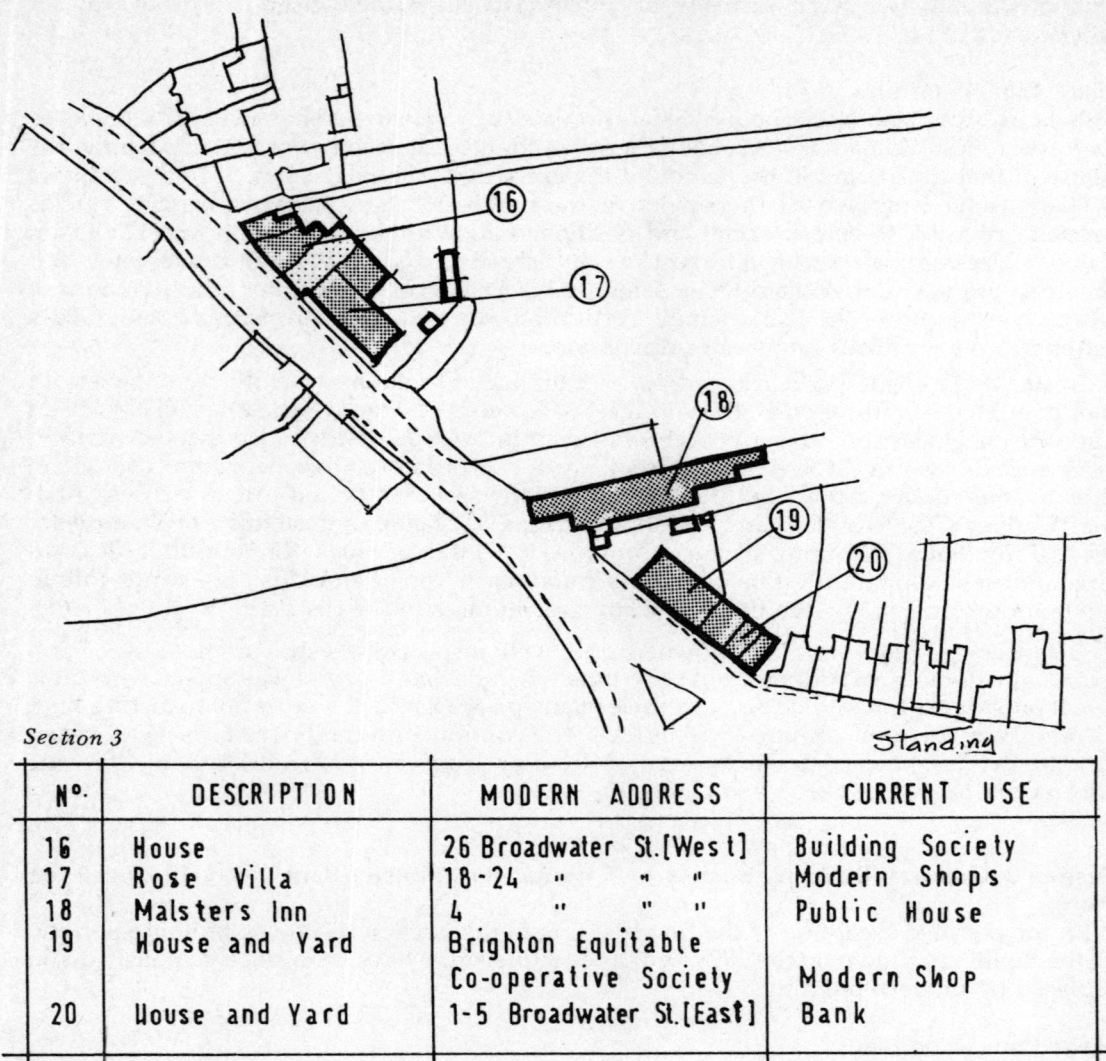

Section 3                                                          Standing

| Nº. | DESCRIPTION | MODERN ADDRESS | CURRENT USE |
|---|---|---|---|
| 16 | House | 26 Broadwater St.[West] | Building Society |
| 17 | Rose Villa | 18-24  "      "   " | Modern Shops |
| 18 | Malsters Inn | 4    "    "   " | Public House |
| 19 | House and Yard | Brighton Equitable Co-operative Society | Modern Shop |
| 20 | House and Yard | 1-5 Broadwater St.[East] | Bank |

   In 1887 it is known that Henry Wheatland established his business as a bootmaker in the building and this might have been when the property was modified or rebuilt into two small gable-ended buildings. By 1898 the Ordnance Survey map shows another building added between the above property and Rose Villa to the south, which appears to have been a dairy. A newspaper report in the *Worthing Herald* dated 23 June 1961 records that Henry Wheatland's son Frederick was invalided out of the Navy in 1914 and was given a cycle business by his father. He started in the shop next door to his father in the former dairy which was a single storey, flat-roofed building. In 1926 this building was demolished along with Rose Villa, and the Wheatland's Cycle business was moved up near the *Cricketers*, next door to W. Appleton's bootmaker's shop. The other building still remained as

Wheatland's bootmaker's shop for many years and survives today as the Gateway Building Society (1982).

*House and Garden/Rose Villa (Tithe No. 143)* (No. 17 on plan)
This house was built in 1810 on Samuel Heather's enclosed piece of ground, probably by Samuel Heather himself as he is shown as the first owner (in the Broadwater Land Tax records), with Richard Whitpaine as the occupier. It was a large flint house with a high-pitched roof having only one front door, which served as the single access to the building, although it was occupied by several families at one time.

In 1812 Mrs. Jane Holman obtained the property, probably by purchase from Mr. Samuel Heather, and the 1821 census still shows her with three children and two other adults. By 1828 the property was in the hands of Mrs. Holman's executors and was empty. From 1832-34 a William Penfold junior owned the property, and two years later Oliver Penfold was the owner.

The 1841 census shows a George Elliott and others as occupiers, and throughout the next ten years there were various occupiers. In 1851 the census shows John Barker, aged 72, a 'gentleman', as the occupier along with his wife Ann, his sister Elizabeth Dennett, aged 60, and 16 year old Jane Bushby, his house servant. From about 1848 and on into the 1860s Mrs. Gregory was the owner, with Thomas Gregory and William Marshall as the occupiers.

In 1880 the house was owned by Bessie Longman and became a convalescent home by 1883. According to the *Local Directory* of 1907 it was known as 'Rose Villa', a name which continued until it was demolished in 1926 when the present block of shops (with flats over) was built on the site.

*Inn/The Maltster's Arms (Tithe No. 145)* (No. 18 on plan)
An inn is mentioned in Broadwater in 1690[15] and, although the references to this are few, the available data suggests that if it was not on the site of the present *Maltster's Arms* it was very near to it. This inn was possibly the copy-hold cottage to which Mary Turnagaine (daughter of Robert Turnagaine, who was issuer of a tradesman's token in the village in 1669–see Chapter Two) was admitted at a Court Baron in 1676 when only eight years old. Her father was appointed as guardian. The token as issued by Robert Turnagaine does not depict a trade, but as a large number of these tokens during the 17th century were issued by tavern or innkeepers it now seems most likely that the token was for that purpose. Robert died in 1679 and as his daughter Mary appears to have had no heirs, the cottage passed to her sister Elizabeth who had married an Ambrose Martin. In 1725 Ambrose Martin and his wife Elizabeth surrendered the property and Thomas Moor of East Grinstead was admitted a tenant.

The next mention of an inn in Broadwater is in a Land Tax list of 1752 when William Humphrey, a maltster, was occupier. It seems most likely that this was the same property for in 1780 a Phillip Moor was the landlord. In 1789 the building was revalued at a higher rate in the Land Tax Record which signifies it was probably rebuilt or enlarged and it may have been when it first adopted the name of the *Maltster's Arms* (the name is known to have been used in 1796). From 1797 onwards a Mr. Gates owned the building and he was probably the Samuel Gates who was the landlord (and probably the owner) of the *Three Tuns Inn* at Steyning. (The local brewery there, which the Gates family later owned, was known for many years as 'Gates' Brewery'). Various members of the Gates family owned the *Maltster's Arms* from 1797 until at least 1900. In 1828 the building was known as the *Millwright's Arms* due to the landlord at the time being a millwright by trade. This name did not appear to be popular for in the following year the building reverted to its previous name.

From the data obtained it would appear that the copyhold cottage was first used as the inn and was probably demolished in 1789, and/or rebuilt into the *Maltster's Arms* which it remained until 1934. This old building (shown on the master map at right angles to the road) was demolished during the road widening scheme for Broadwater Street West. The present building, still on the same site, stands back from the street and is parallel to it. From various records an almost complete list of Innkeepers/landlords has been compiled from 1727 and is reproduced as follows: 1727-1758, William Humphrey; 1762-1771, Peter Penfold; 1771-1780, Phillip Moor; 1781, Samuel Peacock; 1782-4, James Austin; 1785, Henry Dowling; 1786-7, William Baker; 1788, Mrs. Craske; 1789-90, John Craske; 1791-1823, John Lamport; 1824-1826, James Shepherd; 1827-1831, Samuel Stubbs; 1831-1833, George Hinton, 1834-1835, Samuel Stubbs; 1836, George Hinton; 1838-1843, David Meaden; 1846-1853, Edward Goodyer; 1861-1862, Henry Norton; 1864-1871, George Norton; 1872-1889, William Pay; 1889, William Prince; 1892-1894, Walter Wardroper; 1907, J. Purser.

Although not shown on the Ordnance Survey map of 1898 there was originally a building behind the *Maltsters* (to the north) which is clearly shown on the tithe map (tithe No. 144). This building consisted of two tenements which by 1821 were shown as the property of Edward Penfold and in the occupation of two poor families, Edward Baker and John Paskins. By 1839 only one occupant, James Guile is shown. He remained there for many years although Edward Penfold died prior to 1841 and the property was acquired by Charles Roberts. In 1862 the Surveyor's Book described the property as an old cottage which apparently survived until 1883.

D. R. Elleray's *Worthing: A Pictorial History*, plate No. 161, shows the old *Maltster's Arms* in about 1885 with the end of a building protruding from behind it. This building is thatched and appears to be a barn but is on the exact site of the old cottages which by 1885 had gone. It seems quite feasible that these old cottages were probably derelict and were therefore used as a barn which had gone by the time that the 1898 Ordnance Survey map had been prepared. However, the boundaries of the site of this old cottage/barn can be approximated to the small field to the rear of the *Maltster's Arms*, which for many years contained trees and is shown in a number of old pictures of Broadwater.

*House and Yard (Tithe No. 146)* (No. 19 on plan)
The earliest positive identification of this house is in the Church Rate Book of 1818 when it is recorded as being occupied by Frances Nottingham. The age of this property is difficult to determine, as the early photographs and views show the outside of the building to be rendered, but it is almost certain that the building was constructed of flint and that it was probably built in the early 19th century.

By 1839 it was in the hands of John Holden's executors and occupied by Charles Ballard, the miller of Broadwater. John Holden's wife Frances took over the property until 1869, when Charles Roberts acquired it for a period of about 11 years. By 1880 T. F. Wisden was the new owner, but it was still occupied by Charles Ballard and remained so until his death in January 1887 (aged 70), when the new owner-occupier was Richard Ballard, his son, also a miller.

Charles Ballard had occupied the house for at least 48 years, probably even longer, and Richard Ballard is still shown in the property in 1912, according to the directory for that year. It appears that he had also acquired the adjacent property (No. 20 on plan)by 1912, for both cottages were shown as 'Ballard's Cottages'. The cottages survived for many years until they were demolished and the modern brick building was erected on the site which is at present the Co-operative Society's shop (1983).

*House and Yard (Tithe No. 146a)* (No. 20 on plan)
As to the origin of this building, the same comments apply as in the case of the previous property. It is first identified in the Church Rate Book of 1818 when William Inkpen is recorded as the occupier. The 1821 census shows that the property was divided into three tenements, owned by Edward Penfold, with the families of William Inkpen, William Herbert and Arthur Wicks in occupation. The latter two families were described as 'poor'. It is known that by 1839 William Inkpen owned and occupied the property until about 1846 when Frances Holden, wife of the late John Holden, acquired it. William Inkpen, continued as occupier, however, until his death in about 1849.

The 1851 census shows that the house was still divided into three tenements with Jane Inkpen, Abraham Paskins and Frances Bailey named as the three heads of the households. Jane Inkpen, aged 87, was described as 'infirm house-keeper, from Charlwood in Surrey'.

Thomas Gibbard, a carpenter, was the owner in 1851 and remained so until 1865 when it appears that he had died. From 1869 another Thomas Gibbard was shown as the owner, presumably his son, who was originally a law clerk. In 1878 T. F. Wisden acquired the property and it remained in his possession during the Victorian period. By 1912 it was shown as part of 'Ballard's Cottages' and two persons were shown as occupiers. The house was demolished several years ago and the Broadwater branch of the National Westminster Bank now stands on its site.

## Section 4–Northgate Cottages to three houses adjacent to 'Loxwood'
Except for renovations and modifications all buildings in this section are intact, and are those which are shown on the 1898 Ordnance Survey map.

*Houses (Tithe No. 147)* (No. 21 on plan)
The origin of this block of houses is unknown. However, it is thought they were built in the early part of the 19th century. Records and maps of the early 19th century indicate that there were only three houses in the original block, and that a fourth was added to the east end by 1851, for the census of that year shows four houses in the block and records their name as 'Northgate Cottages', no doubt because of their position opposite the north gate of the churchyard. In 1851 the fourth house was occupied by John Price, the parish clerk and sexton, who was recorded there until 1872.

The 1821 census records the property as being owned by John Penfold, senior. By 1839 it was in the hands of the executors of John Holden, and about 1840 it was acquired by Charles Roberts with whom it remained until about 1880. In 1883 the property was shown as in the hands of the 'devisees' of Charles Roberts and by 1885 it was owned by John Roberts, probably the son of Charles, who retained it for virtually the remainder of the Victorian period.

The front facade of these houses has been rendered over for many years but they were originally flint built, as can be seen from the rear of the building. The block still exists but has been modernised with the first two houses converted into modern shops. The name of 'Northgate Cottages' is no longer used. The village school was at the rear of these premises for many years (see section 14). The demolition of the school provided an extra piece of garden for the property.

*House and Yard (Tithe No. 148)* (No. 22 on plan)
This house is shown on the Charles Hide survey of 1838 and appears to be the property recorded in the 1821 census which was owned by Mr. John Penfold, senior, and occupied

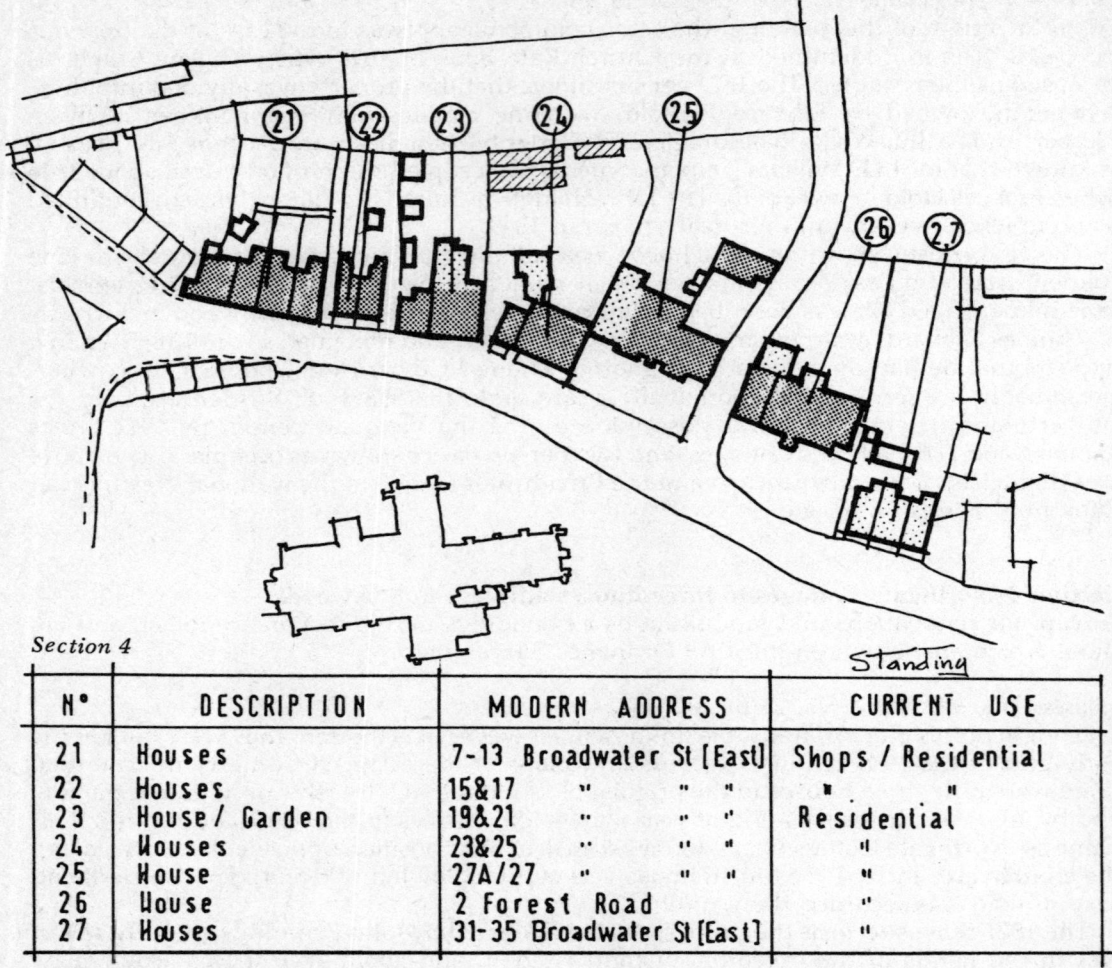

Section 4

Standing

| N° | DESCRIPTION | MODERN ADDRESS | CURRENT USE |
|----|-------------|----------------|-------------|
| 21 | Houses | 7-13 Broadwater St [East] | Shops / Residential |
| 22 | Houses | 15&17 " " " | " " |
| 23 | House / Garden | 19&21 " " " | Residential |
| 24 | Houses | 23&25 " " " | " |
| 25 | House | 27A/27 " " " | " |
| 26 | House | 2 Forest Road | " |
| 27 | Houses | 31-35 Broadwater St [East] | " |

by Thomas and Anne Chipper. The actual date of construction is at present unknown, but it is flint built and appears to be very similar to 'Northgate Cottages', adjacent to it. In 1839 it was in the hands of John Holden's executors and occupied by Sarah Boyce. Two years later George Sharp, an agricultural labourer, and his family are shown as occupiers with the Rev. Peter Wood as owner, and it appears that at this time the property was a single house.

The census of 1851 records that George Sharp and his family were still in occupation. George and his wife Frances had two daughters, both in their early twenties, who were described as visitors in the 1851 census, although born in Broadwater. It is also interesting to note that his granddaughter, Charlotte, aged only 14, was described as an 'Assistant School Teacher'! She would not have had far to travel, as the school at that time was only next door at the rear of 'Northgate Cottages' (see section 14). By 1861 George Sharp was also the owner of the property, and continued to reside there for many years. By about 1876 his daughter Jane was the new owner, presumably after her father's death, and from that date the Surveyor's Books show the property to be two separate houses let to tenants (Jane herself does not seem to have lived there).

In 1883 Mary J. Cecil appears as the new owner and she remained so until at least 1894 and maybe longer. The tenants during this period seemed to come and go fairly rapidly.

The 1907 Worthing Directory shows the property as 'Linden Cottages', numbered 1 and 2, and it appears that this name may have been used from about 1870. Later the cottages were re-numbered as 15 and 17 Broadwater Street East , and directories of the late 1920s show that the front of the first house had been converted into a hairdresser's shop. By at least 1939 the front of both cottages was taken over by the hairdresser and two cottages were shown at the rear as 15A and 17A, each with a separate tenant. Today the shop is 'Broadwater Books' and it can be seen that two modern shop windows have been added. The outline of the front entrance to the old No. 2 'Linden Cottages' can still be seen on the front of the building together with its step still protruding onto the path. The right of way to the two cottages at the rear of the building is on the eastern side.

*House and Garden (Tithe No. 149)* (No. 23 on plan)
A house is shown on this site on the 1720 map and it now seems most likely that it is the same house which still survives today. All the existing evidence suggests that the house belonged to John Parrot, senior which was inherited by his son, also John, on his death in July 1720. The house was described as 'All that messuage and tenement (late Rowlands) with a rood of land there unto belonging . . .'.[16] The rood of land mentioned is undoubtedly the piece of land, recorded in a document, on which the house next door was built (see subsequent notes on No. 24).

The original date of the building is not known but may well have been about 1680 when John Parrot senior married Margaret Heath. There is always the possibility that the house has been rebuilt since 1720 but no evidence has as yet come to light, and so at present it must be considered as the oldest surviving house in Broadwater. The building is constructed of flint and probably had a thatched roof.

There are no further entries relating to the Parrot family in Broadwater's Vestry records after 1720, and it is not until 1818 that a further positive identification of the occupants of this building can again be made. However, a comparison of the probate inventories of John Parrot (Blacksmith) and William Paine (Blacksmith) strongly suggests that Paine took over this property from about 1730, a theory which receives further support from the *Worthing Gazette* of 9 December 1925, where it is recorded that William Paine started his business in a house in Broadwater Street East.

At some time prior to 1818 this property was acquired by Mr. John Penfold, its occupant being Mrs. Elizabeth Penfold who remained there until 1826. In 1827 a person named Phine occupied the property, who was succeeded by Thomas Gibbard in 1828. Three years later, in 1831, William Newman was the new occupier and remained so until about 1843, when Elizabeth Newman was recorded as the occupier. By 1846 the property was in the hands of the executors of Edward Penfold (having been in the Penfold family since at least 1821) and by 1848 had a new owner, Charles Roberts. The 1851 census shows ten people living in the house, the head being Hannah Collyer, aged 60. It appears that part of the premises had now been converted to a shop. It is described as a grocer's shop and Post Office. Hannah's daughter Mary married Henry Blaker, a carpenter, and they lived with their children and Hannah in the premises. Mary is described as a 'shopwoman' and obviously worked in her mother's shop.

In 1861 William Manwaring is shown as the occupier and is recorded as such in the Surveyor's Books until 1894 (it is possible that William Manwaring junior took over, about

1881). Charles Roberts remained as owner until 1870, but it appears that William Manwaring acquired the property in 1871.

During the 1860s bread ovens were added at the rear of the property (shown as an addition on the 1875 Ordnance Survey map) presumably meaning that Mr. Manwaring had added a bakery to his grocery shop. The directory for 1912 shows the property as 'Burndale', occupied by G. Knight, a baker. In 1927 the property was numbered 19 and 21 Broadwater Street East and occupied by G. Knight & Sons, bakers, who remained there for many years. In recent years the shop was a 'Do-it-yourself' shop, but it has now reverted back to a private residence.

*Houses (Tithe No. 150) (No. 24 on plan)*
This property comprised two houses joined together, the smaller of the two being on the west. According to an old document, at present displayed in the smaller of the two houses,[17] the property was originally copyhold. This document, written in a mixture of Latin and English, records that a William Andrews of Broadwater, butcher, built a house and slaughterhouse on one perch (or rood) of land in 1723. This fact is supported by both a map of 1720 which does not show any buildings on this site, and by an extract from the old vestry minutes dated 22 June 1724, when Jeremiah Dodson, Rector 'gave leave to William Andrews, who had lately built a new house in the street, to erect a seat in the south aisle of the Church for himself and family'. The document also records that William Andrews had to pay rent of 6d annually, and plant and preserve seven elm trees, three in the front of the property and four at the rear. By observing and performing these and other services formerly due, of which the details are not given, he was duly admitted as tenant on 1 October 1723. The elms at the front were probably planted on the perimeter of the churchyard opposite the house.

It seems certain that the larger of the two houses was the one erected in 1723. It was constructed with a front elevation of dark red and black bricks with flint sides and rear, the slaughterhouse being erected at the rear. As William Andrews is not recorded in the parish registers, it is not known whether he had any heirs which makes the tracing of the owners and occupiers of the property difficult. It is again positively identified in the Land Tax Record of 1780 when it was owned and occupied by Edward Hide who had married Sarah Singer of Decoy Farm in 1760. The date of 1760 might well have been when the Hides moved into the property. Edward and Sarah had eight children and it seems likely that they may have had the house extended at this time. The small extension is constructed in similar bricks and flint but is not exactly in line with the other building.

It is not until the 1821 census that the property is recorded as two houses both owned and occupied by the Hides, who remained owners of the property until 1895 when the last member of the family to own the houses was Alkemia, wife of Singer Edward Hide. She died in May 1895.

According to the 1907 Directory of Worthing the small house was 'Ivy Cottage' and the larger one 'St Mary's'. When the Hide family were in occupation both houses were treated as one building, with an inter-connecting door between them. The property was called 'Ivy Cottage' before 1887 according to the Hides' old family Bible,[18] obviously due to the house being covered in ivy as many of the old views show. It seems likely, therefore, that the smaller house was re-named 'St. Mary's' after 1895 but before 1907. The names of the two houses remained as such well into the latter half of this century until, for some unknown reason, they were reversed. The larger house has now become 'St. Mary's' and the smaller one 'Ivy Cottage'. A concrete plaque let into the wall of the house renamed 'St. Mary's', refers to a dog which died and was buried there, in 'Ivy Cottage'.

During recent renovations several old oak beams have been uncovered in the house which certainly appear to be old ship's timbers. The old slaughterhouse still remains, and has been used as a workshop over the years. It has now been converted and forms part of the kitchen of the larger house. The smaller house now has been made into a separate residence and has a small garden of its own.

Ivy Cottage is one of 90 buildings in Worthing listed as of 'special' architectural and historical interest under the Town and Country Planning Act of 1947.[19]

### House (Tithe No. 151) (No. 25 on plan)

On the 1720 map a property is shown on this site, but this appears to have been a forerunner of the house that now occupies the site. A document of 1723 records that the house was owned by the Lord of the Manor and at that date was in the occupation of James Watson. The next positive identification of the house is in the Land Tax records of 1780, when the house is shown as owned and occupied by John Harwood. It may well be that the house shown as 'Coate's House', occupied by a Henry Harwood in the earlier land tax list of 1752, is also the same house. In 1791 the house passed to the Shepard family who held it until 1803, when it was once more shown in the possession of the Lord of the Manor, John Newland. It was recorded that he was also the occupier, which probably meant that it was empty and possibly derelict.

By 1818 it had been purchased by Elizabeth Thompson and all the available evidence suggests that the old property was demolished at about this date, and a new house was built replacing it, this being the present house on the site. In 1819 Miss Dorothy Fearn acquired the property and at the time of her death in 1821 the house had been let to a Mr. Arthur Robinson. By 1824 the building was empty and about 1826 a Mrs. Marriott took over the property for about two years, after which it again became empty. In 1832 Richard Bamber acquired the property and became owner/occupier for about the next nine years. The 1841 census shows that John Stringer, a 'gentleman', his wife and daughter were occupying the building together with three servants. At sometime between 1838 and 1848 an extension was added to the west end of the house which also abutted the adjacent building (Ivy Cottage).

The 1851 census shows the property as 'Broadwater Lodge' with John Stringer, aged 70, and his daughter, still in occupation with three servants. By 1861 John Stringer had died and his daughter, Miss A. Stringer, was shown as the occupier but one year later the property was again empty. From then until about 1883 there were a number of different occupiers but from 1832 until 1883 a Richard Bamber was shown as the only owner. During the latter part of the Victorian period Michael King was the occupier and by 1906 it was Miss King, presumably his daughter.

The house was still a single property for at least the first half of the present century but by 1956 the small building was a doctor's surgery. The property is currently two separate residences. The smaller part is No. 27A Broadwater Street East, known as 'Broadwater Lodge', while the larger house has been re-named 'Broadwater House'.

At the rear of the premises was an outbuilding, presumably a small barn or workshop. This still survives but has been converted into a separate private residence known as 'The Studio'.

### House (Tithe No. 152) (No. 26 on plan)

According to the Surveyor's Books this house was built in 1820. The front of the house is of typical Regency style, constructed of cream coloured bricks, which were probably made from the blue clay found on Worthing beach. These bricks were first made by Thomas

Wicks in the 1770s and used in a number of buildings in Worthing. It is interesting to note that a Thomas Wicks lived in Peryers Row (now The Square) in Broadwater in 1809-1810, and may well have been the brickmaker for this house.

The rear of the house, however, is constructed from flint. Originally there were some outbuildings on the west side of the house adjacent to the road (now Forest Road). In the early part of this century the road was widened, and these outbuildings were removed. The wall of the garden was moved back in a line with the side of the house. This alteration can clearly be seen when viewing the layout of the front garden. A semi-circular path from the front door of the house originally led to a gate in each end of the front wall. The eastern gateway is visible in the wall, but filled in. Due to the road widening the western gateway and part of the wall has gone, and the pathway now ends in a gate through the side wall leading into Forest Road.

In 1820 the house was owned and occupied by Miss Dorothy Fearn who also owned the house on the opposite side of Forest Road (Broadwater Lodge). In 1821 she died and by 1822 the house was in the hands of her executors. In 1826 it was acquired by Mr. R. Coffin. It was shown as occupied by the Reverend Peter Wood, rector of Broadwater from 1826 to about 1846, and then it was empty for several years.

In 1864 the new owner was Edward Lucas who retained the house until 1883, during which time there were a number of different occupants. It then appears that the house was acquired by Charles Botting during the latter part of the 19th century. The 1912 street Directory shows the house as 'Rectory Cottage', it was occupied by Rev. E. K. Elliott, the former rector of Broadwater who resigned in 1905. Later Directories of 1927 and after show a Miss Elliott as occupier. The house still exists as a private residence.

*Houses (Tithe No. 153) (No. 27 on plan)*
This block of three tenements was built in 1880, this date being shown in the rendering on the front of the building at second floor level. The first owner of these buildings was Edward Collins, who appears to have died by 1887, as the property was then in the hands of his executors. By 1912 the property was known as 'Church Cottages' and today they still exist as three houses.

Before 1880 there were three other houses on the same site which according to the Land Tax records appeared about 1821. In the 1821 census they are shown as owned by Mr. Tribe from Tarring with three separate families in occupation. By 1843 Mary Tribe was the owner and the occupiers were described as 'Cooter and others'. By 1878 the houses had disappeared, and no views have so far been found of these earlier buildings. No details of their construction is known. However, the eastern end of the building which still exists shows flint work which appears to be ancient, and it is possible that the old buildings may have been renovated rather than rebuilt.

**Section No. 5–Modern high-rise block of flats** (Nos. 28-30 incl. on plan)
This section relates to three groups of buildings which once stood on the site of what is now a high-rise block of modern flats in Broadwater Street East; i.e. 'Alfriston House', 'Steyning House', 'Bury House' and 'Ashington Court'.

*House (Tithe No. 154) (No. 28 on plan)*
This old property is typical of the flint cottages so characteristic of Georgian Broadwater. A photograph of the cottage reveals a plaque over the door which records both the date of its

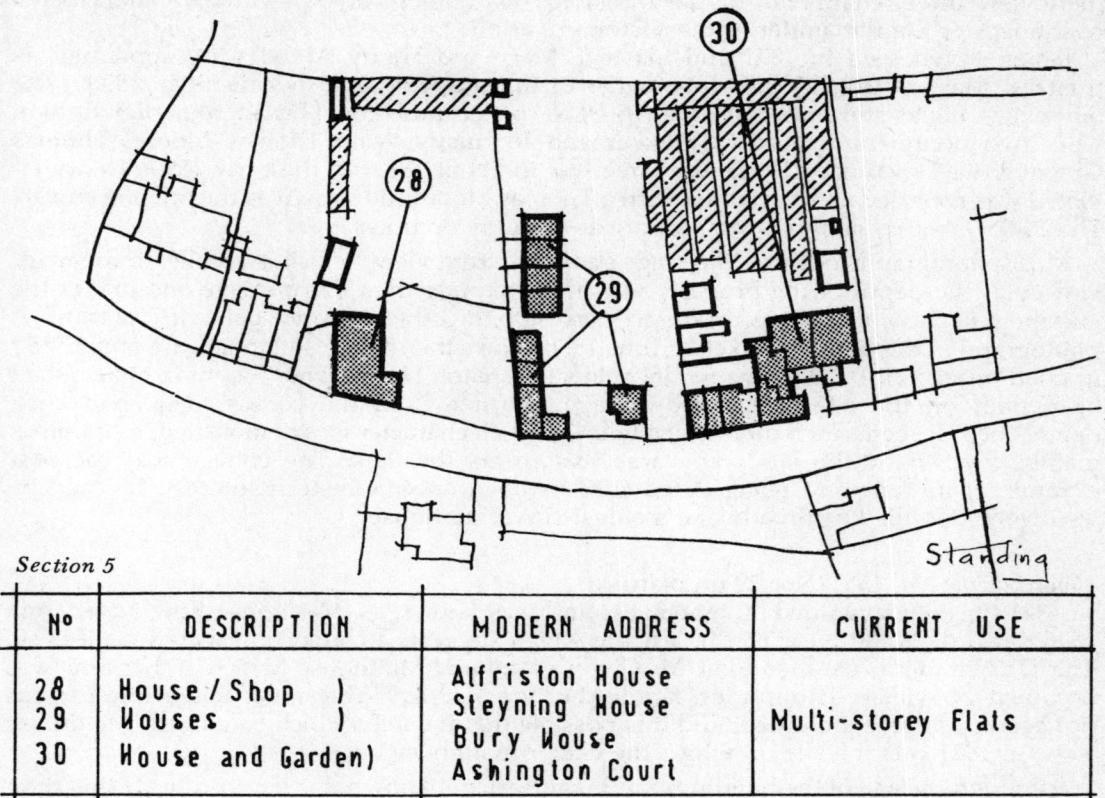

Section 5                                                        Standing

| Nº | DESCRIPTION | MODERN ADDRESS | CURRENT USE |
|----|------------|----------------|-------------|
| 28 | House / Shop ) | Alfriston House | |
| 29 | Houses ) | Steyning House | Multi-storey Flats |
| 30 | House and Garden) | Bury House | |
| | | Ashington Court | |

construction as 1701 and the letters T.B. The authors believe the letters to be the initials of Thomas Backshall (Bagshall) of Broadwater, who was born about 1674 and is shown on the 1712 list of inhabitants as having lived in Broadwater since 1686. By trade he was a cordwainer or shoemaker,[20] and he appears to have been of some repute, for both John Hestead of Broadwater and Richard Hunt were apprenticed to him under common indentures for seven years in 1732 and 1723 respectively.[21]

Thomas Backshall died on 30 December 1748 aged 76 years, leaving a widow, Mary, who is shown on the Land Tax list of 1752 as 'Widow Backshall'. From Backshall's probate inventory,[22] which amounted to £752 14s 1d, it appears his business activities had expanded to that of a mercer (dealer in silk and fabrics) for in his shop, possibly only the parlour of his house, were large quantities of clothes, linen, cotton, worsted caps, stockings, sackcloth, yarn, silk, etc, valued at approximately £200.

Mary Backshall died on 7 December 1752 and it appears that Barnet Backshall, her daughter, inherited the copyhold estate valued at £59. It is not certain what happened to the house for the next few years. In 1759 Barnet married William Rye of West Tarring, and it may well be that the house was then sold. It is not until 1780 that the property is again identified in the Land Tax records, when Thomas Adams was recorded as the owner-occupier. By 1791 the property was owned by John Penfold and remained in the family for many years until 1862, when it was acquired by James Apted. During the 1840s there were three tenants but by the 1860s only two tenants are shown, a situation which continued for the remainder of the Victorian period.

James Apted died in 1871 and his wife Mary and Henry Apted were appointed as trustees. Mary is later recorded as owner of the property until her death in 1890. (The Surveyor's Books still record a Mary Apted as owner until 1894.) During this period there were two occupiers, Thomas Greenyer and for many years Thomas Moore. Thomas Greenyer was succeeded by Louisa Greenyer in about 1881. In the early 1890s Henry G. Apted was recorded as an occupier with a Thomas Moore still shown as the other occupier. The 1907 Directory shows a Mrs. Moore as the only occupier.

Most photographs of this old cottage show the front view, which is parallel to the road. However, the depth of the property was almost longer than the frontage and one of the entrances to this cottage was on the western side,the other entrance being in the front. A photograph of the property taken in June 1960 shows the cottage still intact and apparently in good order, but by 1965 the modern flats ('Alfriston House' and 'Steyning House')had been built on the site of the old cottage's garden, and the cottage itself had been demolished. It seems incredible that a house of such character was demolished, as its site is mainly covered by the landscape area that fronts the flats. The cottage was the best example of its type and being dated (1701) was of specific historic interest. It could be positively identified as Broadwater's oldest surviving house.

### Houses (Tithe No. 155) (No. 29 on plan)

In 1821 this site contained 10 tenements and was known as 'Malthouse Row' (later from 1846 onwards 'Malthouse Yard'), a name which suggests a connection with a malthouse. The 1752 Land Tax list mentions 'Mr Green's land and Malthouse' which at that time was occupied by William Humphries, landlord of the *Maltsters*. The site of this malthouse has not been positively identified, and it is possible that the land which contained 'Malthouse Row' in 1821 was the site on which the earlier malthouse once stood.

Although the age of the buildings on this site are not known it is most probable that they are late 18th or early 19th century in origin. In 1821 they were in the hands of Solomon Sandle, a 'house agent', and the houses were all occupied by the poorer families of the parish, except one which was occupied by Richard Apted and his wife Sarah. (Richard Apted was later described as a baker and moved into a building on the site of which is now *Ye Old House at Home* public house.)

The houses on the site consisted mainly of two rows on the western side at right angles to the road, with two other buildings parallel to the road. The northernmost row consisted of two terraces running north to south, joined back to back to form a double-roofed house which was divided into four (see plan). These were two-storeyed houses. To the south of this terrace was another one, also with two storeys, but smaller in height and containing three houses. There were two buildings facing the road, the easternmost one of which appears to have been called 'Bay Cottage' in the 1912 Directory. In the same directory the row of houses were then known as 'Malthouse Cottages'.

### Houses and Gardens (Tithe Nos. 156 and 157) (No. 30 on plan)

According to the Land Tax records the houses on this site were constructed in 1820. The census of 1821 records that six houses were then in existence. The three on the west of the property were owned by a Mr. Weller, one being described as a house, garden, shop, bakehouse, yard and stables occupied by Solomon Sandle, his wife and two other adults. The other three houses were owned by Elizabeth Stedman, and occupied by poor families.

The Charles Hide Survey of Broadwater in 1838 shows the property as two separate groups of houses, the western group at the edge of Broadwater Street with the other group set back. The houses at this date were still under the same ownership as 1821. When the tithe map was produced in 1848 the property had become one long terrace and was probably very similar to the photographs taken in the early part of this century.

By at least 1860 the western part of the property fronting the street was acquired by James Apted and as the terrace was named 'Alma Cottages', it seems most likely that it could have been taken over in 1854 when the famous Battle of Alma took place and the Russians were defeated. This terrace contained four houses; by 1875 a shop had been added to the eastern end (recorded as a Post Office in the 1907 Directory). This terrace remained in the ownership of the Apted family until at least the end of the 19th century–James, Henry and Emily Apted.

The other part of the property was acquired by Zeph Greenfield about 1843 and remained in his possession until 1864 when Susan Greenfield was recorded as the new owner. In 1878 it appears that George Hayward took over from Susan Greenfield and remained as owner for the remainder of the Victorian period, although there were several changes of tenancy during this period. The houses all survived the first half of the present century, but photographs taken in 1960 show the property being demolished to make way for the new block of flats constructed shortly afterwards.

**Section 6–'Knowles Bakery' area** (Nos. 31-33 incl. on plan)
This section contains the area and buildings which were affected in some way due to the building of the modern Knowles Bakery.

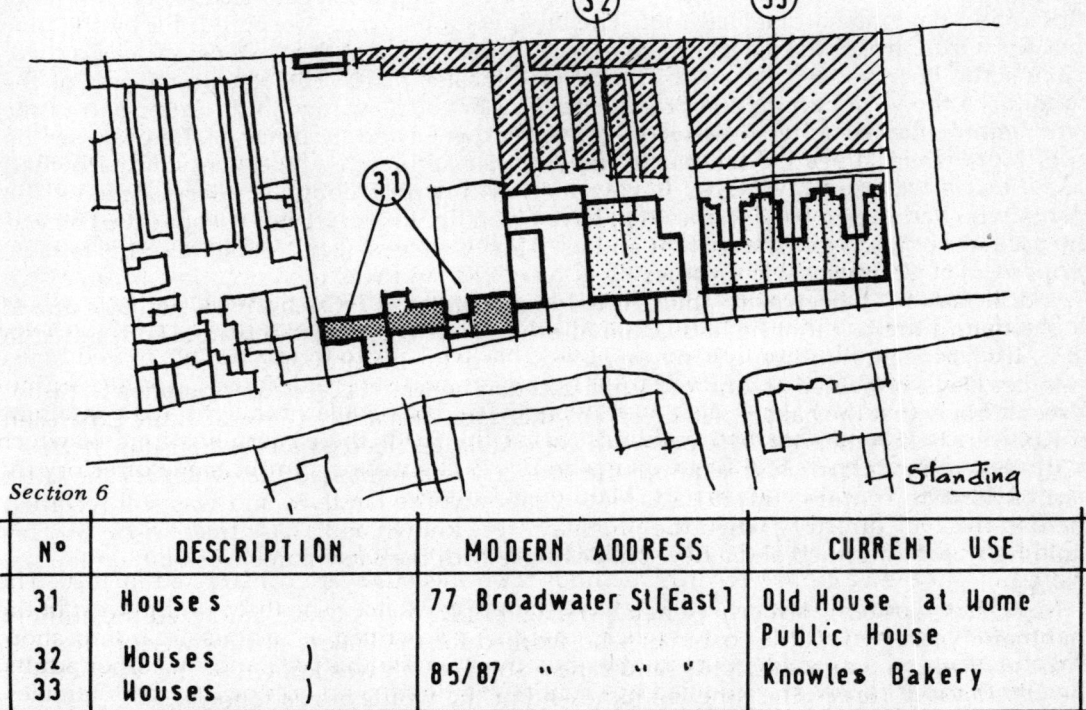

Section 6

| Nº | DESCRIPTION | MODERN ADDRESS | CURRENT USE |
|---|---|---|---|
| 31 | Houses | 77 Broadwater St [East] | Old House at Home Public House |
| 32 | Houses ) | 85/87 " " " | Knowles Bakery |
| 33 | Houses ) | | |

*Houses (Tithe Nos. 158 and 159) (No. 31 on plan)*
This site contained two houses which will be dealt with separately.

a) *House on the west of the site* (Tithe No. 158)

By 1818 this was a garden owned by Richard Apted, formerly known as 'Jacksons'. Richard Apted was an agricultural labourer from Wiston, born in 1772. It is not known for what reason he came to Broadwater but it may have been when he married Sarah, whose surname and parish are unknown. In 1820 a house was recorded on the site in the Surveyor's Books and on the first reliable map (Charles Hide Survey, 1838) a house is shown parallel to the street with an extension protruding to the west.

In the 1841 census Richard Apted, aged 65, is described as a baker and it is quite possible that the extension was a bakery. The census shows a Jane Apted, aged 50, who appears to be his wife and it would therefore seem that his first wife had died and he re-married. By the next census in 1851 his son James, also a baker, had taken over the property which was then described as a beer house. (Apparently his father had also sold beer on the premises for there is a reference in the Surveyor's Books describing the premises as a beer house in 1832.) James, who was born in 1813 in Broadwater, married Mary from Dorking in Surrey, and was living in another property in Broadwater (see No. 66). It would appear that James had learnt to be a baker in order to take over his father's business, for in the 1841 census he was described as a labourer.

James and Mary had a son, Henry, who was born in 1836 and a daughter Mary, born in 1838. In the 1851 census Henry, then aged 15, was shown as a baker following in his father and grandfather's footsteps!

From the few available photograph of the old building it appears to have been built of flint and to have had a thatched roof. The business must have prospered, for by the time that the Ordnance Survey of 1875 map was drawn up, another extension was added, making the beer house into an 'L' shape (see master plan). The remaining part of the building to the west became the Broadwater Fire Brigade's garage in the latter part of the 19th century. James Apted was recorded as the owner and occupier of the premises up until 1868, when James Davis became the occupier, although Apted was still the owner. James Davis was his son-in-law, having married his only daughter Mary. Apted's son Henry who had been a baker appears to have given up this trade, for by about 1860 he was the occupier of a shop at the eastern end of 'Alma Cottages' (see No. 30), also his father's property. The shop was a post office by at least 1907 and was then occupied by an H. G. Apted. It may have been that James Apted had decided to retire by 1868, perhaps due to ill-health and the fact that he had acquired other properties in Broadwater. James died in 1871, his son Henry and wife Mary being executors for his property.

James Davis remained as landlord until 1872 and he was succeeded by Stephen S. Swan. It seems likely that the bakery had ceased by this date, probably as a result of the expansion of Knowles Bakery nearby. The premises were still described as a beer house in 1887.

By 1884 a Mrs. Harris had acquired the property and remained the owner for the latter part of the 19th century. In 1891 a George Guiel was the landlord and was still recorded there in the 1907 directory when the premises were known as *Ye Olde House at Home*. This building was demolished and a new public house with the same name was built on the site in 1925.

Mr. Harry Gosden, formerly General Manager of Knowles Baker, informed the authors that many years ago a little Irishman who worked for the bakery always went to the *Old House at Home* on Saturday nights, and sang a song which was known as the 'Anthem' of the *Old House at Home*. The tune is unknown but the words are as follows:

'On Monday I goes out with Rosy,
On Tuesday I goes out with Jane,
On Wednesday I goes
with a Widow I knows
and her kids follow on down the Lane.
On Thursday I goes out with Ryah,
and Friday I practise the choir,
but on Saturday night I get tiddly-tight
in the *Old House at Home* by the fire!'

After singing this song apparently the Irishman usually ended up in a fight and was thrown out.

The modern public house with the same name still stands on the site.

### b) *House on east of site* (Tithe No. 159)

This building is recorded in the 1821 census as being owned by Mr. Weller of Clapham and consisted of two houses both occupied by poor families of the parish. Very little is known about the origins of this house, but it is likely that it was one of the houses built in 1820 for Mr. Weller. By 1841 the house was in the hands of Mr. Weller's executors and was occupied by James N. Collyer. The 1851 census records that the head of the household is Susan Cooter, aged 67, described as an infirm laundress from Newtimber, Sussex, who resided in the house with her son Thomas, aged 36, her two daughters, both laundresses, and two grandaughters who were shown as 'scholars'. This strongly suggests that the building was used as a laundry.

It appears that by the 1860s James Apted who lived next door had acquired the property and by 1868 it was occupied by Sarah Lindupp. A member of the Lindupp family continued to occupy the house until about 1887, by which time Emily Apted was recorded as the owner. James Apted died in 1871 and his daughter married James Davis, who was shown as the occupier from 1889. The 1907 Directory records a J. Davis and the house is named as 'Laburnum Cottage'. During the first part of this century the house was occupied by Harry Slaughter, and was described in the local directories as a laundry (e.g. 1927, 1934, 1940).

The authors have only been able to locate one reasonable photograph of this house, which shows that it was constructed of flint and brick. Mr. Harry Gosden, who lived next door in 'Sunnyside', informed the authors that it was an old house with ivy on the roof and that it was used as a hand laundry. During the war the roof of the house caved in when tanks went down the road and £10 was paid to the tenant for her to move out. The site is now covered by Knowles Bakery.

### *Sunnyside/Knowles Bakery* (Tithe No. 160) (No. 32 on plan)

As this house represents the final and present site of Knowles Bakery, a brief summary of the early history of the bakery is necessary. The information concerning the origin of the bakery was kindly offered by Mr. Harry Gosden, whose father passed it down to him by word of mouth.

The business was originally founded in 1817 by James Knowles, in a small brick building which once faced the triangle in the middle of the road (see Fig. 27), the site of which is now covered by the present Co-operative building. James Knowles apparently worked in the Broadwater Mill and the water required for making the bread was taken from the well in the triangle. Once made, the bread was delivered by his wife around the village. Apparently the business prospered and was transferred by Knowles to the building which is now the Broadwater Conservative Working Men's Club in Broadwater Street East.

*Fig. 27.  Broadwater, c.1900.*

   This information regrettably cannot be substantiated as there is no mention of a James Knowles or his wife in the parish registers or in the Surveyor's Books. However, it is a fact that in the 1821 census Ford Knowles, his wife and children are shown in a building on the site of the present *Elms* public house (see No. 53). He is recorded as working in agriculture (this could include a miller!) and in about 1828 he actually moved into (and probably had built) the house at present known as the Broadwater Conservative Working Men's Club. He was later described as a family baker and it is therefore quite possible that over the years in passing down the information by word of mouth the name of the person concerned was changed to James.

   The bakery was constructed at the rear of the Conservative Club building and a faggot oven was installed (parts of the outbuildings still exist). Apparently Knowles also became a market gardener and a pioneer in sending tomatoes to the London markets. Ford Knowles died in 1855, surviving his son Bushby, and it appears that his grandson, also Ford, took over as baker, for he is recorded as the first occupier in the house later to be known as 'Sunnyside'. This house was built about 1868 and the property became the site of the new bakery. In 1884 a new steam tube oven was installed and another in 1886. By this time James Bushby Knowles had acquired the bakery but he had retired by 1900 when Mr. Harry Gosden's father took over, eventually owning the bakery. Later a shop was incorporated on the west side of the house. The name of Knowles was still retained for the bakery and eventually Mr. Harry Gosden himself became the owner.

   The house was incorporated into the new bakery buildings when it expanded in the 1950s and the front of the house can still be seen today. Several years ago the bakery was sold to Rank-McDougall-Rose who have retained the old name of Knowles Bakery.

*South Terrace* (No. 33 on plan)
This terrace of six houses was built in 1877 for James Bushby Knowles, the owner of the bakery next door. Behind the cottages were greenhouses, each with a different type of grape grown in them. Eventually the houses in the terrace were all sold, but they were bought back again later in order that the bakery could expand. The terrace was demolished and the bakery buildings extended over the site in the 1950s.

**Section 7–Garden Cottages to 'Jex' the Newsagents** (Nos. 34-36 incl. on plan)
In this section all the domestic buildings still survive as shown on the 1898 Ordnance Survey map, with, of course, any inevitable modern improvements and minor additions.

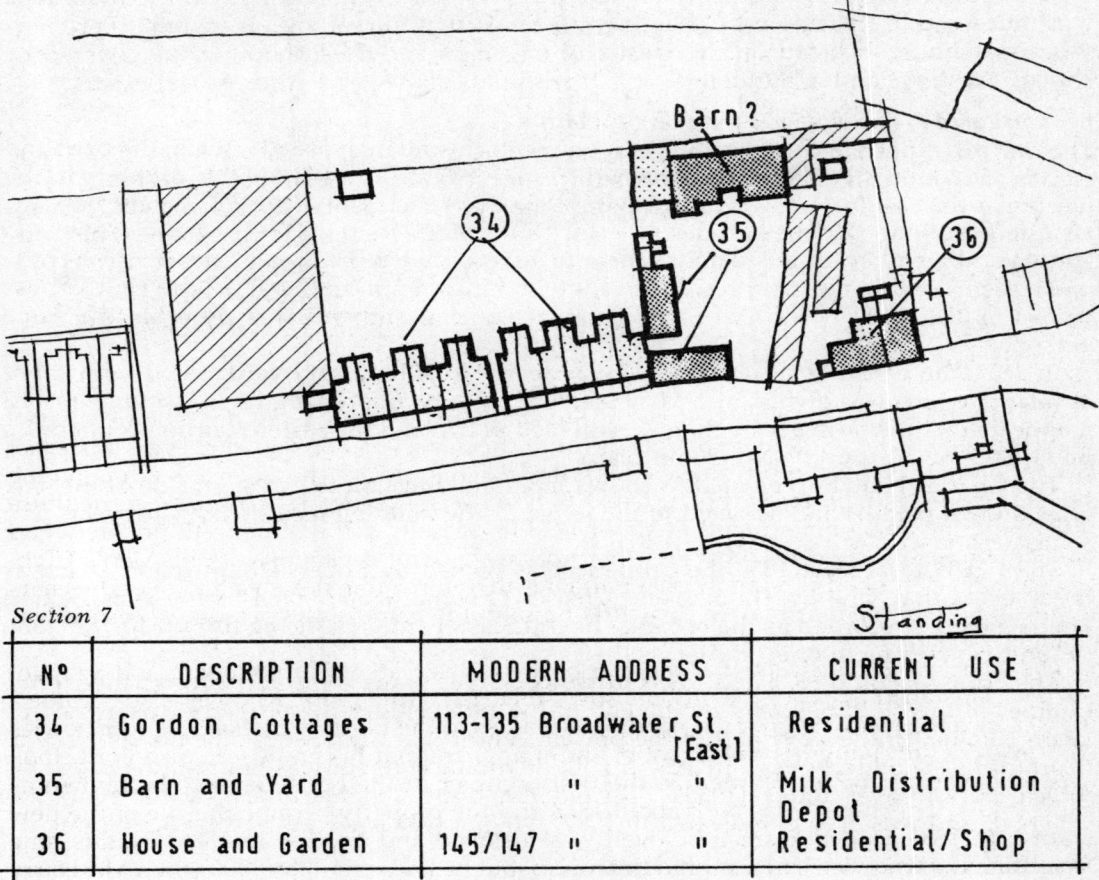

| N° | DESCRIPTION | MODERN ADDRESS | CURRENT USE |
|---|---|---|---|
| 34 | Gordon Cottages | 113-135 Broadwater St. [East] | Residential |
| 35 | Barn and Yard | " " | Milk Distribution Depot |
| 36 | House and Garden | 145/147 " " | Residential/Shop |

*Gordon Cottages (Tithe No. 161)* (No. 34 on plan)
The plot of land on which these cottages were built was described as a garden, and can be traced back to 1780 when it was part of the estate of Thomas Heather. It descended through the Heather family until 1813, when it was acquired by Edward Penfold from Samuel Heather. Mr. Penfold held it for a few years; then it went to Mr. Wyatt, before passing to

William Hill, who was its owner/occupier during the first half of the 19th century. Eventually the site was acquired by James Bushby Knowles, from Brighton, who appeared to be concerned with the business interests of the Knowles Bakery.

In 1885 a terrace of 12 cottages was built on the land from the east end fronting the road. The buildings were in two blocks of six, and were separated in the centre by a through passageway or tunnel, which provided the rear access to the premises. On a stone archway over the entrance to the passageway is an inscription, part of which shows a monogram of an intertwined JBK for James Bushby Knowles. The inscription also tells us that the buildings were erected by A. G. Wright, a builder, no doubt the Albert George Wright who was a tenant in No. 6 for many years. James B. Knowles was also a builder, and probably personally superintended the actual building.

The cottages were undoubtedly named after General Gordon, a hero at the time, who was murdered in Khartoum in 1885, the same year that the cottages were built. For many years glasshouses existed on the west end of the plot, their site now being covered by shops ('Austin's' and a launderette, 1982) with flats above. The cottages still exist.

*Barn and yard (Tithe No. 162) (No. 35 on plan)*
The first identification of this property is on the enclosure map of 1806, when the barn and yard is shown on an old enclosure owned by John Holmes. Adjoining this property to the north was the east furlong which was part of the third allotment of approximately 7½ acres awarded to John Holmes under the Inclosure Act. Neither John Holmes nor any subsequent members of this family appear to be recorded in the Broadwater Parish records and it seems certain that they resided in another parish. From 1801-1809 a John Holmes was shown as the occupier of Old Salt's Farm in Lancing and this was probably the same person.

In 1821 the census still describes the property as a barn and yard, rated with other farmland, which was owned by a Mr. Holmes from New Shoreham. From the same record it appears that the property by then was divided in two and the eastern portion contained a house (see next property–No. 36 on plan).

The Charles Hide Survey of 1838 shows more buildings on the western side of the site. One, shown parallel and adjacent to the street, is the building recorded in later years as a slaughterhouse.

From 1839 to at least 1850 the property was owned by Robert Holmes, and as it was occupied at that time by Thomas and Charles Groome, it may well be the same Robert Holmes who is recorded as the occupier of Old Salt's Farm in Lancing from 1810-1828 (son of John Holmes mentioned earlier).

The Tithe Map and 1875 and 1898 Ordnance Survey maps show very little change in the outlines of the buildings, and by the end of the 19th century the property was owned by George Paine. In the early part of the present century directories describe the property as 'Cornford's slaughterhouse'. In 1947 a milk distribution depot was built on the property, which still survives today (1983). The old flint-built slaughterhouse by the road was retained, and was only demolished in 1982, when it was replaced by a brick building.

*House and Garden (Tithe No. 163) (No. 36 on plan)*
This house was built on part of a site owned in 1806 by John Holmes. The 1821 census indicates the building contained two tenements, which were occupied by George Lisher and Thomas Emery respectively. According to the Church Rate Books Thomas Emery first appears in 1819, and this is probably the date when the house was built. In 1821 the property was owned by a Mr. Holmes and from 1839 to about 1851 a Mr. Robert Holmes, possibly the same person.

Very little is known about the house, other than that it was constructed of flint, for no pictures or views appear to have survived. One of the two tenements was let to the poorer families of the parish.

Thomas Emery and family occupied one of the tenements until 1828 when Job Paskyns became the new tenant. He was shown as such until the early 1850s. The first tenant recorded in the other tenement was George Lisher and his family, in 1821, but by 1839 Sam Baker was in occupation, whose family resided there until about 1850.

There were several changes of tenancy in both tenements in the latter half of the 19th century, during which time the ownership of the property also changed hands a number of times. From 1861 Charles Groome was the owner. He was succeeded by C. A. Elliott from 1866 to 1873. His executors held the property from 1874 to 1877, but by about 1880 A. M. Webb was in possession. Between about 1882 and 1886 George Paine, who also owned the barn and yard adjoining to the west of this property, owned it.

The building now standing on the site is dated 1887 with the initials A. G. W., which undoubtedly represents Albert George Wright, a builder who occupied one of the tenements in 1886.

It would appear at first sight that the two houses were built in 1887, but a closer inspection and further research suggests that the original building may well have had a 'face lift' of flint and bricks. It is also quite probable that in 1887 the eastern end of the building was converted into a shop and sold to Charles Edwards, who was recorded as the owner in the latter part of the 19th century. The eastern end of the building still retains quite old flint-work which strongly suggests that the original building was modified.

By 1907 the Worthing directory shows the building named as 'Elm Lea' and the shop as used by a greengrocer. The building still exists but the shop is now 'Jex', the newsagents and confectioner's shop. The father of the present owner had a similar shop at the end of Southfield Road (see No. 39).

### Section 8–Sompting Road (Western side)
This section contains many buildings which were demolished when the Sompting Road was widened and the new roundabout was added. The resultant site was re-developed and the layout as shown on the 1898 Ordnance Survey map is now almost unrecognisable.

*Houses (Tithe No. 164)* (No. 37 on plan)
Directly adjoining the previous property, lying at right angles to the road, there were two semi-detached copyhold premises. In a deed of 1900 (held by Worthing Borough Council, File A558), this building was described as an 'ancient tenement' and was, in about 1810, part of the estate of Isaiah Stone and subsequently held by William Parsons (see also No. 38). It would appear that William Parsons had died by 1821 for from the census we see that both parts of the premises were now held by Frances Parsons, his wife (referred to as Fanny in No 38), who occupied one half while William Cave occupied the other. Very little information has been found for the intervening period between 1821 and 1841, although the previously-mentioned deeds record that the will of Samuel Dudney, dated 13 March 1844 (proved on 18 November 1848), reveals that he held the property. After his death it was to be bequeathed to his wife and then to George Dudney for life.

This is supported by the Surveyor's Books for they show Samuel Dudney as owner and John Best and John Blake-Geer as occupiers in October 1843. In the Tithe Award of 1851 Margaret Dudney is specified as the owner, she was presumably Samuel's wife. On 30 September 1872, George Dudney was formerly presented at a Court Baron of the Manor

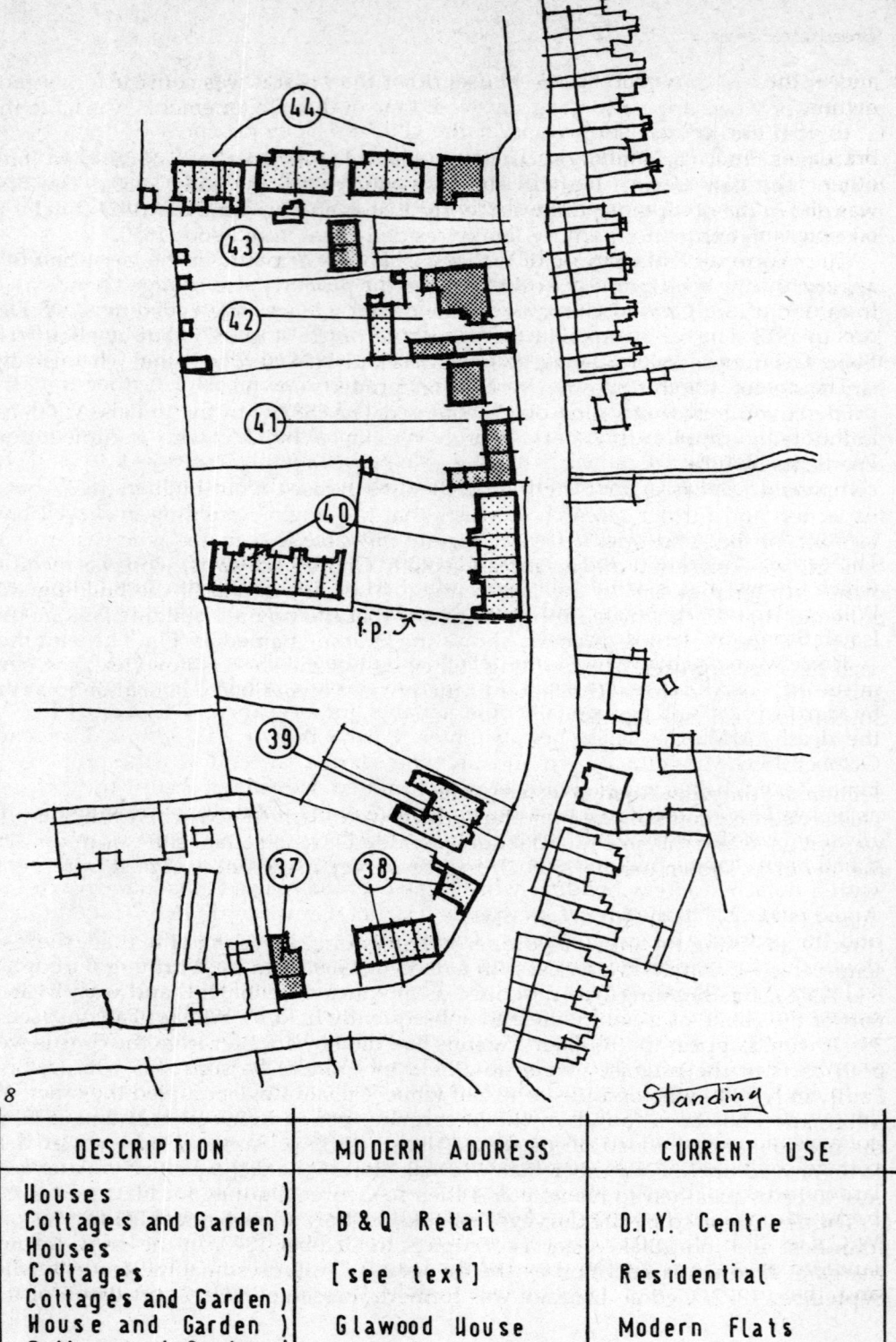

Section 8                                    Standing

| N° | DESCRIPTION | MODERN ADDRESS | CURRENT USE |
|----|-------------|----------------|-------------|
| 37 | Houses ) | | |
| 38 | Cottages and Garden ) | B & Q Retail | D.I.Y. Centre |
| 39 | Houses ) | | |
| 40 | Cottages | [see text] | Residential |
| 41 | Cottages and Garden ) | | |
| 42 | House and Garden ) | Glawood House | Modern Flats |
| 43 | Cottage and Garden ) | | |
| 44 | Houses | 82-94 Kingsland Road | Residential |

and in the last Surveyor's Book of 1894 it is recorded that a George Dudney was still the owner.

In 1841 the census shows one of the cottages to be occupied by John Blake-Geer, a bricklayer, and his family with Henry Tomsett, a miller's labourer and his family in the other. John Blake-Geer (the father of Elias who became a builder and purchased No. 39) was shown as occupying the property until at least 1864 and his wife was still shown as occupier in 1894.

The Worthing Directory of 1907 names the cottages as 'Cooks Cottages', and as there appear to have been no owners of that name it is reasonable to assume that the name came from one of the previous tenants. The Surveyor's Books show George Cook as being an occupier of one of the cottages from about 1869 to about 1890, next door to Mary Blake-Geer, and it seems likely that the cottages derived their name from this person.

The cottages were still copyhold in 1921. After a number of further transactions the property was held from 1948 to 1969 by Marriott's Garage Ltd., who conveyed it to the local authority. During this time the cottages were demolished and the site was conveyed to the Worthing Borough Council. The site was subsequently conveyed to a development company and 'B & Q' the 'Do-it-yourself' store was built on this site by 1972.

*Cottages and Garden (Tithe No. 165)* (No. 38 on plan)
The earliest mention of this copyhold property found to date is in an 'Abstract of Title'[23] which shows that Martha Mills was admitted at a Court Baron upon the surrender of William Parsons, carpenter and Fanny his wife in 1817. It was formerly part of the estate of Isaiah Stone, by then deceased.

There were originally two semi-detached buildings on the site with a garden formed by means of a quick-set hedge separating it from an old orchard. The cottages were occupied by Martha Mills, and occasionally other tenants, for 36 years until 6 October 1853 when, on the death of Martha Mills, her daughter Martha Brown was admitted as a tenant. In October 1858 Mr. John Brown and his wife Martha surrendered the property, and Mr. James Apted, baker and beer brewer, was admitted. He did not occupy the cottages himself as he lived and worked in a building on the site of the public house now known as the *Old House at Home* in Broadwater Street East. By 1862 the property was unoccupied, and by 1864 it had been demolished and a terrace of four new cottages was built on the site, together with a detached larger building which was eventually used as a laundry. In 1866 James Apted paid £228 to the Misses Newlands (Harriet, Francis and Emily), for enfranchisement and the property became freehold. These cottages became known as 'Elm Cottages', no doubt due to their location opposite 'Elm Villa'.

James Apted died on 5 May 1871, and his wife Mary and son Henry were appointed as trustees for the property. According to the Surveyor's Books,[24] an Emily Apted was shown as the owner of the property, although on 21 May 1890 when Mary Apted died her will showed that the property was left to her daughter Mary Davis.

In 1901 sale particulars including a 'plan and conditions of sale'[25] show that the site contained four cottages and a larger building used as a laundry. The description of the cottages indicates that they were constructed of brick, flint and slate, and tile healed. Each cottage contained a front sitting room with fireplace, kitchen with range, coal cupboard, larder and copper (one cottage did not have a copper), front bedroom with fireplace and back bedroom. There was a large rear garden to each cottage in which were two brick built W.C.s used in common. The cottages were let to weekly tenants at 4s 6d per week. The landlord paid the rates, the rental of the laundry being £8 per annum. Water was laid on and the property had recently been main-drained (1901). The auctioneers, Messrs.

Patching & Co. drew the attention of builders and others to the desirability of the site for the erection of first-class business premises in a commanding position in a rapidly-developing district.

Information kindly supplied by Mr. Charles Virgoe (the Honorary Archivist of the Methodists) throws some light on the early history of the building used as a laundry, which was referred to in the 1901 sale particulars. It was originally a stable behind No. 4 Elm Cottages, and in April 1876 the Rev. Thomas Griffiths Dyke (the first Primitive Methodist Minister in Worthing) accepted the offer of a ten-year lease for the cottage, the stable at the rear and the adjoining ground. The stable was converted into a chapel for an approximate cost of £40 and used as a place of worship for the Primitive Methodists. It was almost certainly the preaching room mentioned in the *Victoria County History*.[14] The ten-year lease seems to have been extended, for in 1889, when the chapel was no longer required, it was offered to the Baptist Church who apparently did not take up the offer. At some time between 1889 and 1901 this building was converted into the laundry previously referred to.

After a number of conveyances during the 20th century the property was purchased by the local authority in December 1964. An article in the *Worthing Herald* of 1 December 1967 shows the houses almost demolished and states that the first phase in building a new large traffic roundabout was due to start in 1968 for £80,000. The second phase, including widening of Sompting Road, further to the north, was scheduled for the following year (1969) at a cost of a further £80,000. In 1971 the property was conveyed to a development company and 'B & Q' the 'do-it-yourself' store was built on the site by February 1972.

*Houses (Tithe No. 166)* (No. 39 on plan)
This piece of land was part of a small copyhold estate owned by a Mr. Carlton from at least 1752[26] until 1792 when George Newland was admitted.[27] In 1806 John Newland senior, the Lord of the Manor of Broadwater, died. In his will he left Carlton's estate, together with other land, to one of his sons, Richard Newland, the owner of Decoy Farm.[28] Information contained in deeds show that by 1807 the property had been enfranchised.[29]

The 1821 census shows that the property comprised a house, garden and village school (for school see section 14) with Henry Nicholls and his wife, described as poor, being tenants. The Land Tax List of 1752 shows that Mr. Carlton had a house, and it would be fairly reasonable to assume that it was located on his land. The map of 1720 shows a house on the same site as the house described in the 1821 census and, if still surviving then, it may well be the same building. However, at the time of writing this has not been proven. A number of different tenants occupied the property until about 1856, when Thomas Burtenshaw, an agricultural labourer, aged 49, occupied the house with his wife Caroline and his son Thomas. At this time William Newland was the new owner of Decoy Farm and it is most likely that Thomas Burtenshaw was employed by him. Mr. Burtenshaw's tenancy came to an end in 1862 and his wife Caroline remained until 1868 when Elias Blake-Geere, a builder, took over the property. By 1881 the property was demolished and 1 and 2 Eastern Villas were built on the site, presumably by Elias Blake-Geere himself! These two houses are clearly shown on the 1898 Ordnance Survey map.

Elias died in 1899 and his will shows that he left his property to his wife Harriet, and on her death, to their daughter Harriet Jane Duffield. In 1902 one of the houses was granted to George Duffield, and in 1903 the other one to Daniel Carter.

A Directory of 1907 shows that another four houses were also built on the site, to the north of Eastern Villas, and were known as 'Duffield's Cottages'. However, a later photograph shows them to be renamed 'Eastern Terrace' and the last building on the South-East corner of Southfield Road was a shop, for many years 'Jex' the newsagents and sweet shop. These buildings have now all been demolished, and the site covered by 'B & Q' the 'Do-it-yourself' store in 1972.

## Stonewall Croft/Clifton Cottages (Tithe No. 167) (No. 40 on plan)

This piece of land is not shown separately on the enclosure plan of 1806 but is part of an old enclosure of Richard Newland. The descent of the ownership of this piece of land is the same as Tithe No. 166, i.e. William Carlton, George Newland, Richard Newland, William Newland and Elias Blake-Geere.

It is described in the Broadwater Tithe Award of 1851 as a pasture with the name of Stonewall Croft, and the first buildings appeared in 1869 when six cottages, known as 'Clifton Cottages', were built by Elias Blake-Geere. Six more houses were also built on this parcel of land in 1880, and serviced originally from Broadwater Street by a footpath. These six cottages still exist, and today form part of the north side of Southfield Road. 'Clifton Cottages' were demolished in the late 1960s when the road was improved.

## Cottages and Garden (Tithe No. 168) (No. 41 on plan)

According to the Land Tax Records for Broadwater, buildings were on the site by 1809, owned and occupied by George Parsons who later occupied the *Sea House Hotel* in Worthing. The 1821 census describes three houses and gardens on this site all owned by George Parsons. One of the houses was occupied by Parsons himself while the other two were occupied by poor of the parish. From 1822-32 John Newman is shown as the owner; by 1841 he had been replaced by Soutton Waterman.

A member of the Waterman family continued to own the houses until 1869 when Walter Greenfield took over the properties; four years later T. F. Wisden was recorded in the Surveyor's Books as being the new owner. The 1898 Ordnance Survey map shows the site virtually unchanged by the *Household Compendium for Worthing* of 1907 shows that the buildings must have been demolished, for there were four new buildings on the site known as 'Fern Villas'. These in turn were demolished when the Sompting Road was widened and the new traffic roundabout installed. On a map of Worthing, revised in 1973, 'Glawood House' is shown as occupying the site together with the properties shown as Nos. 42 and 43 on the plan.

## House and Garden (Tithe No. 169) (No. 42 on plan)

This ancient house, shown on the Tithe map, is recorded in the Land Tax Record as belonging to, and occupied by, Mr. Thomas Baker from 1780-1792. There is a house shown on the 1720 map in a very similar position and it may well be the same house, but as yet this cannot be verified . From 1793-1803 the owner was Mrs. Baker, probably the wife of Thomas, while from 1805-1823 a Mr. Buckley owned the property. The Tithe Award of 1851 describes the property as a house and garden owned by a Mr. Rowland (no Christian name shown) and occupied by James Long, a gardener, his family and others. During the 1860s a James Rowland is shown as owner until 1883, probably the same person as in the Tithe Award, with James Long still in occupation along with others. In about 1876 this house became the home of Daniel Carter (as tenant), a baker with Knowles Bakery. In 1884 Carter's Bakery was established here; Mr. Carter left the employment of Knowles Bakery when they installed a new steam oven which he regarded as 'a new fangled thing', which he wanted nothing to do with.[30] He purchased the house which was known as 'Briar House' and the outbuildings became his bakery, all of which were demolished when Sompting Road was improved and the site is now under part of 'Glawood House'. Carter's Bakery was re-sited in modern premises in Penfold Road where it still exists today (1983).

*Cottage and Garden (Tithe No. 170) (No. 43 on plan)*
This site was part of the land belonging to descendants of the Heather family from
1780-1806. Samuel Heather gave up a croft of 3 rods 37 perches in 1810 when it formed part
of a parcel of land awarded to John Holmes. The first positive identification of a building on
the site is shown on the Charles Hide Survey of 1838 and is also given in the Surveyor's
Book of 1841, when it is described as a house in the occupation of George Cooter, Joseph
Munnery and William Bailey. This information is verified by the 1841 census.

    Two of the occupiers, Munnery and Bailey, are shown to be in the building until 1864,
Cooter continuing until the late 1860s. Robert Holmes was the owner from 1841 to 1849,
while during the 1860s Charles Groome was recorded (the occupier of Lyon's Farm). In the
early 1890s Daniel Carter bought the property, being adjacent to his bakery, and by 1907
they became known as 'Carter's Cottages'. The cottages remained until the 1970s when the
site formed part of the 'Glawood House' re-development.

*Houses and Gardens (Tithe No. 171) (No. 44 on plan)*
The 1898 Ordnance Survey map shows this property containing a number of separate
buildings which will be dealt with separately (see Fig. 29).

    The 1806 enclosure map shows the property as an old enclosure owned by Mary
Greenfield with a large field on the north also shown as 'Greenfields'. At the time it would
appear that there were no buildings on the old enclosure.

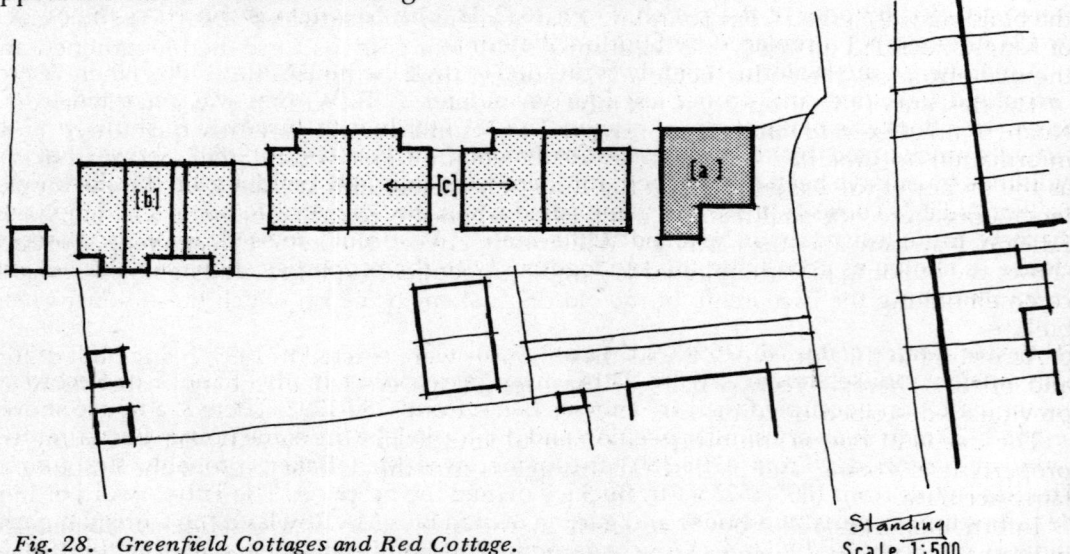

Standing
Scale 1:500

*Fig. 28.   Greenfield Cottages and Red Cottage.*

a) *House and Garden*
The 1821 census records that this building was divided into three parts, two of which were
empty at the time of the census, and one part occupied by William Bamfield and Rachel
(presumably his wife), two other adults and one child. The house was owned by Jane
Greenfield. The Church Rate books show that a William Banford was in the property from
1819 to 1822 and it seems that one of the spellings of the name was wrong. There were a
number of occupants recorded over the next few years: John Slaughter in 1828 and 1829,

after which it was empty in 1830. By about 1831-33 Henry Goble was installed. Henry May took over in 1832 and 1833 and was succeeded by Robert Duley in 1834. During that year it became empty, but between 1836 and 1839 Charlotte Duley lived there, as well as Sarah Longley. By 1839 Noah Smith Lee had acquired the property which he retained until about 1875, his executors holding it from about 1875 until 1881. The property then appears to have passed to Jane Searle by 1886, who was still recorded as the owner in the last Surveyor's Book of 1894.

Between 1839 and 1881 the property was still divided into three parts with many changes of occupants, too numerous to mention in detail. However, by 1886 there appeared to be only one family group in occupation until at least 1894. The 1907 Directory of Worthing names the property 'Red Cottage'. This property remained until the road widening took place in the late 1960s and early 1970s. Very few details of the origin of this house are known, but it seems likely that William Banford was the first occupier in about 1819. The house was no doubt built of flint and bricks.

b) This building, which still survives, was erected in 1866 according to the date on the outside of the building. Above the date ar the letters 'N. & J.L'. The N.L. is almost certainly the initials of the first owner, Noah Lee, while the 'J' probably represents his wife's or perhaps a brother's Christian name. The house was built of flint and bricks and divided into three tenements. The outside of the building is now rendered over.

The address of the building is now Kingsland Road, but before this road was constructed the building was served from Sompting Road (originally Broadwater Street). The formation of Kingsland Road ensured that the former small rear gardens were then lengthened and the rear entrances have now become the modern front entrance.

The descent of this property is not too clear, but from 1866 to 1875 it was in the hands of Noah Smith Lee and after that, his executors until 1881. From this date there is no information documented in the Surveyor's Books until 1886 when Jane Searle was shown as the owner of the easternmost of the three tenements until at least 1894. The other two tenements were not documented until 1893, when the central tenement was owned by Edward Harrison and the other by William Greenyer. The 1907 Directory of Worthing shows the building to be numbered 6, 7 and 8 'Greenfield Cottages', the name presumably commemorating the ownership of the old original enclosure on which these houses were built.

c) According to the Surveyor's Books these houses were erected in 1885, being built of flint and bricks. There were two pairs of these buildings erected in the space between the previously-described buildings.

The deeds of one of the properties refer to land to the north and west (including the property itself) being sold in 1884. This suggests that the date of 1885 for the buildings is fairly accurate.

Information received from a resident in the area, who has lived there all his life, indicates that the buildings were erected originally for the use of the workers in Carter's Bakery, south of this property. This again tends to support the original date of 1885 as the bakery started in 1884. The buildings have long gardens to the north, but these remain as rear gardens, as there is a passage to the south which still leads to the front doors. In 1907 these buildings are shown as Nos. 2 to 5 Greenfield Cottages. Their modern address is now Kingsland Road.

**Section 9–Sompting Road (Eastern Side)** (Nos. 45-51 incl. on plan)
This section contains a number of late Victorian buildings which were unaffected by the Sompting Road widening project and, with one exception, all survive today.

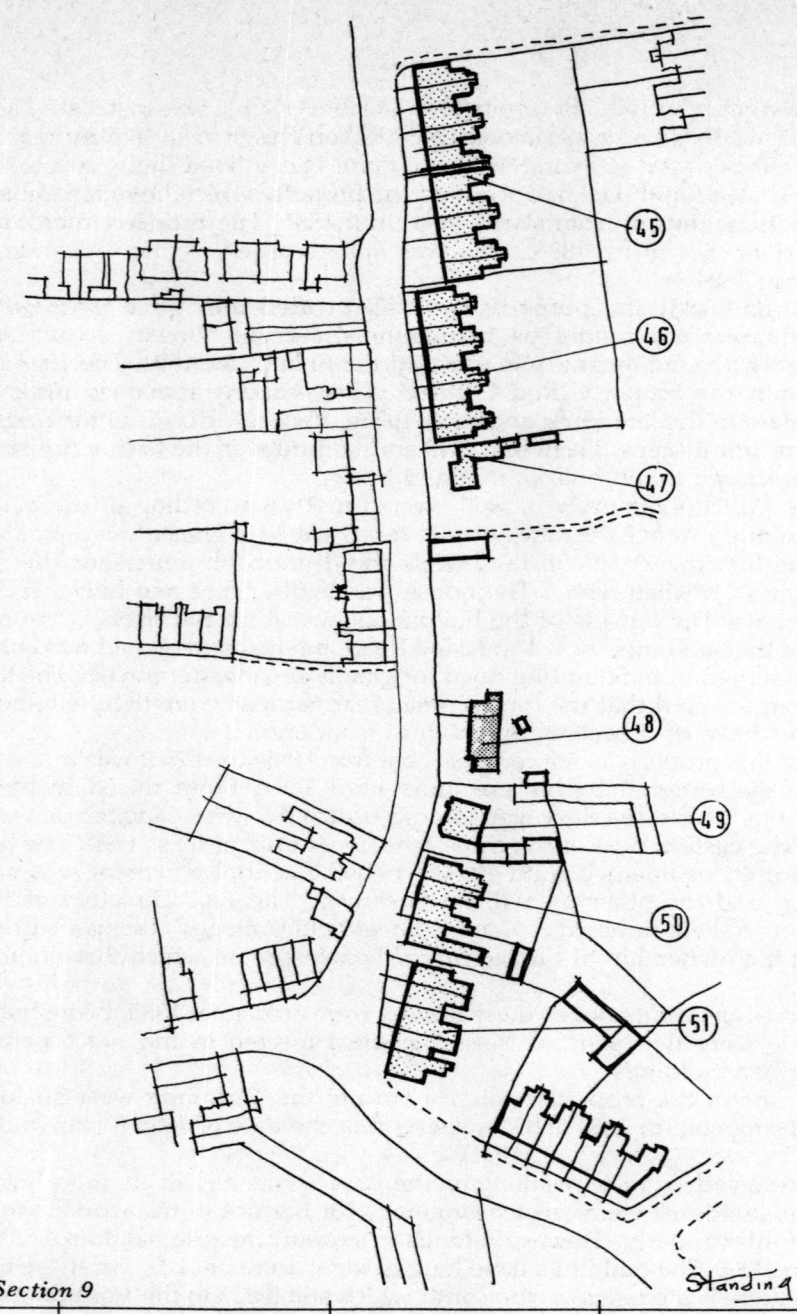

Section 9

Standing

| N° | DESCRIPTION | MODERN ADDRESS | CURRENT USE |
|---|---|---|---|
| 45 | Briar Terrace | 60-78 Sompting Rd. | Residential |
| 46 | Northbrook Cottages | 44-58 " " | " |
| 47 | Lyons Cottage | 42 " " | Unigate Dairy |
| 48 | Cyprus Cottage | 22 " " | Residential |
| 49 | House | 20 " " | " |
| 50 | Oxford Terrace | 12-18 " " | Residential/Commercial |
| 51 | Terrace of Houses | 2-10 " " | " " |

*Briar Terrace (Tithe No. 174)* (No. 45 on plan)
This block of ten houses, in a typical late-Victorian style, was built in 1893 by J. A. East and
named 'Briar Terrace'. They were built for Daniel Carter who lived almost opposite, in Briar
House (hence the name of the terrace) and owned Carter's Bakery. This terrace still exists
but the road has been renamed Sompting Road in the early part of the present century.

*Northbrook Cottages* (No. 46 on plan)
This terrace of eight houses was built in about 1885 presumably for George Cooper and
William Greenyer, who were the original owners. George Cooper owned the three
northernmost houses in the terrace and occupied the first house himself for several years.
By about 1888 Ruth Cooper was the new owner, possibly the wife or daughter of George.
   The other five houses in the terrace were the property of William Greenyer. He lived in
the second house from the southern end and was still there in 1907. The houses are still
standing in 1983.

*House (Tithe No. 175)* (No. 47 on plan)
At the time of the tithe map this parcel of land did not contain a building, but was described
as a garden owned by Mr. Henry Tribe and occupied by Elias Blake-Geere. By 1875 the
Ordnance Survey map still shows no buildings on the site, but the 1898 Ordnance Survey
map reveals a building which, in the 1907 Directory, is recorded as 'Lyons Cottage' and
occupied by C. Lillywhite. The exact date of the building is not known and as it does not
appear to be recorded in the Surveyor's Books, which finish in 1894, it is therefore quite
probable that it was built between 1894 and 1898. The cottage is still recorded in directories
of Worthing in the first half of the present century (in 1949 it is recorded but no occupier
shown). The cottage no longer exists and the Unigate Dairy covers the site.

*House and Garden (Tithe No. 176)* (No. 48 on plan)
This house was built on an old enclosure, shown on the enclosure map as occupied by
Joseph Spicer. By 1818 the Church Rate books record that a house and garden was occupied
by Susan Spicer. Later, in 1820, a Mary Spicer is shown as the occupier. By 1821 the census
records the house and garden as still owned by Spicer but occupied by Spicer with Elias
Geere and his family. From 1822 it seems that Elias was the new owner and remained as
such for some considerable time. Both the census for 1841 and 1851 record him still in
occupation, but by 1841 a son also called Elias and a daughter, Esther, are shown. In 1868
the Surveyor's Books show that a house and workshop were built to the south of his
property (see No. 49). It appears that Elias moved into this new house in 1873 and let his
other house to a tenant, Charles Grevatt. The records do not clearly show which Elias is the
householder. However, Elias senior was born in 1786 and by 1873 would have been 87
years old and hardly likely to have built a new house for himself!
   In 1880 his house was then shown as owned by Esther, his wife, while an Elias (probably
the son) had moved into the property to the south (see No. 50) which the family acquired in
1869 from Charles Groome. In 1881 a new owner, Mr. Henry Tribe, is recorded in the
Surveyor's Books and remains there until 1892, with his executors still shown in possession
until 1894. During the period of Mr. Tribe's ownership there were a number of tenants. The
Directory for 1907 shows the house to be called 'Cypress Cottage' and occupied by W. M.
Boxall. The house still exists and although the original date of construction is not known, a
building is shown on Yeakell & Gardner's map of 1780, and it seems quite likely that it is
the same. A building also shown on a map of 1720 in a similar position, which could also be
the same house, but this at present cannot be verified. The existing building has a rendered

facade but is almost certainly flint built. As the house is not mentioned in the land tax records it also seems probable that it was copyhold at some time.

*House, Workshop and garden (part of Tithe No. 177) (No. 49 on plan)*
As previously mentioned this building first appears in the Surveyor's Books in 1868 under the ownership of Elias Blake-Geere (probably the son of Elias senior). For about four years it is shown as empty, but in 1873 Elias Blake-Geere moved from his house next door (No. 48) into this new house and workshop. He remained there until about 1880 when he again moved, this time into his other property to the south (see No. 50). His wife is shown as the owner from 1881 until 1889, during which time a possible lodger is shown, George Stone. It then appears that her son Elias (junior) returned to the house for a short period (probably on her death) for he is recorded as owner and occupier for the next four years. In 1894 a new tenant, W. Dabbs, is recorded. This person is still recorded as the occupier in the 1907 Directory when the house is referred to as 'Hibernia', a name which can still be seen on the house today on a glass panel above the door. As with the previous house it has been rendered on the outside but no doubt it is built of flint.

*Oxford and Cambridge Terraces (part of Tithe No. 177) (Nos. 50 and 51 on plan)*
Both of these buildings are typical late Victorian brick-built terraces, dated between 1894 and 1898. Oxford Terrace is built on the site of two old cottages which certainly are shown on a map of 1780 and may well be the buildings shown on the 1720 map. Cambridge Terrace was built on the site of an old barn and both of these Terraces still exist today.

**Section 10–Broadwater Street East (South side)** (Nos. 52 to 54 incl. on plan)
The area contained in this section has been considerably altered through re-development and is basically chosen on geographical grounds. It is the area between two well-defined roads, the modern Dominion Road and the start of the Quashetts that leads to the Square from Broadwater Street East.

*House and Garden (not shown on 1898 O.S. map) (Tithe No. 128) (No. 52 on plan)*
There is evidence to indicate that this property is very old, for the 1720 map shows a house of a similar size and shape which faced in the same direction as the house shown on later maps. A thorough search of the Parish Registers, wills and probates show that Peter Price, a yeoman of Broadwater, born in 1643 lived in Broadwater from 1662 and died on 6 December 1713 'at his dwelling house at Broadwater'.[31] In 1712 he is shown on a list of inhabitants of Broadwater . He married Elizabeth (nee Thirston), a widow of Steyning, on 6 September 1705 and they had two sons, Peter and John, and two daughters, Mary and Elizabeth. Both of the sons were dead by 1721 and Mary was shown as a beneficiary in her father's will with a one-third share of all goods and effects. Elizabeth appears to have been the sole survivor of the family and inherited the dwelling house, which is almost certainly the house and garden shown as No. 128 on the tithe map. On 16 May 1744 Elizabeth Price married Daniel Denn. She later had three children, the eldest of whom was Daniel (baptized in 1745). The records show that Daniel married and in turn had a son, another Daniel, who was baptized in 1792. This Daniel is the person shown living in the property with his wife Diana and children in the 1821 census. By the 1851 census the property was owned by William Newland of Decoy Farm but the occupier was still Daniel Denn, aged 69 and his wife, aged 68, with a Jane Denn, aged 20, shown as a seamstress (presumably their daughter). Daniel lived to a ripe old age, for he was still shown as an occupier in 1868 (by

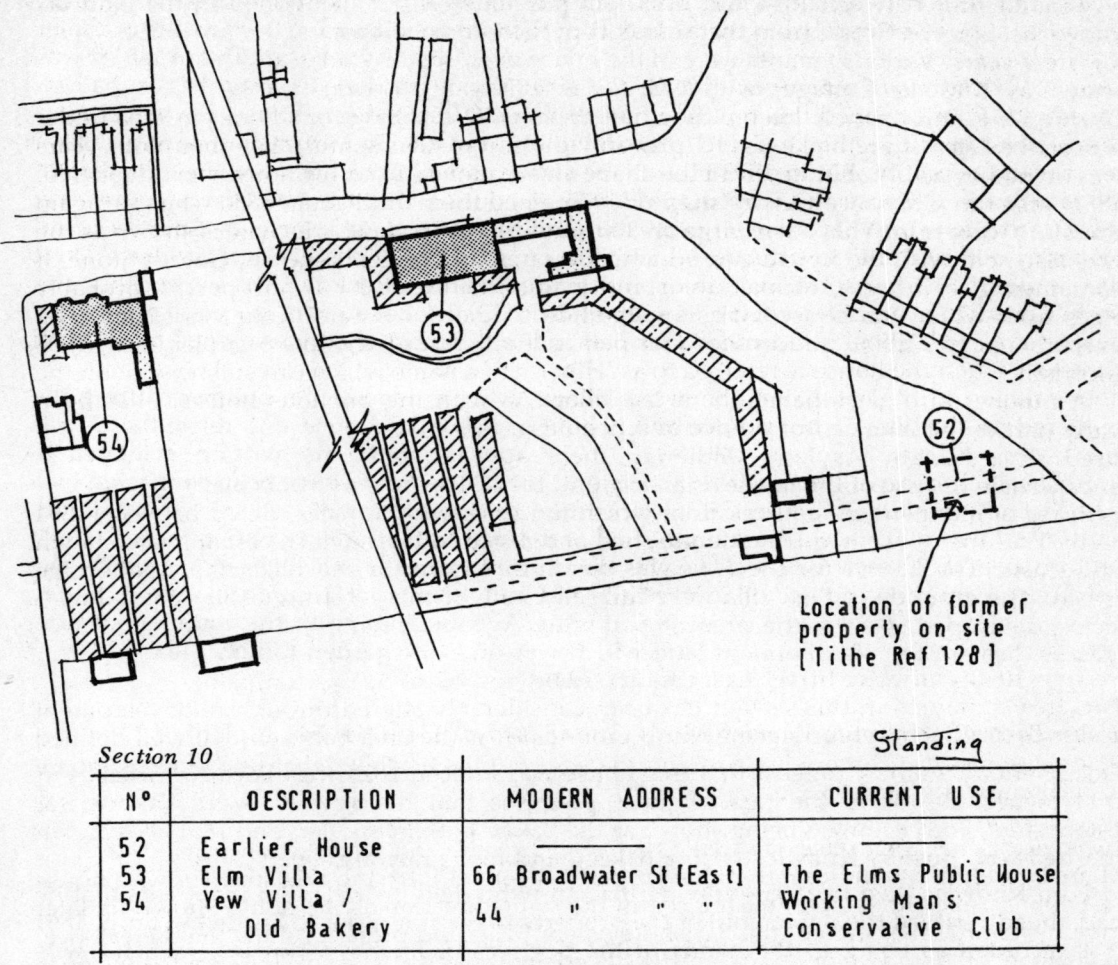

Location of former
property on site
[Tithe Ref 128]

*Section 10*                                                    Standing

| N° | DESCRIPTION | MODERN ADDRESS | CURRENT USE |
|----|-----------|----------------|-------------|
| 52 | Earlier House | ——— | ——— |
| 53 | Elm Villa | 66 Broadwater St [East] | The Elms Public House |
| 54 | Yew Villa / Old Bakery | 44  "  "  " | Working Mans Conservative Club |

then he was 86 years old). Just prior to 1875 the house was demolished and on the 1898 Ordnance Survey map a windpump is shown on the site. Very little is known about the construction of the house for there appear to be no known photographs or illustrations existing.

*House and Garden/Elm Villa (Tithe No. 130) (No. 53 on plan)*
The first mention of this house is in the 1821 census when it is described as a 'House and Garden' belonging to Richard Newland of Decoy Farm, the occupants being Ford Knowles, his wife Sarah and their two children. It is most likely that the original house was a copyhold tenement belonging to Decoy Farm, and may also have been the house shown on or near the site on the 1720 map, but this has not been substantiated. Ford and Sarah were described as 'poor' in the 1821 census and the family were employed in agriculture. Later (about 1828) Ford Knowles and his family moved out of the house and a Thomas Burtenshaw is identified as the tenant in the 1841 census.

At some time between 1844 and 1846 Ford purchased the house and surrounding area, known as 'Spicer's Croft', from the executors of Richard Newland and became the occupier for a few years. Various tenants were in the house over the next ten years and in 1851 it was known as 'Knowles Cottage', with a Mrs. Harriet Taylor and her daughter in occupation. During 1851, and possibly later, it may have been used as a lodging house, for Mrs. Taylor is described as a 'Lodging House Keeper' in the 1851 census. By 1861 the house and garden was owned by a C. A. Elliott. From the shape and situation of the house on the tithe map of 1851, and the Ordnance Survey map of 1875, it appears that the house was completely rebuilt to form 'Elm Villa'. The large area around the old cottage known as 'Spicer's Croft' was also sold with the house and became the large and spacious gardens of Elm Villa; it contained glass houses, formal lawns and gardens, an orchard and trees (probably elm trees from which the house took its name). By 1877 the house was in the hands of the executors of Mr. Elliott and in the latter half of the 19th century it was owned by William Morris.

A number of older inhabitants of the village, who remember the building during the early part of the 20th century, have described it as the 'Mad House' and relate that it was used as a Lunatic Asylum. Although there appears to be no written evidence to substantiate the use of the house as an asylum, the fact seems to have been confirmed by a number of independent sources from which the statements came.

By 1927 the house had been demolished and replaced by the *Elms* public house, which still exists. The licence for the *Elms* was transferred from the old *Engineer's Arms* by the green. The grounds of Elm Villa were utilised as allotments for a number of years before being developed. Part of the present Sompting Avenue leading to the roundabout now passes through the old allotment land which was once the garden to Elm Villa.

### *House/Bakery/Conservative Working Men's Club (Tithe No. 131)* (No. 54 on plan)

Documentary sources suggest that this house was built in 1828 with Ford Knowles as its first owner. It was to the rear of these premises that the new Knowles Bakery was established, Ford Knowles being shown as the Baker, both in the 1841 and 1851 census. His married son, Bushby Knowles (also a Baker), and his family also lived there.

Ford Knowles died in 1855 outliving his son (who died in 1851), but it appears that he had already passed the ownership of the property to his son, prior to his death, for in 1861 it is recorded as being in the hands of the devisees of Bushby Knowles, with his wife Elizabeth shown as the occupier. Later the house passed to C. A. Elliott, the owner of Elm Villa, and it is most likely that he was responsible for naming the property Yew Villa. By the end of the 19th century it was owned by Mr. Redford and occupied by Joseph Greenyer. During 1924 it was turned into the Conservative Working Men's Club, which still exists. The main fabric of the building is flint, a typical building material of this period, and is today disguised below a covering of render.

### Section 11–Broadwater Street East (Southside) (Nos. 55 to 58 incl. on plan)
This section contains the area between the Quashetts and the eastern edge of the churchyard.

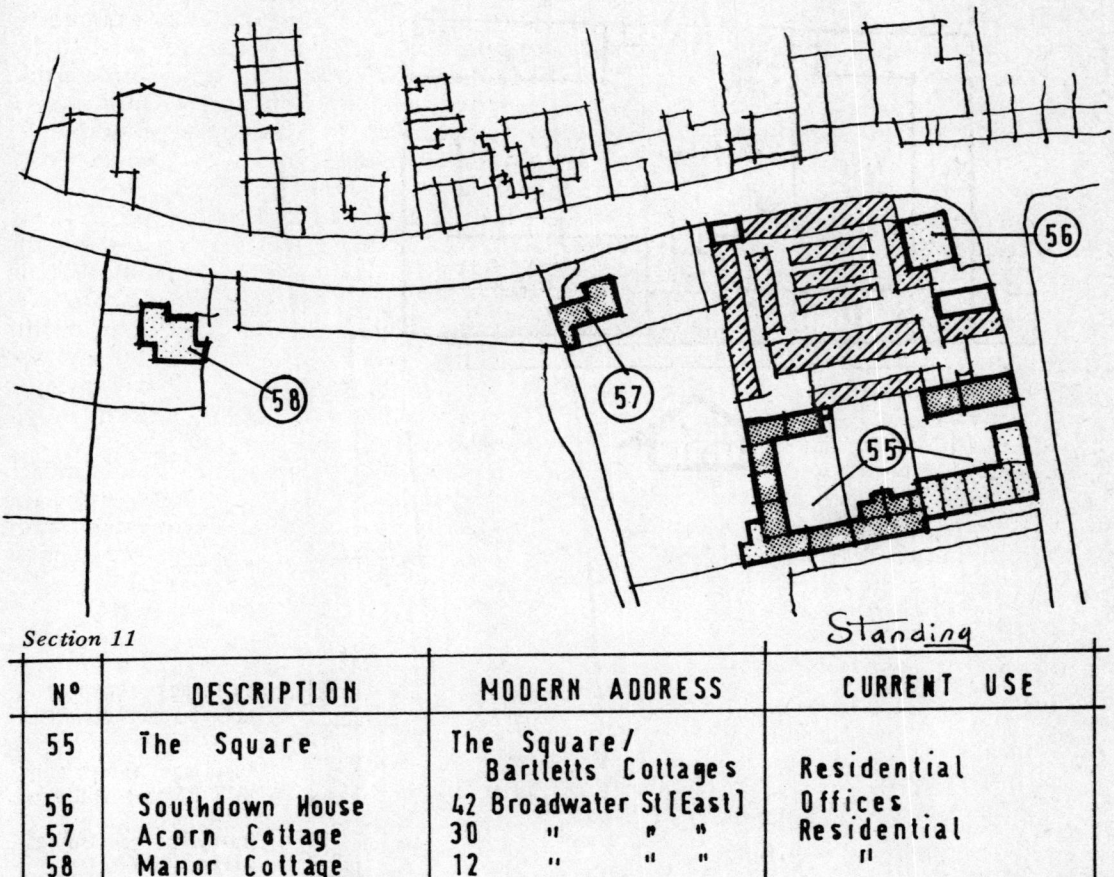

Section 11    Standing

| N° | DESCRIPTION | MODERN ADDRESS | CURRENT USE |
|----|-------------|----------------|-------------|
| 55 | The Square | The Square/ Bartletts Cottages | Residential |
| 56 | Southdown House | 42 Broadwater St [East] | Offices |
| 57 | Acorn Cottage | 30 " " " | Residential |
| 58 | Manor Cottage | 12 " " " | " |

*Houses/Peryers/The Square (Tithe No. 132) (No. 55 on plan)*

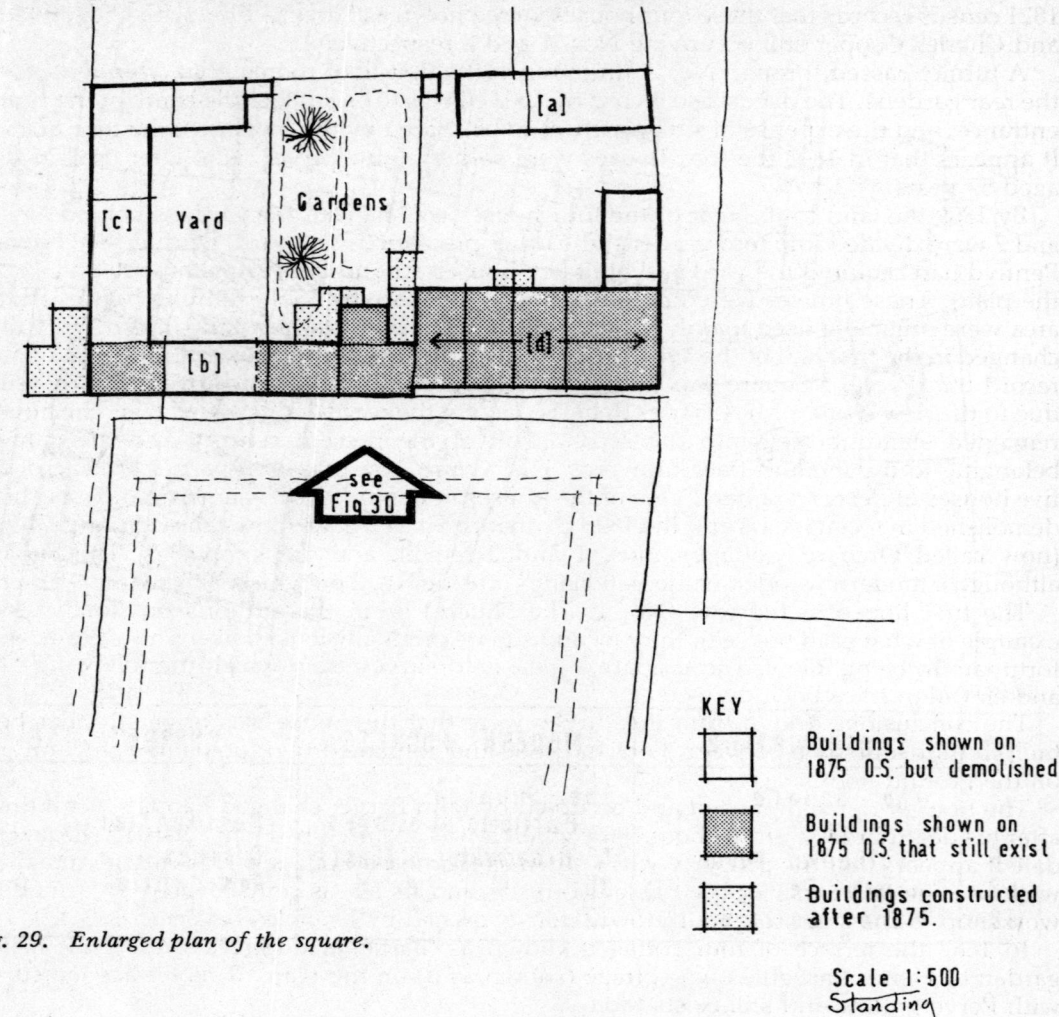

KEY

Buildings shown on
1875 O.S. but demolished

Buildings shown on
1875 O.S. that still exist

Buildings constructed
after 1875.

*Fig. 29.   Enlarged plan of the square.*

Scale 1:500
Standing

The Land Tax Records indicate that the first house built on the above piece of land was in
1789, and is that shown as a) on the above plan, owned and occupied by John Peryer.
However, the deeds of the property [32] confuse the issue as they record that the *house and
land* was purchased from Robert Vaughan in 1747 by Thomas Peryer, cordwainer of
Broadwater. If this is so then the house recorded as Thomas Peryer's in an early Land Tax
list of 1752 may well be the same one. The land was divided into two portions, the
westernmost part being a garden plot. By 1803, the deed (previously mentioned) shows
that John Peryer, only son and heir of Thomas Peryer (deceased), cordwainer of
Broadwater, had acquired the property and built the four houses on the garden plot,
shown as b) on the plan. The deeds also reveal that the four houses were previously
occupied by Messrs. Burstow, Champion, West and Braby but by 1803 were in the

occupation of Gideon Hook, Charles Cooper, William Puttock and Elizabeth Plowman. The 1821 census records that these four houses were known as Peryer's Row with Gideon Hook and Charles Cooper still occupying Nos. 1 and 2 respectively.

A tunnel passed through No. 2, underneath the first-floor rooms, that offered access to the rear gardens. The deeds also record that a well was to be sunk to the south of the tunnel entrance, and the expense of sinking it was to be shared by the owners of the four houses. It appears that in 1803 the four houses were sold by John Peryer, who later died in 1807 aged 57 years.

By 1809 the land to the rear of the four houses was halved, the gardens behind Nos. 1 and 2 were divided into four gardens, the other piece forming a yard. During 1809 Edward Penfold had acquired the yard and built five houses around the perimeter (shown as c) on the plan). These houses were known as Peryer's Square by 1821. All nine houses in this area were originally used mainly to accommodate the poor people of the Parish. Very little changed in the first half of the 19th century but during the early 1860s the Surveyor's Books record that Peryer's Square was known as 'Ready Money Square' for two years, possibly due to the new owner, Mr. Charles Roberts, having the ready money available! The houses remained standing well into the second half of the present century and the garages belonging to the modern flats known as 'East Court' now stand on part of the site of the five houses of Peryer's Square. One of the houses in Peryer's Row, namely No. 3, has been demolished in recent years and the 1898 Ordnance Survey map shows an addition on No. 4 (now called Orchard Cottage). Nos. 1 and 2 remain and are known as 'The Square' although a modern wooden nameplate hangs outside No. 2 on which is the name 'Peryers'.

The first house in the row (No. 1, The Square) is, in the author's opinion, a good example of what each house in the row and square originally looked like. The authors were fortunate in being allowed to prepare a measured survey from which the following plan and elevation have been derived.

The conclusions drawn from the survey were that the house was originally thatched, built in flint sometime between 1790 and 1800 and contained two rooms upstairs and one on the ground floor.

The house originally owned and occupied by John Peryer changed hands several times after his death in 1807, until about 1867, when it was acquired by Henry Bartlett. From that date it appears that the property was known as 'Bartlett's Cottage'. This cottage remained well into the latter half of the present century and its site is now covered by a modern workshop to the south of 'Southdown House' owned by Knowles Bakery.

In 1867 the terrace of four cottages known as 'Bartlett's Cottages' were built in the garden of Henry Bartlett's own cottage (shown as d) on the plan). This terrace joined up with Peryer's Row and still exists today.

*Southdown House (Tithe No. 133)* (No. 56 on plan)
This house was built in 1868 and was owned by James Apted who moved from the house almost opposite (that being the forerunner of the *Old House at Home* public house). He was described as a baker and beer brewer and when he moved he left his previous house in the occupation of his son-in-law, James Davis. James Apted died in May 1871 and the property passed to his wife Mary until her death in 1890. A William James Apted, possibly her son, then took over.

There are several glass houses shown in the gardens of Southdown House on the 1898 Ordnance Survey map and it appears that William James Apted was a horticulturist and grower and that he sent potatoes to Brighton Market. The house was first shown as 'Southdown House' in the 1907 Directory (a name which it retains) and that W. J. Apted

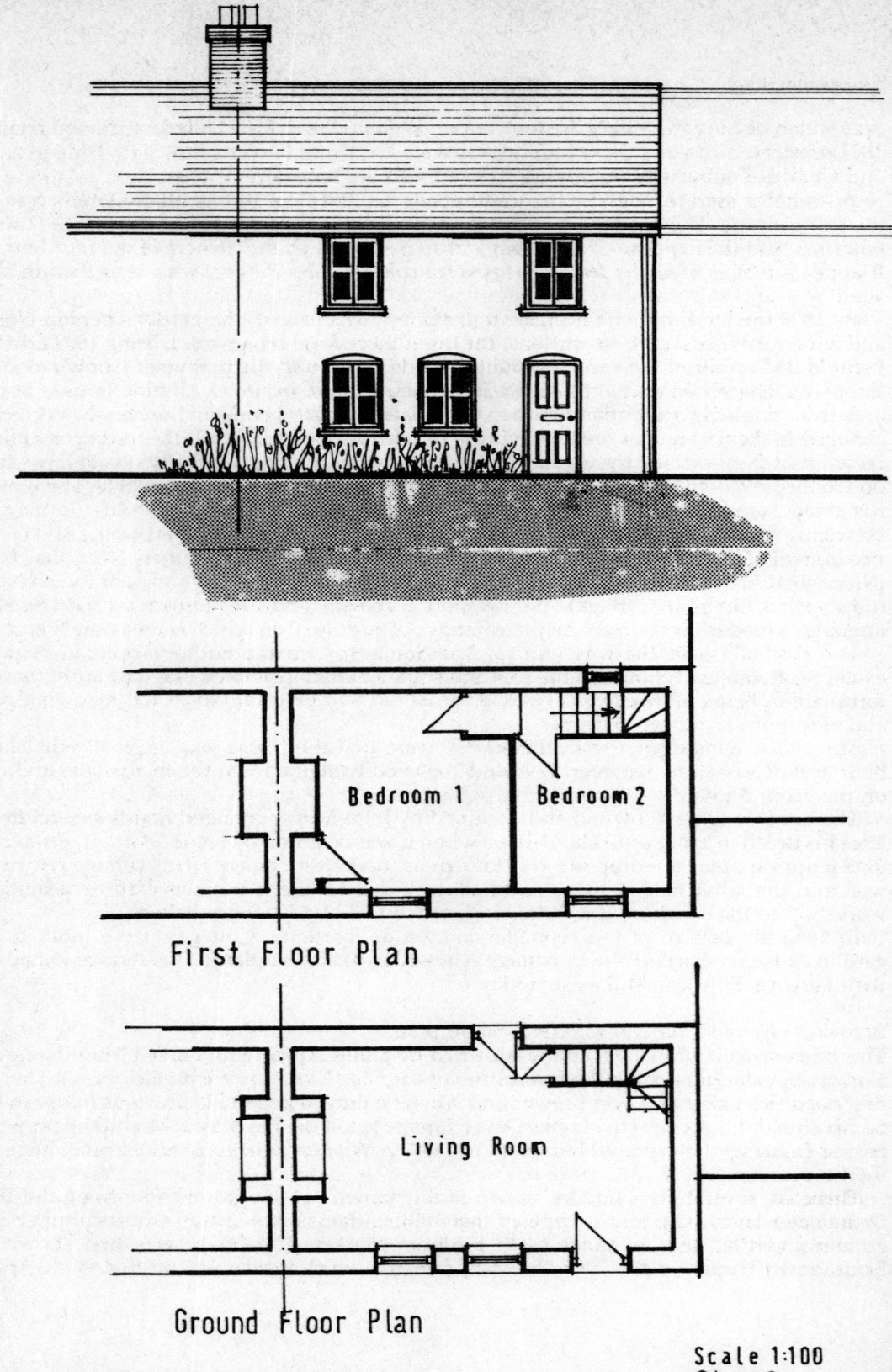

Bedroom 1

Bedroom 2

**First Floor Plan**

Living Room

**Ground Floor Plan**

Scale 1:100

Standing

*Fig. 30. Measured survey of No. 1, The Square.*

was still in residence. During the first half of the 20th century the Apted family still retained the property.

The house still exists but was converted into six flats several years ago, retaining the same exterior appearance. It has recently been modified for use as offices (1983).

### House (Tithe No. 134) (No. 57 on plan)

The origin of this house is somewhat confusing for the front and sides are faced with large flints typical of the mid- or late Victorian period, whilst the rear of the house shows smaller flints in lime mortar which strongly suggests a much earlier period (1800 or earlier). Even though a house is shown on this site on the 1720 map of Broadwater, the early Land Tax records do not record a house for the period 1780 to 1832. This may well be because the house was copyhold and not necessarily shown in such records.

It is first positively identified in the 1821 census when it is recorded as being occupied by Edward Burtenshaw, his wife Lucy, one other adult and a child. The owner was John Newland, the Lord of the Manor, supporting the suggestion that it may have been copyhold. In the 1851 census Edward Burtenshaw, aged 83, is shown as the occupier with his servant. By 1861 James Burtenshaw is the occupier, the house is still owned by the Newland family. The 1907 Worthing Directory shows a James Burtenshaw still in occupation with the name of the house shown as 'Acorn Cottage', the name by which the existing house is still known.

It is the authors' opinion that the house was originally the one shown on the 1720 map and that it has been continually modified or rebuilt over the years, culminating in a last major 'facelift' when the front and sides of the house were faced (or rebuilt?) with large flints, probably in the 1850s or 1860s. Other minor modern extensions and modifications have been carried out since.

### House (part of Tithe No. 125) (No. 58 on plan)

This house was built, sometime between 1894 and 1898, adjacent to the east wall of the churchyard, and shows a pleasant front aspect constructed of large flints. By 1912 the Worthing Directory shows it as 'Manor Cottage', presumably due to its proximity to Broadwater Manor House, which was by then used as a Preparatory or Day School. Its use as a school lasted well into the late 1920s, although it has now returned to being a private residence.

### Section 12–Broadwater Church Area (Nos. 59 and 60 on plan)

This section covers the area containing the church and the buildings on the northern side of the churchyard.

### Broadwater Church (No. 59 on plan)

The church of St Mary's is, typically, the oldest building in the village. The Domesday Survey reveals there was a church at Broadwater in 1086,[33] and although no part of the original structure is now visible, a church is thought to have existed in Saxon times. The Saxon church might have been constructed of timber by the local lord. The nearness of the Manor House to the church has in many villages born witness to such a close relationship.[34]

The present church was commenced some time after 1100, and from the first it was constructed to last; it was the one building upon which the village community at Broadwater lavished time and money, generation after generation. It is a large cruciform building, constructed largely of flint, partly Norman and partly Transitional but chiefly English with some decorated work, consisting of a chancel, nave, transepts and north and

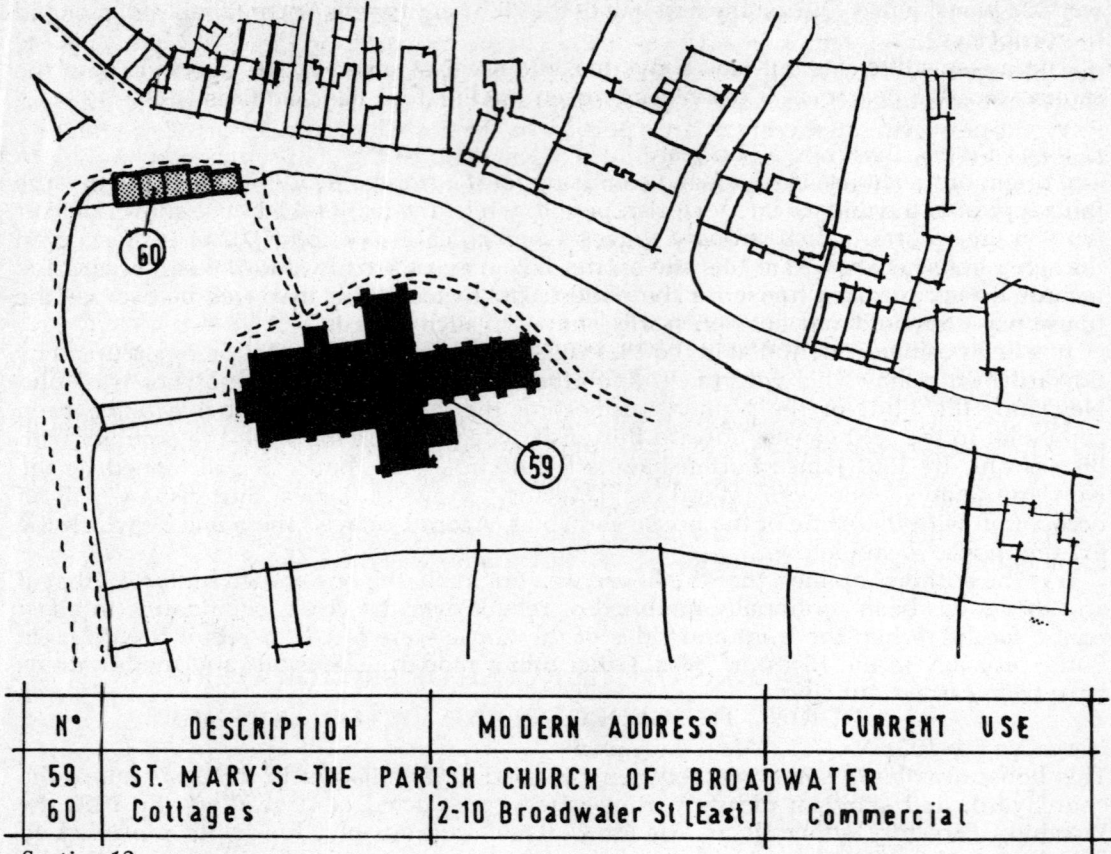

| N° | DESCRIPTION | MODERN ADDRESS | CURRENT USE |
|----|-------------|----------------|-------------|
| 59 | ST. MARY'S – THE PARISH CHURCH OF BROADWATER | | |
| 60 | Cottages | 2-10 Broadwater St [East] | Commercial |

*Section 12*

west porches.[35] The massive Norman tower rising nearly 140 feet is impressive, and the rounded Norman Chancel arch, seen from the nave through a pointed arch with Norman carving is a very rare sight. It is thought that this nave arch supporting the tower, became unstable in the 14th century, and was taken to pieces and rebuilt in the new style with the old stones.[36] At the western end of the church, and in the north porch, are some beautiful examples of knapped flint work. The flints have been chipped or knapped into small squares fitting together almost as accurately as bricks. On the south side of the church are two crudely made crosses in flint, said to be the only examples of their kind in West Sussex, though they are common in Suffolk.

When first constructed, as well as using the church for daily worship, its parishioners used the nave as a communal 'village hall'. The parish notices still posted in the church porch act as a reminder that the porch was the usual place for the transaciton of civil business from earliest times, deliberations and discussions on legal and economic matters, especially those connected with agriculture and questions of tenure.[37]

The Rev. P. Wood, when presented with the living in 1797, found the church in a very neglected condition, which was typical of most of the properties in the village at the end of the 18th century. Nearly 30 years later, in 1826, the church was extensively repaired. The short spire was taken down, and a corner turret and battlements were substituted, the Rev. P. Wood personally defraying a large portion of the costs incurred.[38] Further restoration was required in 1866, when it was found that the walls of the chancel were beginning to bulge outwards. Henfry Smail records the restoration works as follows in his book the *Notable Houses of Worthing No. 2*, (p. 89):

'The roof was stripped and iron rods were passed through the walls across the chancel and bolted outside to baulks of timber. The rods were then heated by coal braziers placed beneath, causing them to expand, when they were bolted tightly against the timber baulks. This process was repeated until the walls were once again drawn back into an upright position when they were underpinned and buttressed. At the same time the existing decorated chancel windows consisting of a pair of trefoil lancets with a quatrefoil over, were removed and replaced by the present Victorian Early English lancets.'

The supervision of this restoration was undertaken by Mr. Charles Hyde. A relation of his, Mr. T. R. Hyde, relates his earliest childhood recollections of this activity:

'. . . of watching the workman from a window of my father's cottage opposite the church, watching carpenters working on the restoration wearing top hats and white jackets'.[39]

The clock now installed in the tower, was presented by the parishioners in 1903 to commemorate the jubilee of the Rev. E. K. Elliott who was then rector.

## RECTORS OF THE PARISH OF BROADWATER
## DURING THE GEORGIAN AND VICTORIAN PERIOD

| | | | |
|---|---|---|---|
| 1684 | William Wade | 1781 | Richard Russel, M.A. |
| 1714 | Jeremiah Dodson, M.A. | 1797 | Peter Wood, M.A. |
| 1745 | Samuel Terrick, M.A. | 1853 | E. K. Elliot, M.A. |
| 1762 | Richard Bassett, M.A. | 1905 | Ed. Jas. Elliot, M.A. |

*Cottages* (No. 60 on plan)

These three very old cottages were originally very picturesque as shown on the many drawings, pictures and sketches which survive today. They were built of flint and originally had thatched roofs. The cottages were in a row, with a smaller building on each end and a central long building. The date of their construction is not known, although one is mentioned in the will of John Parrot (senior)[40] whose daughter Margaret inherited, on the death of her mother 'all that messuage or tenement adjoining to the churchyard'. At the time of her father's death, in July 1720, the cottage was occupied by William Parrot, her uncle, and she inherited the cottage in December 1721, when her mother died. This particular building was probably the central one of the three.

Another mention of the cottages occurred in the vestry minutes, of 22 June 1724, as follows: 'This evening Henry Travies Esq. the undoubted Patron of the living of Broadwater was pleased to declare in the company of Mr. Young Wills, Mr. Penfold and Mr. Henley that he really believed that the three houses which stand on the north side of the churchyard, are built on the Lord's waste, and that there is no tresspass on the Church ground by them'.

It is interesting to note that the map of 1720 does not show any cottages on the site, and since the map shows all the property of the Lord of the Manor, and the cottages were built on his property, it could mean that the map was slightly earlier than 1720 and the cottages were actually built in 1720. It is of course well known that some early maps do not always show all buildings, as this depends on the reason for the maps' preparation. Further research is necessary to determine the actual date of the buildings, although the very early views do indicate that the estimated date of 1720 could be accurate. As they were built on the Lord of the Manor's property it is most likely that they were originally copyhold. Records for the early years of their existence are very scanty, but by using what is available, together with some logical reasoning, it is possible to gain some ideas about the cottages and their inhabitants over the years.

a) *Cottage by the North Gate of the Churchyard*
This cottage is shorter in length, but taller than the other two, and has a small window high up in the gable end on the west that looks out over the roofs of the others. An early sketch shows it with a door at the eastern end, with steps up to it and a hand rail. There were two windows shown, one at ground level and one at first floor level. As yet, no positive information has been found regarding the occupiers or owners during the 1720s, but it is almost certain that the cottage was the one occupied by John Hide and his wife Hannah, probably from 1731, when they were married. One of his daughters, also named Hannah (1740-1811), did not marry and it appears that she inherited the cottage from her father, for her will recorded 'I give devise and bequeath to my sister Sarah Penfold, wife of Mr. John Penfold of Broadwater aforesaid, all that my freehold messuage Tenement and premises situate lying and being at Broadwater aforesaid abutting to the Churchyard to have and to hold the said messuage or Tenement and Premises'. Now it appears that Sarah Penfold died in 1809 and the cottage passed to her brother Edward Hide, for the Church Rate books from 1819 to 1824 show him as the owner, with Thomas Holcombe and his wife Hannah as occupiers. Between 1839 and 1849 the owner was George Olliver with Mary Legatt as occupier.

During the early 1850s Olliver is still recorded as the owner but the cottage is shown as empty. From 1861-1869 William Palmer was the tenant with a George K. Olliver the owner (possibly the same Olliver as shown earlier!). By 1870 Mrs. Newland had acquired the property and retained it for at least the next three years. There is a gap of several years in the Surveyor's Books before Willim Foard Tribe is shown as the owner/occupier in 1883. Later in 1886 a new occupier, Henry Hatchard, is shown and remained there until the end of the Surveyor's Books in 1894. The Worthing Directory of 1907 shows that the cottage had been converted into a shop and was in the occupation of J. H. W. Pollicutt, tobacconist and stationer. Other directories of 1927 and 1932 show the same occupier but describe it as only a stationer's. By 1939, however, Pollicutt had moved next door and the shop was shown as the 'Modern shoe repair Service Ltd'.

Today the building is still in existence with most of its original fabric still visible and is used by a Building Society.

b) This cottage is the long central one of the group of three, and from the early sketches appears to have two storeys with a door in the front at each end.

The earliest mention of this cottage is in 1720 (as described in the introduction to the cottages) when William Parrott was occupier and John Parrott, his brother, was the owner. The cottage was inherited by John's daughter, Margaret in 1721 after the death of her

other. There is a large gap in the records from this point until 1821 when John Newland, the Lord of the Manor, is shown as the owner. John Best and Anne, his wife, and William Ward are shown as the occupiers. From 1824 to 1836 John Holden is shown as occupier of a property, rated the same value as the cottage, and it appears that he was the occupier of this particular cottage. John Holden died in 1838 and in 1839 the Surveyor's Book records the cottage as owned by the executors of John Holden, with Thomas Gibbard as the occupier.

Thomas Gibbard acquired the property in 1840 and remained as the owner until about 1862 occupying it himself for the first six years. From 1847 to 1851 Mr. Manwaring is shown as the occupier . In about 1864 Gibbard died, for the property was shown as owned by Gibbard's Mortgagees. Edward Braby was recorded as the occupier from at least 1861 until 1884. Around 1875 it appears that T. F. Wisden acquired the property and became the owner for the remainder of the period of records (until 1894). During this time there were several occupiers, the property by now being divided into two residences, and in 1884 an Edward J. Thompson is shown as the occupier of the eastern part. In 1907 he was still there, shown as a saddler with a shop. The other part had several occupiers but had become a shop by 1907, occupied by an E. E. Long, who was shown as a 'confectioner'.

By 1907 (and probably earlier) the property appears to have been split into three separate residences, Nos. 4, 6 and 8 from the east. In 1927 a directory shows that in No. 4 was M. & W. Thompson, fruiterers, and in Nos. 6 and 8, Mrs. Long, confectioner. By 1931 J. H. W. Pollicutt had taken over No. 4 with Mrs. Long still next door, but by 1939 Pollicutt occupied the whole property. The property still exists as shops.

c) This cottage was the easternmost one of the three and is similar to the others in construction, as seen on early sketches and views. It was a two-storey building, similar in height to the central cottage with a small lean-to structure at its western end.

The earliest reference to inhabitants so far uncovered for this cottage is from 1818 to 1836 when Francis French is shown as owner and occupier with his wife Anne and one child. By 1839 Francis had died, for the property was in the hands of his executors and was shown as empty. There appear to be no further records of this property, although it is still shown on the tithe map of 1848. The 1875 Ordnance Survey map shows that this cottage had been demolished and its site today can be identified as the site of 'Trendsetter's' the modern jeweller's shop.


**Section 13–From the Old Rectory to Paine Manwaring's** (Nos. 61 to 70 incl. on plan)
This section includes the old Rectory and all the buildings on the west side of Broadwater Street West, most of which were demolished when road widening took place in the early 1930s.

The authors are indebted to the Managing Director of 'Paine and Manwaring' for allowing them to research the company's deposited deeds and other documents, many of which proved invaluable for much of the information contained in this section.

*The Vicarage/Rectory (Tithe No. 91)* (No. 61 on plan)
The 1720 map of Broadwater shows a rectory on the same site as that shown on the 1898 Ordnance Survey map. However, by reference to their shapes one can see that they are not the same building.

The *Victoria County History* (p. 78) informs that there was reference to a rectory in 1554 and that in 1662 it was called the Vicarage and contained 11 hearths. In Evans *Picture of Worthing* (1804) it is recorded that a handsome parsonage-house was situated in Broadwater and was occupied by the Rev. Peter Wood. This is the rectory shown on the

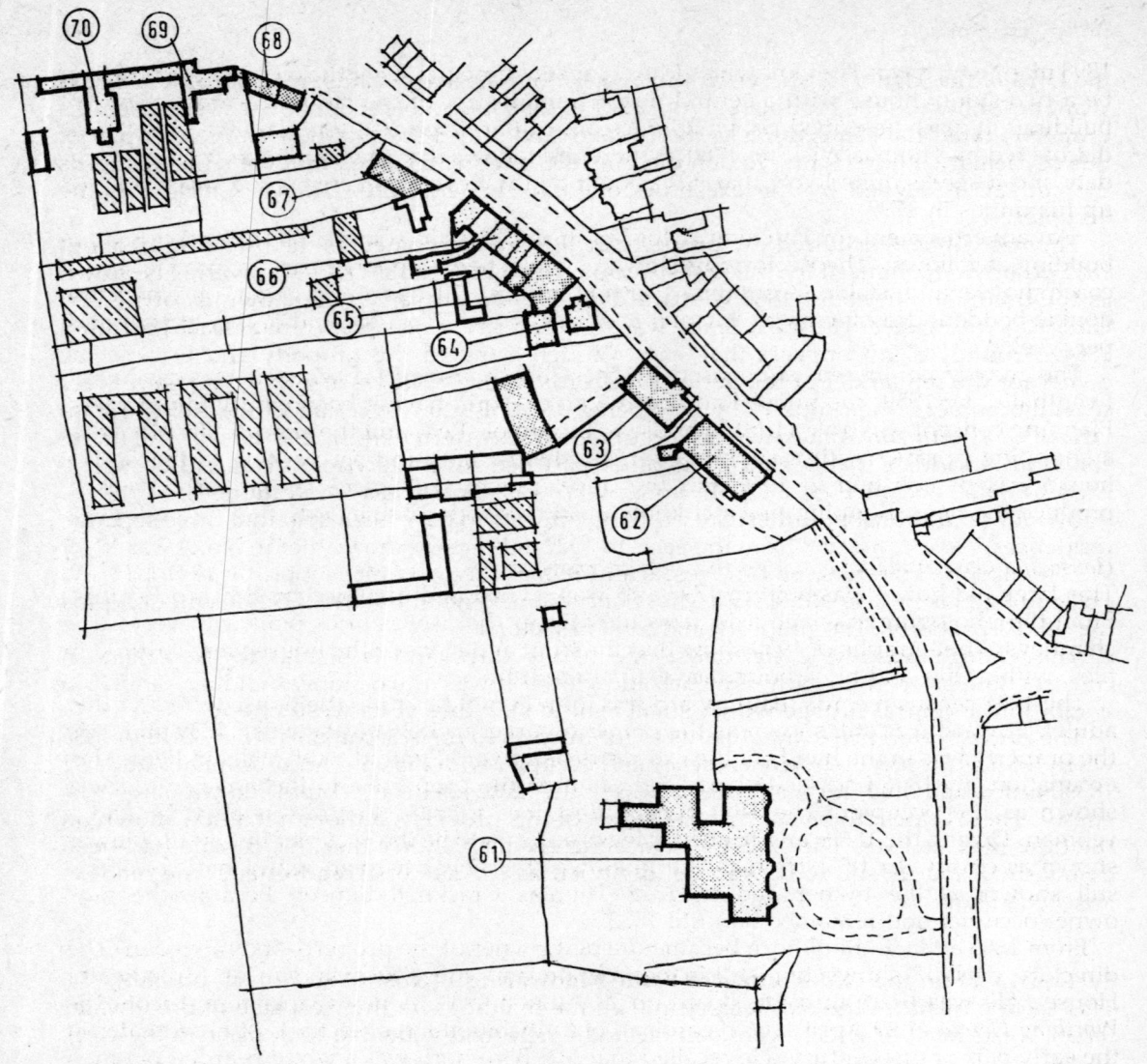

Section 13                                          Standing

| N° | DESCRIPTION | MODERN ADDRESS | CURRENT USE |
|---|---|---|---|
| 61 | Rectory | Broadwater Boulevard | Commercial |
| 62 | House and Garden | 25/27 Broadwater St [West] | " |
| 63 | House | 35/37 " " " | " |
| 64 | Cottage | 39 " " " | " |
| 65 | Bath House | 41/43 " " " | " |
| 66 | Jubilee Cottages | 45/49 " " " | " |
| 67 | House and Shop | 53 " " " | " |
| 68 | House and Garden | 1 Ardsheal Road | " |
| 69 | House/Engineers Arms | 3 " " | " |
| 70 | Paine, Manwaring and Lephard P.L.C. | " " " | " |

1898 map, which was later known as Muir House. Photographs of the old rectory show it to be a two-storey house with a central porch, reminiscent of the late 18th-century style of building. It was described as built of cream-coloured bricks, the clay for which was discovered by Thomas Wicks in 1780. It therefore follows that the house was built after this date and it seems quite likely that it was built by the Reverend Peter Wood when he took up his duties in 1797.

An advertisement for Patching & Jordan in the *Worthing Gazette* of 1883 describes the building as follows: 'The Rectory, Broadwater: Detached with large garden, croquet lawn, coach house and stable. Contains 4 sitting rooms, 10 bedrooms (four of which are double-bedded) dressing room, kitchen & offices. To be let till the end of July at 8 guineas per week'.

The rectory continued to be used by the Church until 1924 when it was given up. Eventually, by 1959, the house had become an eyesore, having been empty for 12 years. Planning consent was given for the house to be demolished, and the site was developed as a shopping precinct with a supermarket, residential flats and car-parking facilities. The house was demolished in 1959 and the development took place in the early 1960s to produce the new shopping precinct known as Broadwater Boulevard.

*House and Garden (Tithe No. 135)* (No. 62 on plan)
This large old house was built in 1797 and was owned and occupied by Edward Penfold. From the photographs which exist it would appear that it was brick built with very large chimneys. Photographs of 1930 show that the front and sides of the house were covered in tiles, with a flint and brick boundary wall at the front.

The 1821 census records that Edward and John Penfold lived in the house with six other adults. Edward was still shown as the owner/occupier in 1836 but between 1839 and 1843 the property was in the hands of the executors of Edward Penfold, with William Penfold in occupation. By 1846 Charles Roberts had acquired the property and Richard Penfold was shown as the occupier. The 1851 census describes Richard Penfold as aged 75 and a yeoman. During the 1860s an Elizabeth Meggs appears to be the occupier but by 1871 it was shown as empty. In 1872 Thomas Cracknell was the new occupier, with Charles Roberts still shown as the owner and in 1878 Thomas Cracknell himself became the new owner/occupier and remained so until 1883.

From 1883 a Mr. E. Blinkhorn became the new owner of the property and moved in. The directory of 1907 shows him still in occupation and the house known as 'Broadwater House'. He was there until his death on 27 August 1930. A newspaper report from the *Worthing Herald* of 29 April 1966 records an old inhabitant's recollections of Broadwater in the early part of this century. He recalled that Mr. Blinkhorn was a white-bearded old man who had a Spanish wife and rode around in Broadwater on an outlandish tricycle. Apparently Blinkhorn always carried a bag of sweets in his pocket for the local children, but unfortunately it was the same pocket in which he kept his pipe, thus giving the sweets a tobacco flavour!

Edward Blinkhorn left the property to his wife Ramona, who died on 14 August 1931, and her executors conveyed the property to Worthing Corporation on 13 August 1932. By 1933 road widening had started in Broadwater Street West and 'Broadwater House' was demolished. For many years the narrow road from the old *Maltster's* public house going northwards had become a dangerous bottleneck and so road widening was considered the answer. In order to carry this out, all the buildings on the west side of Broadwater Street West (from Broadwater House to the Green) were eventually demolished during the early 1930s. Mr. Ray Herbert of Broadwater recalled to the authors that when he was a small boy one of his weekend pursuits was connected with the old narrow road. Apparently, opposite the old *Maltster's* public house was a telegraph pole, and when two motor-coaches passed each other there was just about enough room, except that most of the brass handles from the side of one of the coaches were removed by the telegraph pole as it went by. Mr. Herbert used to go to see how many brass handles he could find embedded in the telegraph pole at the weekends.

The site of the old house is approximately under the modern Woolworth's shop but nearer the road.

*House (Tithe No. 136)* (No. 63 on plan)
This old Georgian house was built in 1800 either by, or for Thomas Richardson. It was a large house, according to old photographs, and it appears to have a coat of render on the outside thus disguising the basic building material. It is most likely, however, that it was built of flint and bricks.

It appears that up until 1817 Thomas Richardson was the owner, with occupiers as follows: from 1800 to 1803, Thomas Richardson; 1804 to 1811, John Street; 1812 to 1816, Thomas Richardson; and in 1817 Richard Penfold.

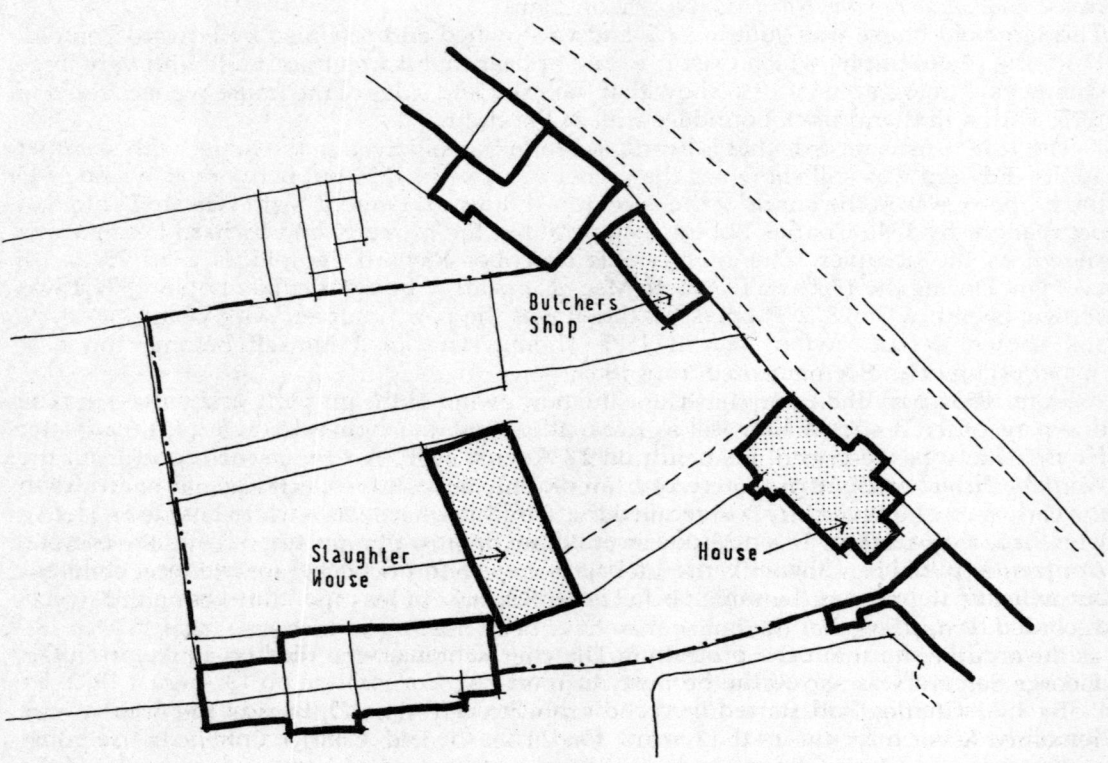

*Fig. 31. Layout of property No. 63, c.1838.*

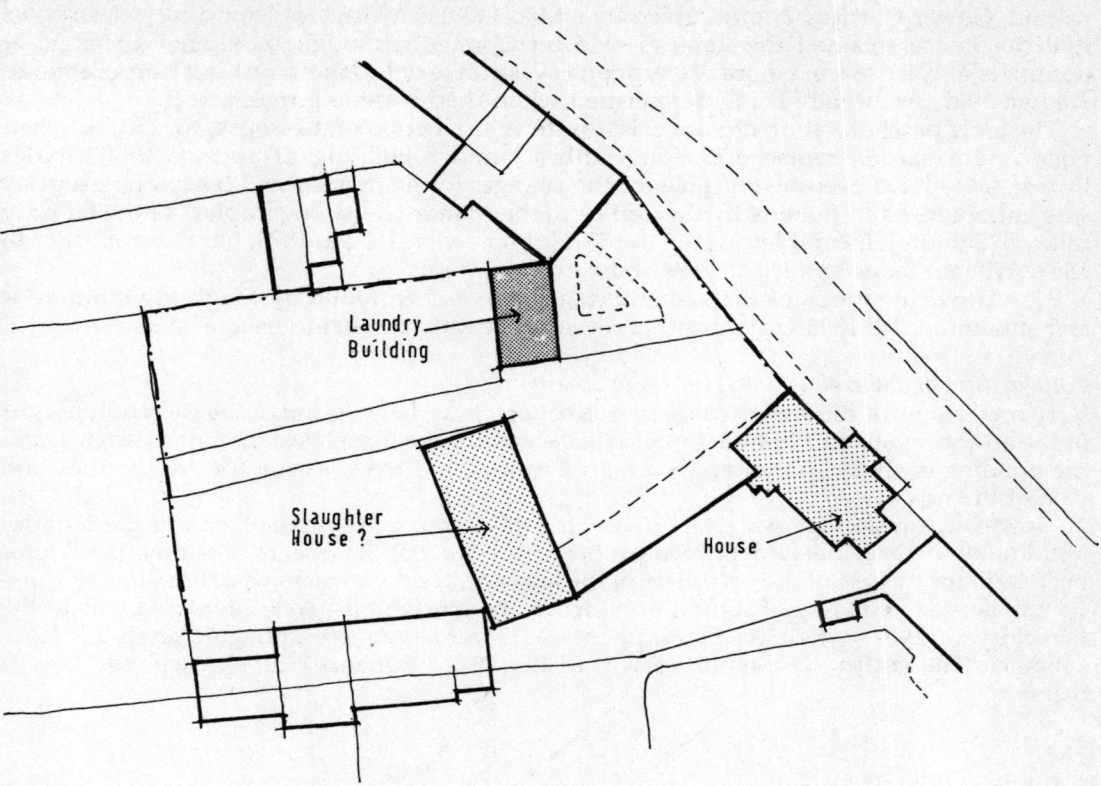

*Fig. 32.  Layout of property No. 63 from 1875 O.S. map.*

In 1818 a Mr. Borrer, possibly from Fittleworth, was the new owner with Richard Penfold shown as the occupier. This situation continued until 1820 when the occupiers were recorded as 'Penfold, Hazelgrove & Redman', in the Land Tax Records, and continued to be described as such until 1830. However, the 1821 census is much more specific and it records that there was a house, butcher's shop, slaughterhouse and garden on the site, owned by a Mr. Borrer and occupied by (Richard) Hazelgrove and John Holden (probably the butcher). The 1838 survey of Broadwater by Charles Hide shows the layout of the property (see Fig. 31) while the later tithe map shows no change. Mr. Borrer remained as owner of the property until 1851 during which time at least two different occupiers are recorded. It appears that the house may have been used as a beerhouse from 1830 to 1849 as the occupier for that period was John Thatcher, who was described as a brewer! In 1850 George Sargent was shown as the next occupier.

By 1861 Charles Roberts acquired the property and Mary Duke was the occupier and remained as such for the next 12 years. On 23 March 1883 Charles Roberts died and the property was in the hands of his devisees and by 1886 his wife, Mary. During this period two other occupiers were recorded, Linfield and Walter William Wells. At the close of the Surveyor's Books in 1894, F. Manwaring was shown as the occupier and had been so from at least 1891. The owner was still Mary Roberts. The Directory of 1907 shows the house named 'Gower Cottage' and occupied by a Miss Lewis. A study of later directories shows that the house retained the name of 'Gower Cottage' although there was a change of occupiers at least twice, before the property was conveyed to the Worthing Corporation in August 1932, eventually being demolished when road widening took place.

The early butcher's shop did not exist for the entire period of the house, for in 1862 it had gone and a garden replaced it along with a laundry building. It appears that Charles Roberts may have been responsible for the change, for he then owned both. The property was enfranchised to Roberts by the Ladies of the Manor. A list of occupiers of the laundry follows (although incomplete): 1863 to 1871, John Fowler; 1872 to 1873, Job Pyecroft; 1883 to 1889, William Skindle; 1890 to 1894, Edward Blinkhorn.

No further mentions of the slaughterhouse have been found although the building is still shown on the 1898 Ordnance Survey map. It was later being used as a barn.

*Cottage (part of Tithe No. 136) (No. 64 on plan)*
Very few details of the construction of this cottage have been found, as all the photographs of the area in which this building is situated seem to have been taken at various angles, and the building is always obscured by a high flint wall and trees, except for the chimney and part of the roof.

However, the cottage was built in about 1880 in the garden area fronting the laundry building of the previously-described property (see No. 63). It appears that it may well have been built for the use of the occupiers of the laundry, for the owners were the same as those for the laundry building. The first occupier of the cottage positively identified was in the Directory of 1907, when A. E. Phippen was recorded in the cottage shown as 'Farm Cottage'. The cottage is plainly shown on the 1898 Ordnance Survey map (see Fig. 33 below).

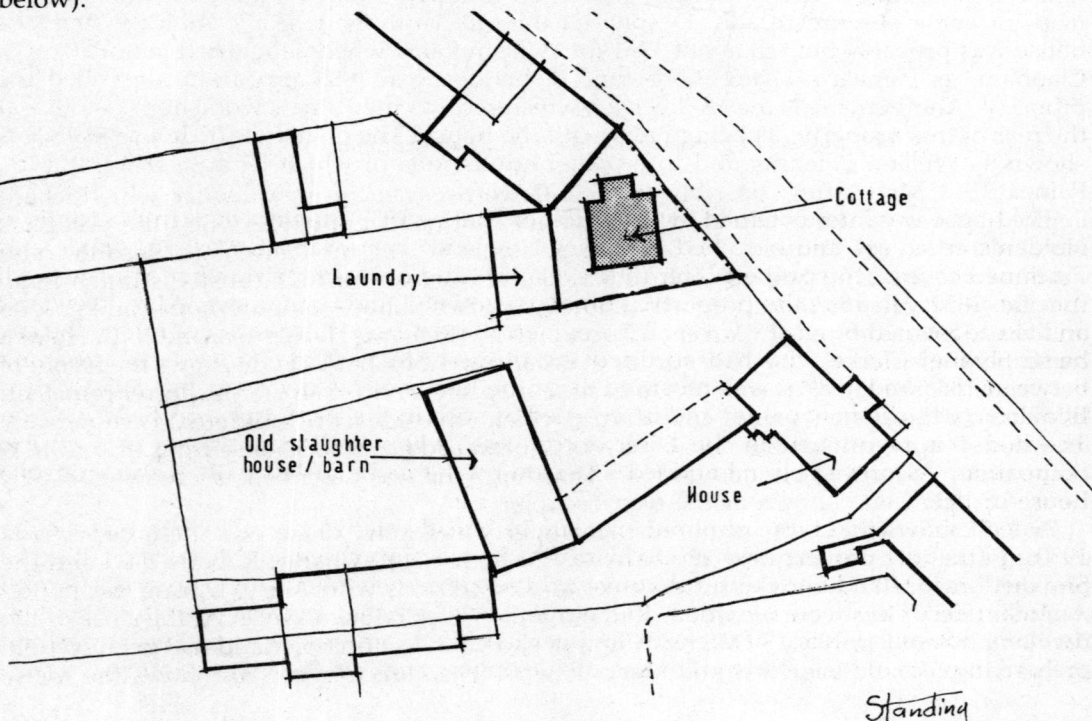

*Fig. 33. Layout of property No. 64 from 1898 O.S. map.*

From at least 1912 the occupier was W. H. Mole who was gardener for Mr. Edward Blinkhorn of 'Broadwater House' (see No. 62). This is interesting, for the occupier of the laundry, in about 1890 and after, was Edward Blinkhorn himself. This fact plus the lack of any information concerning the occupiers of the cottage from 1880 to 1907 tends to confirm the previously-mentioned idea that perhaps the occupiers of the laundry and cottage were one and the same. This cottage was also demolished when the road was widened, after having been conveyed to Worthing Corporation in 1932. It appears that the laundry had become a dairy by 1932.

*House (Bath House) (Tithe No. 137)* (No. 65 on plan)
This old building was tall with a very high pitched roof incorporating a garret, indicating that it was almost certainly thatched when it was originally built.

The origins of this property have been difficult to determine. One item which has confused the issue was an article from the *West Sussex Gazette* dated 30 June 1934, in which it is recorded that the house was erected in the early part of 1600, and that it formed a retreat for the widows and the orphaned younger sons and daughters of the Manor. Apparently Captain Pitt said his statements were substantiated by the deeds of the property and that in the early 1700s the house was occupied by members of the Pitt family, descendants of which were the last to occupy the house in 1933.

There are a number of discrepancies in this article. Firstly, there are no mentions of any of the Pitt family in the parish registers, and secondly, although a Captain Pitt is shown in the house in the years prior to its demolition in 1933/34, there are no Pitts either owning or occupying the property from at least 1821 to 1894. The other fact is that no house is shown on the 1720 map of Broadwater, although of course this does not entirely prove that the house was not in existence. It could have been copyhold premises and not shown on the map for some obscure reason. Despite all this, the authors' research indicates that the house was probably built in about 1761 for William Paine when he married Jane Parson of Clapham, as Paine's probate at the time of his death in 1880 appears to described the property. Another clue is the 1821 census which records the Paine's workshop, possibly at the rear of this property, as being rated with the house. The owner of the house in 1821 is shown as William Patching and three other adults, one of which is most probably Mrs. Paine.

The house was later obtained by John Holden and by 1839 was shown as in the hands of Holden's executors and occupied by James Newland. It appears that Messrs. Hide and Patching acquired the property from the executors and held it for a number of years, well into the 1850s. In 1861 the property is shown as owned and occupied by Mary Newland and after 1868, although she was still the owner, there were a number of occupiers, the last being Samuel Clarke who had acquired the property himself by 1883. Clarke died and between 1886 and 1889 it was recorded as in the hands of his devisees. By 1893 Edward Blinkhorn was the new owner and is recorded as such in the last Surveyor's Book of 1894. The house is mentioned in the Directory of 1907 when W. Pitt is shown as being in occupation. As previously mentioned a person by the name of Pitt is then shown in the house in 1931/2.

A deed shows that Edward Blinkhorn, late of 'Broadwater House' (No. 62), had died in 1930 and that the property was left to his wife who was appointed sole executrix in his will. She died in 1931 and her executors conveyed the property to Worthing Corporation on 13 August 1932. The deed describes the property as 'All that messuage or tenement or dwelling house with yard or backside and garden (then formerly described as garden and orchard or piece of Meadowland) there unto belonging and lying behind the same and then known as 'Bath House' and also all that cottage (sometime since an outhouse) and the pig pound also situate behind the said cottage (Bath Cottage)'. The property was eventually demolished when road widening took place.

*House (Tithe No. 137a)* (No. 66 on plan)
The Directories of 1907 and 1912 show these six buildings to be 'Jubilee Cottages', a name which suggests they were possibly built in 1887 or 1897 (both Jubilee years of Queen Victoria). However, a study of the Surveyor's Books for the whole period shows that there were other buildings, similar in number, on the site prior to those dates. The 1875 Ordnance Survey map shows the buildings in a different formation. Without further information it can only be stated with reasonable certainty that Jubilee Cottages were built between 1875 and 1898.

Houses existed on the site in 1821 when the census records that they were owned by Mr. William Patching and occupied by two poor families of the parish. The Land Tax Records show a piece of Mrs. Paine's property being acquired by Mr. Patching in 1820 and this would seem to be the piece on which these two houses were built. In 1825 John Holden took over the property and after his death in 1838 it was shown as being held by the executors of J. Holden until 1843. By 1846 John Belchamber was the owner and he occupied one of the premises. He was shown as the owner until the late 1870s by which time Edwin and Arthur Henty took over. During the early 1880s Robert Stather acquired the property and held it for many years during which time the authors believe that the old houses were pulled down and 'Jubilee Cottages' built. A deed shows that the property was acquired by Worthing Corporaion on 25 September 1933 and was demolished later when the road widening took place.

*House and Shop (Tithe No. 138)* (No. 67 on plan)
The origin of this property is unidentified, as yet, but is believed to be early 19th century in the authors' opinions. The 1838 survey shows the building near to and parallel to the road, with another building at the rear which was a workshop. A photograph taken of the house in the early part of this century shows the house to be old, small and flint built.

The house is first positively identified in the 1818 Church Rate Book when John Hipditch is shown as owner/occupier. The 1821 census records much more information when it describes the property as a 'House, Shoemaker's Shop and Garden' occupied by John and Catherine Hipditch and their seven children. The house was rated at £1.00 and was also owned by John Hipditch. He was a cordwainer by trade (shoemaker), hence the shoemaker's shop which was probably the workshop. John Hipditch was shown in the house until 1846 when he appears to have died, for the house is then shown as owned by the trustees of John Hipditch. In 1849 and 1850 the house was acquired by the devisees of Richard Weller, during which time Henry Beach, a carpenter, was the occupier. In 1851 John Belchamber took over the ownership but by 1861 Henry Beach, the occupier had apparently purchased the property and he remained there as owner until 1889. In 1890 Edward Patching was the new owner but Henry Beach was still in occupation. The workshop disappeared sometime between 1875 and 1898. Edward Patching was still the owner in 1894 when the last Surveyor's Book was compiled for Broadwater.

The Directory of 1907 shows the house named as 'Dulce Domum' and occupied by W. Brown. However, by 1912 F. C. Knight was the occupier and it appears that he was a motor engineer by trade, and had established his business in the adjacent property to the north (see No. 68). Edward Patching died on 26 June 1919 and his two sons, being his executors, sold the property to Charles Henry Forte on 9 July 1921. Parts of this land belonging to the property were sold to Alfred Borrer on 22 September 1927. It appears that the cottage may well have had its name changed to 'Hawthorn Cottage' prior to its eventual demolition, when the road was widened in the early 1930s.

*House and Garden (Tithe No. 139)* (No. 68 on plan)
The origins of this old house are not known but the authors believe that it is early 19th century, when Broadwater began to expand as a result of the spin-off from the increased prosperity of Worthing.

The census of 1821 shows that the house contained two sets of inhabitants; George Baker, his wife and four children in one part and Hannah Mansell with her six children in the other. These families were described as 'poor' and the house was owned by Mr. Margesson of Offington. The next identification of the house is in 1836 when Joseph Vaux was shown as one of the occupiers. He remained there until at least 1851, and in 1841 Joseph King was the other occupier, remaining there until 1861. During this period Mr. J. B. Daubuz was the owner having taken over Offington from Mr. William Margesson.

In 1862 Thomas Wisden acquired the property and remained as owner at least until the last Surveyor's Book in 1894.

There were a number of tenants in the building up until 1894 and as it appears that the house was divided into two the tenants are listed as follows: in one half, Joseph King, 1861; George Poor, 1862-c.1875; James Slaughter, by 1877; George Slaughter, by 1880-1894: the other half, Richard Till, 1861-64; – Heryet, 1865-68; empty, 1869-70; Mrs. Clements, 1871-74; empty, 1875; John Gould, by 1877-1894. The Directory of 1907 shows F. Elliott and Arthur Batchelor in occupation.

The tithe map shows a possible outbuilding near the road, south east of the house. This outbuilding had disappeared by the Ordnance Survey map of 1875. The Surveyor's Books show that a workshop was built on part of this land in about 1877 and William Carpenter is shown as the occupier until 1894. By 1912 the premises were recorded as 'F. C. Knight, Motor Engineers' in the local directory. The later Directory of 1927 shows that the buildings had all been demolished on the site and Boorer's Garage built. A garage still exists on the site in 1982 but discontinued as such by early 1983.

*House/Engineer's Arms (Tithe No. 140)* (No. 69 on plan)
The site of this property was originally part of an ancient copyhold called 'Horley's'. After the Inclosure Act it became part of the 'West Parsonage' and William Borrer was admitted as tenant at a Court Baron on 17 February 1818, when the property was described as a garden. On 5 April 1848 William Borrer surrendered the property and Daniel Marner was admitted as the new tenant. A house was built on the property just prior to this date by Marner, who lived there with his 24 year-old wife Alice and 2 year-old son Benjamin.

By 1851 the census shows that Daniel had two more children since moving to the new house, William aged 4 and Olive aged 2 and he also employed a 13 year-old girl, Harriet Floyd, as a house-servant. The Surveyor's Record Books for Broadwater show that Daniel was the owner of the house until his death in 1862, after which his daughter Olive took over.

On 7 June 1877, John Bright Marner, painter, the youngest son of Daniel Marner was admitted to the property, as was the custom in Broadwater, but by 18 March 1881 it had been surrendered to Robert Stather, who was later described as a grocer and beer retailer. From this date the property is shown in two parts; firstly as a beerhouse, shop and garden owned and occupied by Robert Stather, and secondly as a house and garden owned and occupied by William Marner, son of Daniel. On 14 September 1888 enfranchisement was given to Robert Stather at a cost of £112 10s 0d, and the property was then no longer copyhold. The property was immediately conveyed to William Cloves Tamplin of Brighton. It eventually became part of 'Tamplin's Brewery of Brighton' and was named the *Engineer's Arms*,[41] probably due to its near proximity to the engineers building of Paine, Manwaring and Lephard. In 1890 William Pay was the landlord, having previously served at the *Maltster's Arms* from 1872 to 1889. The *Engineer's Arms* was closed by 1928,[42] and the licence transferred to the *Elms* public house which was built in 1927.

Tamplin and Sons sold the property to Raymond Wells on 12 April 1928, and he sold it in December 1929 to Harold Daniel Tribe of Broadwater. Some three years later it was conveyed to James Richard Bewell who sold it on 22 February 1938 to Messrs. Paine Manwaring and Lephard Ltd, who were the owners of the adjacent property to the west. It then became absorbed into the expansion of that Company.

During the years 1928 to 1938 plans for a new front line to the property were adopted and the property converted. It appears that the property was split into two pieces, north to south, the western piece known originally as 35A Broadwater Street West but eventually 3 Ardsheal Road.

## Paine, Manwaring & Lephard (No. 70 on plan)

The precise date that the Paine family moved to the village of Broadwater is not known, but by 1731 a William Paine had acquired either freehold land or premises, for he is recorded in the list of freeholders of that date (see full text in Chapter Two). He had married at West Tarring by licence, on 30 March 1725, Ann Weston, a maiden of that parish. The marriage licence reveals that his occupation was a blacksmith, and declares that his parish was Broadwater.[43] William and Ann had five children, three sons and two daughters. His youngest daughter, Elizabeth, married Philip Moor in 1755. He was the landlord of the *Maltster's Arms* between 1771 and 1780. William Paine (senior) died on 18 December 1855, and his wife Ann became his sole executor and beneficiary.[44]

As stated earlier, in the text for property No. 23, it is recorded in the *Worthing Gazette*, published on 9 December 1925, that William Paine started his business in a house in Broadwater Street East.[45] The comparison below of William Paine's Probate Inventory, with that of John Parrot, strongly suggests that William Paine had acquired, prior to 1730, the premises of John Parrot as subsequent to that date no further entries relating to John's branch of the Parrot family have been discerned in the parish of Broadwater.

| Probate Inventory[46] John Parrot (Senior) | | Probate Inventory[47] William Paine (Senior) | |
|---|---|---|---|
| *Ground floor* | Smithy shop | *Ground floor* | Smithy shop |
| | Kitchen | | Kitchen |
| | Brewhouse | | Brewhouse |
| | Hall | | Parlour (Hall?) |
| | Buttery | | Celler/Celery (Buttery?) |
| | | | |
| *First floor* | Hall chamber | *First floor* | Parlour chamber |
| | Mye chamber | | Middle chamber |
| | Kitchen chamber | | Kitchen chamber |

William Paine's probate return also provides an interesting insight into the trade of the 18th-century blacksmith, for the following tools and materials were listed as being in his smith shop:

|                                                              | £  | s  | d |
|--------------------------------------------------------------|----|----|---|
| Iron 6:3:0 @ 22 shilling per hundred                         | 7  | 8  | 6 |
| Horseshoes 1:0:10 @ 28 shillings per hundred                 | 1  | 10 | 6 |
| A pear of Coal Grates                                        | 0  | 16 | 0 |
| Box pin                                                      | 0  | 17 | 0 |
| 3 pears of Visses & black Iron                               | 1  | 10 | 0 |
| Old Iron and tools                                           | 0  | 5  | 0 |
| Steakes                                                      | 0  | 2  | 0 |
| Anuells and bellows                                          | 6  | 0  | 0 |
| Weights                                                      | 1  | 0  | 0 |
| 35 pound of horseshoes and a parcel of od goods              | 0  | 14 | 0 |
| A Grindstone and all belonging to                            | 0  | 13 | 0 |
| 6 Chaldren of Coal                                           | 9  | 0  | 0 |
| A Broom & Skearls                                            | 0  | 3  | 0 |
|                                                              | 30 | 0  | 0 |

The family business was continued by his eldest son, also William, who was baptised on 14 March 1731. He married at Clapham, by licence, Jane Parson of that parish on 2 September 1761[48] and they had eight children (four sons and four daughters). William junior died on 6 July 1800 and his probate return[49] clearly reveals that the property he occupied at his death was very different to that of his father. He probably occupied Bath House, where the authors consider he may have moved immediately after his marriage. As was the custom at Broadwater, Richard Paine, William's youngest son, together with his wife Sarah, inherited both Bath House and the family business, 'as lawful and natural heir'.[50] Richard Paine died in 1814, when his successor in the family business, his son, also a William, was 10 years old. It appears that Sarah Paine continued to occupy Bath House until some time after 1834 when William Pain had moved to Hadley House (property No. 15).

George Paine, the youngest son of William Paine apparently took over his father's business in 1863 after the death of his father on 10 October 1863. George was born in 1845 and in the 1851 census was recorded as a scholar, aged six, the youngest of seven children of William and Eliza Paine. His two elder brothers were shown as Henry, aged 14, a blacksmith's lad and William (junior), aged 18, a blacksmith. Unfortunately William junior died very young (aged 23) but according to a *Worthing Herald* report in 1925 he is credited with making ornamental ironwork which formed the upper part of the east window of Broadwater church. This piece of work was described as an exceedingly commendable piece of ironwork for a village forge.

In his younger days George Paine played cricket for Broadwater cricket club and John Marshall in his book *Sussex Cricket* describes him as a flamboyant, massive blacksmith and hefty hitter. He wore a top hat whilst playing cricket and was described as rolling from tent to wicket always wearing his hat.

The family business was carried out in the small workshop on the green (see No. 73) and in 1874 Frank Manwaring joined the business when there were only five people employed. Up until George Paine took over, the blacksmith's business had been solely carried out by members of the Paine family, apparently in an unbroken line since 1725.

The business prospered and expanded into general engineering, for in 1883 an advertisement recorded George Paine as a machinist of Broadwater who sold his 'Counter Balance Continuous Ventilator Stays' for greenhouses (see No. 15). This small firm was originally known as 'Paine & Manwaring'.

George Paine also had interests in another small firm, eventually known as 'Lephard & Paine'. This firm originated when Mr. Edwin Lephard took on Mr. George Wood as a partner in the threshing business, which was then carried out with horse-drawn machines. Later these old portable machines were replaced by steam apparatus and George Wood, thinking possibly that he could do better at farming, left the firm and took a farm at Poling. Mr. Lephard then joined forces with George Paine and they continued with the threshing and haulage firm.

The property at present owned and occupied by 'Paine & Manwaring' was, in 1873, an orchard owned by Charles Roberts who died in 1883, leaving it to his wife Mary. She died in 1889 and a John Roberts conveyed the property to Frank Vornberger in 1897, when the property contained 'a messuage, shop and other buildings'. On 24 April 1902 the trustees of Mr. Vornberger sold the property to George Paine (described as a machinist), who had by this time become a respected member of the community, with many friends. Following his death, in June 1903, it was decided to combine the various joint enterprises into a small limited liability company under the title of 'Paine, Manwaring and Lephard Ltd'. The company was incorporated in December 1903, and Frank Manwaring was the first Managing Director.

The personal representatives of George Paine (deceased) conveyed, on 8 February 1904, the property described as a 'messuage, shop, stabling, greenhouses and other buildings' to Paine, Manwaring & Lephard Ltd thus establishing the company on their present site.

It appears that the house on the site was occupied by Frank Manwaring in 1907 and is recorded as 'Queensmere'.

The forge and workshop on the green remained until 1938 when the workshops were transferred to the rear of the present property. Other alterations and extensions were also carried out as can be seen in an advertisement recorded in a booklet of 1938,[49] which describes the company as 'General Heating and Ventilating Engineers, Ironmongers, Tool Merchants, Horticultural Sundriesmen'. A notice was also shown in the advertisement as follows: 'Extensive alterations and additions to the works and showrooms are being carried out and clients will find their instructions executed expeditiously and efficiently by experienced mechanics, under personal supervision and the showrooms replete with all the requirements and labour saving devices necessary to maintenance of the modern home, workshop and garden, and at prices that compare favourably with those quoted elsewhere'.

It is quite certain that the extensions were made possible by the acquisition of the old *Engineer's Arms* site in February 1938 (see No. 69). The company are still trading on the same site and as such must be regarded as the oldest firm in the vicinity.

### Section 14–Broadwater Green
This section contains the S.E. part of Broadwater Green on which had been built, by 1898, the Old Pound House, Broadwater School and the Smith Shop.

*House* (No. 71 on plan)
This house was built in 1789, according to the Land Tax Records, on a parcel of land which was formerly described as part of Broadwater Green. The house was originally owned by Ayling Shepherd. The occupier was recorded as Robert Piper, who was born in 1739, and

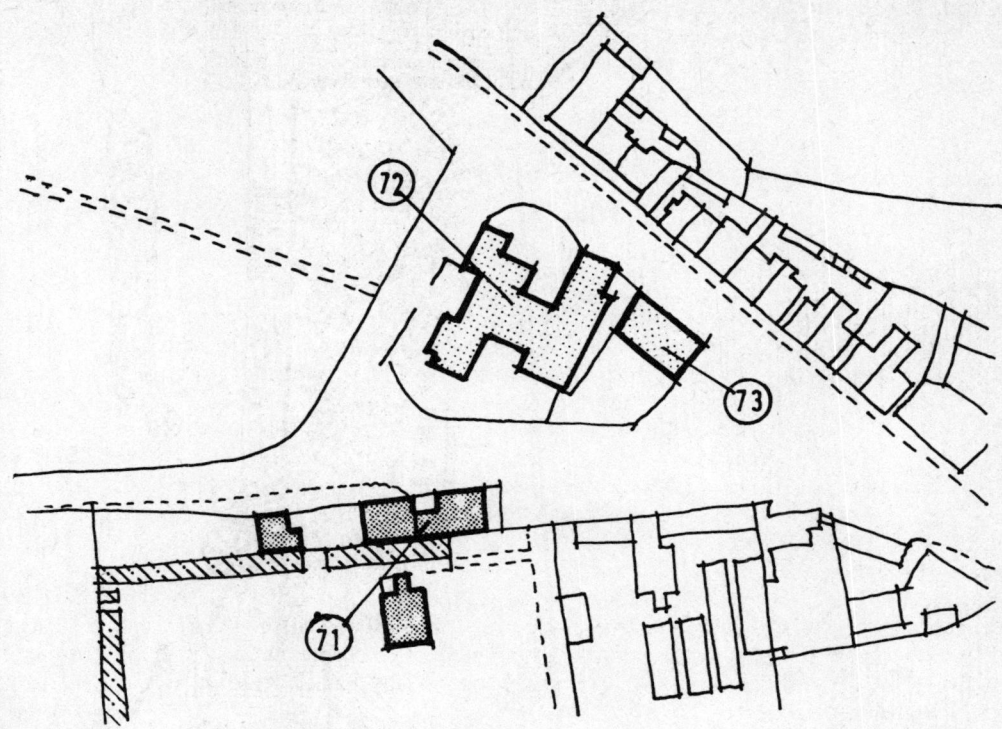

*Section 14*                                                                        Standing

| N° | DESCRIPTION | MODERN ADDRESS | CURRENT USE |
|----|------------|----------------|-------------|
| 71 | Pound House | 41 Ardsheal Rd. | Residential |
| 72 | Village School | ———— | } Broadwater Green |
| 73 | Smithy shop | ———— | |

his wife Ann, born in 1737. He died the year in which he occupied the new house (1789). They had a daughter, Ann, who was baptised in 1778. Robert Piper died in November 1803 and it appears that another member of the Piper family, a Mrs. Piper, acquired the property from Ayling Shepherd, for she is shown as both the owner and occupier in 1804. From this date there are no further entries in the Land Tax Records until 1818, when James Piper is shown as the owner and occupier. However, the 1821 census informs us that there were two Piper families in occupation; James and Frances, and Richard and Mary, plus their children. James and Richard were almost certainly brothers. Another lodger is shown, named William Manton.

This delightful old house which still exists opposite the modern Green is built of flint. A rear, long, narrow garden is surrounded by a high flint wall and there is a low flint wall enclosing a very small garden to its front. At some time prior to 1848 a section at the end of

Fig. 34. Wheelwright's shop on Broadwater Green, c.1870.

the rear garden was used as the parish pound, where stray animals were kept until their owners reclaimed them, usually on payment of a small fine. Both the tithe map and the Ordnance Survey map of 1875 record this part of the garden as the pound.

James Piper continued as owner/occupier, according to the Surveyor's Books, until 1850, after which date Richard Piper took over as owner until 1870. He was described as a wheelwright. It appears that James was also a wheelwright for a wheelwright's shop was shown opposite on the Green from at least 1839 to 1873 (see Fig. 34).

At some time during the 1850s the house was occupied by Phil Holmes and later in the 1860s, 1870s and 1880s by Mrs. M. A. Holmes. During the early 1890s a Mr. Holmes was the occupier. From 1871 to 1894 there were a number of owners, as follows: J. N. Nye, 1871-75; J. S. Sherley, about 1876/7; William Stanbridge, by 1880 to about 1883; Amy Guile, about 1886-1894.

The 1898 Ordnance Survey map shows outbuildings on the property, one immediately to the rear of the house and one at the end of the garden, where the parish pound used to be. By 1912 the house was occupied by Miss L. Woodford and the property was the 'Temperance Laundry'. According to a newspaper report in the *Worthing Herald* of 29 April 1966, the old drying grounds for the laundry were on the greensward in front of what is now the fire station.

The house still exists with its flint walls, and the exterior shows very little change from photographs taken many years ago. It is now overlooked, however, by a block of flats.

*Broadwater School* (No. 72 on plan)
The building shown on the 1898 Ordnance Survey map is Broadwater school. This, however, was not the first school recorded in Broadwater. The 1821 census describes a property at the eastern end of the village as a 'House and garden and village school' (see Fig. 35A).

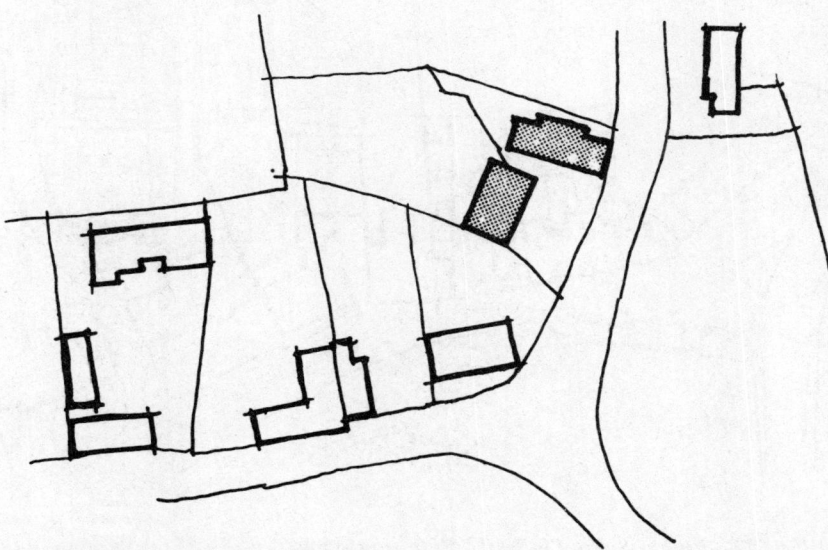

*Fig. 35A. The Village School in Georgian times.*

An Infants' School was established in Broadwater in 1817[51] and, together with those in Worthing, was claimed to be one of the earliest of such schools in England. It is almost certain that the 1817 school was established on the same site as that shown in 1821. In 1818 there were approximately 40 boys and girls attending the school, which was supported by both the parish and W. Davison, Chaplain of the Worthing Chapel of Ease. The Reverend William Davison is known to have taken an active part in the affairs of the Town of Worthing, but his most notable achievement was in connection with the education of the poor of the Parish. It was to this cause that he devoted much of his energy and the Davison School, in Chapel Road, Worthing, is a fitting monument.

The conditions in this early school must have been rather primitive for a deed of 1868[52] informs us that 'All that cottage or tenement with the Barn formerly used as a school . . .'.

From 1821 to 1848 the Reverend Peter Wood (Rector of Broadwater) also appears to have been connected with the school, for in 1826 the north transept of Broadwater church was converted for the use of the school.[53] This may have been for use as an 'overflow' building or perhaps while temporary repairs were taking place to the barn, for the tithe award (prepared in 1851) still shows the barn as the village school.

In 1833 the school was supported by subscriptions and school pence. Later in 1840 a building grant was received and by about 1847 the school was united with the National Society. (This society was formed in 1811 and provided day schools in which Anglican instruction was given.) In 1849 the school was moved to another converted barn north of the church at the rear of Northgate Cottages (see Fig. 35B). The Ordnance Survey map, surveyed in 1873, shows this as the 'National School (boys and girls)'. The outline of this building can still be seen in the gardens at the rear of Northgate Cottages, where part of the barn's walls are still in situ, acting as boundary walls for the gardens.

Analysis of the 1851 census returns for Broadwater indicate that 74 per cent of the 138 children listed in the parish between the ages of five and 15 years attended a school.

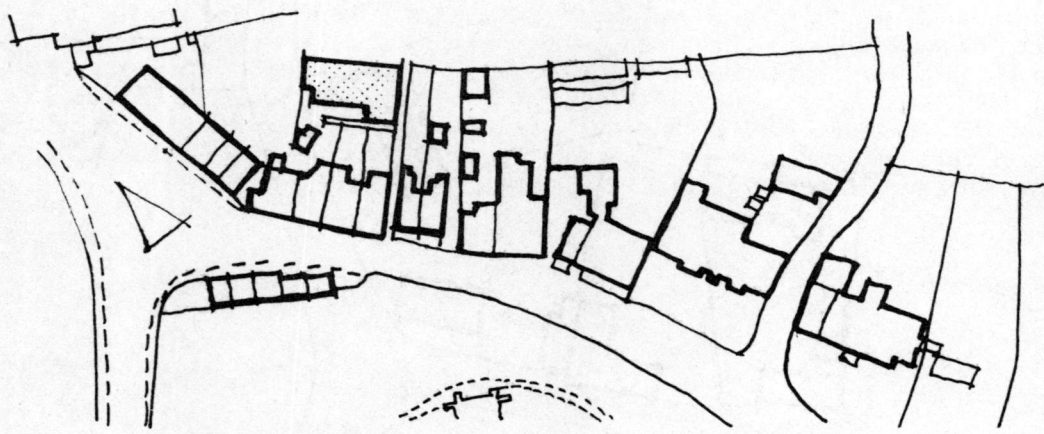

*Fig. 35B. The Village School in Early Victorian times.*

The Elementary Education Act was passed in 1870 and provided that school boards were to be elected with powers to establish and maintain elementary schools by levying rates, charging fees and receiving Government grants. This Act was probably the reason for the new school for infants and older children being built on the south-eastern corner of Broadwater Green in 1873.[54] It was opened on 10 November 1873 and the average attendance was 99, rising to 113 on the role in June 1874. Admission to the school was by payment of the 'school pence', collected on Mondays, according to the entry in the old log books of Broadwater School. In November 1887 a child was sent home for being 6d in arrears of school fees, while in 1889 the Trustees provided the means for the Governors to refuse admission to the school to any child if they were more than a fortnight in arrears of school pence. Apparently no fees were charged in 1893.[55]

There are a few entries in the Log Book which nowadays would tend to be regarded as amusing: 'June 1896–sent child to fountain to wash his hands–he failed to return'. 'March 1905–A pupil sent home to be cleaned'.

Other entries show that there was absenteeism resulting from cases of typhoid fever in 1899, while in 1915 the Infants' School was closed due to an outbreak of measles and in 1920 for whooping cough. One child died in 1884 of scarlet fever and another in 1896 of diphtheria.

The school was finally demolished in 1937 when the majority of the pupils transferred to the present Broadwater Church of England School in Rectory Gardens. Some of the children transferred to Ham Road School, now Downsbrook, which was opened in 1910.

*Smith Shop* (No. 73 on plan)
The Charles Hide Survey of Broadwater of 1838 shows a smith shop on the south-east corner of Broadwater Green. This small shop was erected in about 1834 for William Paine's blacksmith's trade. It was originally a one-storey building, according to a picture shown on the menu for the bi-centenary commemoration dinner given by Paine Manwaring and Lephard Ltd in 1925. This picture shows a group of people in front of the building, one of whom is George Paine, another being Frank Manwaring, both very young. This picture must be dated after 1874, which was the date when Frank Manwaring joined the firm.

The original small firm of Paine and Manwaring expanded and in 1885 the small smith shop and forge was replaced by a much larger one, a familiar sight on Broadwater Green until 1938, when it was demolished together with the school behind it and the land conveyed to Worthing Corporation. Paine Manwarings' built new workshops at the rear of their present showrooms, opposite in Ardsheal Road, where the firm was then trading as 'Paine Manwaring & Lephard Ltd'.

# References

## Abbreviations used in the References

V.C.H.: *Victoria History of the County of Sussex* Vol. VI, Part 1; Bramber Rape (Southern part), ed. by T. P. Hudson (1980).

W.S.R.O. West Sussex Record Office, Chichester.

S.N.Q.: 'Sussex Notes and Queries'. A quarterly journal of the Sussex Archaeological Society, Barbican House, Lewes.

S.R.S.: Sussex Record Society publication.

S.A.C.: *Sussex Archaeological Collections relating to the History and Antiquities of the County*, published by the Sussex Archaeological Society, Barbican House, Lewes.

B.W./P.R.F.: Broadwater Parish records deposited in the Worthing Town Hall Archives.

Field: *English Field Names, A Dictionary* by John Field (1972).

**Chapter One**
1. Ordnance Survey Area Book, 1876.
2. V.C.H., p. 67.
3. J. R. Armstrong, *A History of Sussex*, p. 16.
4. R. J. Devoy, 1982, 'Analysis of the geological evidence for Holocene sea-level movements in South East England'. Proceedings of Geologists' Association, Vol. 93, Part I, 1982.
5. E.P.N.S., pp. 192 and 193.
6. R. G. P. Kerridge, *A History of Lancing*, 1979.
7. Henfry Smail, *Offington, Broadwater & Charmandean*, p. 49.
8. Report on a site investigation at Oakleigh Nursery, Dominion Way, Worthing, carried out by Southern Testing Laboratories, September 1979 (by kind permission of B.I.C. Ltd.).
9. Henfry Smail, *Offington, Broadwater & Charmandean*.
10. V.C.H., p. 67.
11. J. R. Armstrong, *A History of Sussex*, p. 20.
12. Ibid, p. 21.
13. Goodman MSS., (Worthing Library).
14. V.C.H., p. 67.
15. Worthing Museum handlist 'Cissbury'.
16. E. C. Curwen, *The Archaeology of Sussex*, 1954.
17. Worthing Museum Handlist, 'Cissbury'.
18. S.N.Q., Vol. XI, pp. 142-5, 161-7; I. Margary, *Roman Roads in Britain*, 1973, p. 63.
19. Marian Frost, F.L.A., *The Early History of Worthing*, p. 35.
20. John Morris, Gen. ed., *Domesday Book, Sussex*, (Phillimore, 1976, 13.30).
21. V.C.H., p. 69.
22. J. R. Armstrong, *A History of Sussex*, pp. 50 and 51.
23. V.C.H., p. 69.
24. Ibid, p. 73.
25. J. R. Armstrong, *A History of Sussex*, p. 54.
26. Sussex Fines (ii), S.R.S., Vol. VII, p. 126.
27. V.C.H., p. 67.
28. S.R.S., Vol. X.
29. Ibid, p. 62.
30. Ibid, pp. 162 and 163.

31. Ibid, p. 276.
32. S.R.S., Vol. 56.
33. Ibid, Vol. 5.
34. W.S.R.O., E. 179/258/14ff., 17-18v.

**Chapter Two**
 1. V.C.H., p. 68 [W.S.R.O., Ep. I/29 Broadwater 103].
 2. S.R.S. Vol. 4, A Poll for knights of the Shire for the County of Sussex, p. 38.
 3. B.W./P.R.F./Volume I.
 4. S.R.S., Vol. XII, Sussex Marriage Licences, Archdeaconry of Chichester, 1575-1730.
 5. S.R.S., Vol. IX, Sussex Marriage Licences, Deanery of Chichester, Pagham and Tarring.
 6. W.S.R.O., STC/I/32 f.223.
 7. Ibid, STC/I/31 f.433.
 8. Ibid, STC/I/32 f.334.
 9. Ibid, STC/I/31 f.491.
10. S.R.S., Vol. XXVIII, p. 93.
11. Wor. Ref. Library, List of Freeholders from original poll book in Lewes Library.
12. W.S.R.O., STC/41 f.22.
13. S.R.S., Vol. XXVIII, p. 94.
14. S.R.S., Vol. XXII, p. 236.
15. S.R.S., Vol. XXVIII, p. 148.
16. W.S.R.O., STC/III/Q f. 67.
17. S.R.S., Vol. IX, p. 286.
18. BW/P.R.F./Vol. I.
19. S.R.S., Vol. XXXII, p. 62.
20. Ibid, p. 46.
21. Ibid, p. 65.
22. W.S.R.O., STC/III/Q f. 67.
23. V.C.H., p. 68.
24. Dr. Sue Farrant, *Georgian Brighton, 1740-1820*, p. 9.
25. Worthing, Brookfield.
26. D. Robert Elleray, *Worthing: A Pictorial History*, 1977.
27. S.A.C., Vol. 35 .
28. *Sussex Coast Mercury*, 29 June 1887.
29. Dallaway's *Sussex*, Vol. 2, pt. 2, p. 33.
30. Henfry Smail, *Worthing Parade No. 1*, Wor. Pag. Series.
31. Henfry Smail, *Worthing and its Coaches*.
32. Henfry Smail, *Worthing Map Story*, 1949.
33. Henfry Smail, *Worthing and its Coaches*.
34. WB/PRF/II, meeting 1 November 1822.
35. Ibid, meeting 19 February 1823.
36. V.C.H., p. 97.
37. John Lowerson, *Victorian Sussex*, p. 31
38. V.C.H., p. 76.
39. Ibid, p. 76.
40. Ibid, p. 114.
41. Ibid, p. 76.
42. Worthing Town Act; 43, Geo III c.59.
43. Edward Snewin and Henfry Smail, *Glimpses of Old Worthing*, 1945, p. 43.
44. Ibid, p. 43/44.
45. B.W./PRF II.
46. Wor. Ref. Library, Overseers Accounts, 1662-3.
47. B.W.PRF/II, Reports to the Poor Law Commissioners, 6 September 1834.
48. V.C.H., p. 77.

49. B.W./PRF III.
50. B.W./PRF IV.
51. F. G. Emmison, *Archives and Local History*.
52. B.W./PRF/II.
53. Ibid.
54. Ibid.
55. Ibid.
56. B.W./PRF/III.
57. B.W./PRF/III, Report to the Poor Law Commissioners, 6 September 1834.
58. B.W./PRF/II.
59. B.W./PRF/III.
60. V.C.H., p. 62.
61. Ibid, p. 77.
62. B.W./PRF/II.
63. Wor. Ref. Library.
64. B.W./PRF/IV.
65. Wor. Ref. Library.
66. S.N.Q., Vol. 13, pp. 249-54, 'The Occupations of the People of Sussex at the end of the 18th century', H. C. Brookfield, B.A., PhD.
67. V.C.H., p. 67.
68. V.C.H., p. 68.
69. V.C.H., p. 75.
70. Detailed information on Broadwater tokens taken from 'Trade Tokens issued in the 17th century', ed. by George C. Williamson, 1889-1891 (Vol. 3, 1967 reprint), pp. 163/164.
71. Dr. Sue Farrant, *Georgian Brighton, 1740-1820*
72. V.C.H., p. 75.
73. Analysis of 1851 Census, M. R. Standing (not yet published).
74. V.C.H., p. 67.
75. John Lowerson, *Victorian Sussex*.
76. Victorian and Edwardian Sussex from old photographs.
77. *Worthing Gazette*, 14 November 1945, 'Centenary of the Railway coming to Worthing'.
78. V.C.H., p. 68.
79. V.C.H., p. 67.
80. Calendar of Assize Records, Sussex Indictments Elizabeth I, H.M.S.O.
81. V.C.H., p. 80.
82. Winston Churchill, *History of the English Speaking Peoples*.
83. B.W./PRF/4.
84. Edward Snewin and Henfry Smail, *Glimpses of Old Worthing*, 1945.
85. Report to the General Board of Health on a Preliminary Inquiry into the sewerage, drainage and supply of water and the Sanitary Conditions of the Inhabitants of the Town of Worthing in the County of Sussex. By Edward Cresy Esq, Superintending Inspector, 5 July 1849.
86. Edward Snewin and Henfry Smail, *Glimpses of Old Worthing*, 1945, p. 43.
87. Worthing Borough Council Minutes, 25 October 1892.
88. Dr. Theodore Thomson's official report to the Local Government Board on an epidemic of Enteric Fever in the Borough of Worthing, and in the Villages of Broadwater and West Tarring, 1894, p. 11.
89. Report on the epidemic of Enteric Fever in 1893 by Charles Kelly M.D., F.R.C.P. (1894), Table III, p. 11.
90. Dr. Theodore Thompson's Report, p. 2/3.
91. Dr. Theodore Thompson's Report, Table VII, p. 12.
92. Wor. Ref. Library Press Cuttings, *Daily Graphic*, 25 and 26 August 1893.
93. Report on the epidemic of Enteric Fever in 1893 by Charles Kelly, M.D., F.R.C.P. (1894), p. 41.
94. Dr. Theodore Thompson's Report to the Local Government Board, 1894, p. 17.
95. Dr. Charles Kelly, M.D., F.R.C.P., Report on the epidemic of Enteric Fever in 1893, p. 29.
96. V.C.H., p. 166. [L.G.B. Prov. Orders Conf. Act 1902, 2 Edward VIII C.209 (Local).]

## Chapter Three

1. Map of Broadwater Manor, *c.* 1720, held in Worthing Reference Library.
2. Worthing Borough Council Deeds, File A222.
3. Marian Frost, F.L.A., *The Early History of Worthing*, 1929, p. 67.
4. Worthing Borough Council Deeds, File A222.
5. V.C.H., p. 68 (W.S.R.O., Par. 29/13/1).
6. Worthing Borough Council Deeds, File A222.
7. V.C.H., p. 69 (Ed 7/123- *Worthing Herald*, 15 January 1960, 27 June 1975; Smail, op. cit. 66-70).
8. Ibid, (Bor. of Worthing (Part of Broadwater Green) Appropriation Order, 1959, ex inf. Mr. D. R. Elleray).
9. Ibid, (H.F. & A.P. Squire, *Henfield Cricket* (1949), 249; J. Marshall, *Sussex Cricket* (1959), 3, 10-11; *Sussex Life*, September 1971, p. 5; Elleray, *Worthing*, pls. 136-7).
10. V.C.H., p. 76 (references 22-30 inc.).
11. Ibid (e.g. G. A. Walpole, *New British Traveller* (1784), p. 51; *Univ. Brit. Dir.*, iv (1798), p. 580; Young, *Agriculture of Sussex*, pp. 428-9).
12. Ibid (Smail, *Offington, Broadwater, Charmandean*, pp. 63-5).
13. Ibid (Chichester Diocesan Kalendar (1903), p. 64; ex inf. Mrs. D. R. Soper; *Worthing Herald*, 20 June, 4 July 1975).
14. Peter Brandon, *The Sussex Landscape*, 1974, p. 102.
15. Field, p. 231.
16. Ibid, p. 20.
17. Ibid, p. 34.
18. Ibid, p. 54.
19. Ibid, p. 167.
20. Ibid, p. 205.
21. Ibid, p. 140.
22. Henfry Smail, *The Worthing Map Story*, 1949, p. 53.
23. Field, p. 125.
24. Ibid, p. 135.
25. Ibid, p. 43.
26. Ibid, p. 148.
27. R. G. P. Kerridge, *A History of Lancing*, 1979, p. 63.
28. Ibid, pp. 69-79 inc.
29. Peter Brandon, *The Sussex Landscape*, 1974, p. 111.
30. V.C.H., p. 66 (Weston Abbey Mun. 5469, ff. 8v, 32v; cf. S.N.Q. v.241n; xiii, 153-6).
31. V.C.H., p. 68 (B.L. Add. Rolls 31307-8).
32. Ibid (B.L. Add. Ch. 47111).
33. S.A.C., Liii, pp. 143, 149, 171.
34. Field, p. 176.
35. Ibid, p. 119.
36. Peter Brandon, *The Sussex Landscape*, 1974, p. 114.
37. V.C.H., p. 73 (Westminster Abbey Muniments 4072; 5469, f.25).
38. Ibid, p. 74 (B.L. Add. Ch. 18897).
39. Petworth House Archives, 3263.
40. Field, p. 94.
41. G. Mantell, *The Geology of the South East of England*, 1833, p. 19.
42. Ibid, p. 20.
43. V.C.H., p. 75 (V.C.H., Suss i, 447).
44. Ibid (Westm. Abbey Mun. 4072).
45. Ibid (Inq. Non. (Rec. com.), 389).
46. Ibid (Westm. Abbey Mun. 5469, f. 26).
47. Ibid, p. 76 (W.S.R.O., Ep I/25/3 (1616, 1635)).
48. Ibid (W.R.L., Biddulph v Newland, brief for plaintiff, f.2v).
49. Ibid (ibid, f.7).

50. R. G. P. Kerridge, *A History of Lancing*, 1979, p. 67, diagram 2.
51. M. A. Lower, *A Compendious History of Sussex*, 1870, Vol. I, p. 87.
52. V.C.H., p. 73 (W.S.R.O., Ep I/25/3 (1616, 1635)).
53. Field, p. 96.
54. Ibid, p. 181.
55. V.C.H., p. 66 (Shearsmith, *Worthing*, 59-61; W. R. L., notes from Newland Diary, 1816-20).
56. Worthing Borough Council Archives.
57. V.C.H., p. 66 (Worthing and Lancing Rd. Act, 7. Geo. IV, c.10 (Local and Personal); W.S.R.O., QDP/W 58).
58. Henfry Smail, *Offington, Broadwater & Charmandean*, p. 64.
59. V.C.H., p. 70 (W.S.R.L., Add. MS. 13445, ff 64-8; W.R.L., valuation of Broadwater Estate, 1792).
60. V.C.H., p. 74 (Clough and Butler Archives, c54/7135 nos. 3-4).
61. Henfry Smail, *Offington, Broadwater & Charmandean*, p. 64.
62. V.C.H., p. 70 (References 81-84 inc.).
63. Ibid (B.L. Add. MS. 39489, f.138).
64. Ibid, (cf. Smail, *Offington, Broadwater, Charmandean*, p. 73).
65. Ibid.
66. V.C.H., p. 74 (Suss. Subsidies (S.R.S.x), 62; Cal.inq. p.m. xiii, pp. 150-1; B.L. Add. MS. 5685, f.39; Westm. Abbey Mun 5469, ff.9, 12, 25, 33).
67. Henfry Smail, *The Worthing Map Story*, 1949, pp. 47 and 49.
68. V.C.H., p. 75 (Snewin and Smail, *Glimpses*, 135).
69. V.C.H., p. 74 (W.R.L., Valuation of Broadwater Estate, 1792; W.S.R.O., Clough and Butler MS. 185, ff.4v-7; C.P. 43/911 roll. 12, 22d-25).
70. V.C.H., p. 75 (W.R.L., sale cats. 1880-4, no. 62; O.S. map, 6 inch, Suss. LXIV. SE. (1899 and later edns.)).
71. V.C.H., p. 72 (Suss. subsidies (S.R.S.x), 62; P.N. Suss. (E.P.N.S.), i 202; B.L. Add. Ch. 8823, 8837; cf. J.I.1/925 rot.7.).
72. S.R.S. Vol. x., p. 62.
73. S.A.C., Vol. 98, p. 55.
74. V.C.H., p. 72 (Suss. Fines, iii (S.R.S. xxiii), pp. 296-7).
75. Ibid (Suss. Fines 1509-1833, i (S.R.S., xix), 288; Elwes and Robinson, W. Suss., facing p. 267).
76. Ibid (B.L. Add. Ch. 18828; ibid. Add MS. 5685, f.178).
77. Ibid (B.L. Add. Ch. 18866).
78. Ibid (Ibid. 18879).
79. Ibid (Comber, Suss. Geneal. Horsham, 48-9; V.C.H. Suss. iv. 16; C66/2535 no. 33; C66/2564 no. 8; cf. S.A.C. Lxix. 119).
80. Ibid (B.L. Add. Ch. 15874).
81. Ibid (W.R.L., will of J. Penfold).
82. Worthing Borough Council Archives.
83. Ibid.
84. V.C.H., p. 72 (references 83 and 84).
85. Worthing Borough Council, File A.42.
86. V.C.H., p. 72 (Kelly's Dir. Worthing (1940 and later edns.).

**Chapter Five**

  1. V.C.H., p. 68.
  2. Worthing & District Blue Book, 1927, p. 73.
  3. *Worthing Herald*, 14 January 1955.
  4. Household Compendium for Worthing, 1907, p. 99.
  5. Abstract of the title of the Trustees for sale under the will of the late Mr. George Paine to freehold land and two cottages known as 'Belle Vue' situated in Broadwater Street, Broadwater, Sussex, Lot 10, 1904. (Verrall & Sons, Worthing.)
  6. Worthing Museum Publication No. 3, *Worthing—a brief account of the history of the town from Neolithic times to the present day*, ed. by L. M. Bickerton, F.L.A., F.M.A., 1963, pl. 7.

7. 'The Worthing Monthly Record and District Chronicle for Arundel, Littlehampton, Shoreham, Steyning, Storrington and places adjacent', 31 August 1853, MI.

8. John Richardson, *The Local Historian's Encyclopedia*, R.24, p. 270.

9. *The Country Life Book of the Living History of Britain*, consultant editor Professor E. W. G. V. Balchin.

10. Mark Edward Perugini, *Victorian Days and Ways*, p. 124.

11. V.C.H., p. 68 (Kelly's Dir. Suss. (1878)).

12. Mark Edward Perugini, *Victorian Days and Ways*, p. 125.

13. *The West Sussex Gazette and South of England Advertiser*, 6 May 1982, John Batten, p. 13.

14. V.C.H., p. 80.

15. V.C.H., p. 68 (W.S.R.O., Ep.I/29 Broadwater 103).

16. W.S.R.O., STC/i/32 f.334.

17. Copy of a Court Baron document in Latin.

18. Old family bible of the Hide family in the possession of Miss Hilary Hide of Guildford.

19. Article in the *Worthing Herald* of 14 February 1955.

20. S.R.S., Vol. 28, p. 93.

21. S.R.S., Vol. 28, pp. 93 and 101.

22. W.S.R.O., EPI/29/133.

23. Worthing Borough Council, Deeds, file A355.

24. Worthing Borough Council, BW/P/118.

25. Verrall and Sons, Solicitors, ex. inf. Mr. H. Divall.

26. Land Tax List, 1752, Overseers Records, Worthing Borough Council.

27. Land Tax Records, W.S.R.O.

28. Broadwater Inclosure award, Worthing Borough Council.

29. Deeds, file A554, Worthing Borough Council.

30. Ex. inf. from Mr. Gosden (retired General Manager of Knowles Bakery).

31. Will, W.S.R.O. STC/I/31f-433, Probate, W.S.R.O. E/29/199.

32. Deeds belonging to the owner of No. 1 The Square.

33. V.C.H., p. 79.

34. Edwin Smith, Olive Cook, Graham Hutton, *English Parish Churches*.

35. Horsfield, Vol. 2, p. 199.

36. Arthur Mee, *The King's England—Sussex*, p. 35.

37. Smith, Cook, Hutton, *English Parish Churches*.

38. *Notable Houses of Worthing*, No. 2, pp. 59-89.

39. P. A. Barrow and the Rev. V. C. Mowll, M.A., *The Story of the Parish and Church of Broadwater*.

40. W.S.R.O., STC/I/32 f.334.

41. V.C.H., p. 68.

42. Ibid.

43. S.R.S., Vol. ix., p. 271, Sussex Marriage Licences.

44. W.S.R.O., Admin. STC/III/Q f.62.

45. *Worthing Gazette*, 9 December 1925, kindly supplied by the Managing Director of the present 'Paine & Manwaring' from the company archives.

46. W.S.R.O. Probate Inventory E.P.I./29/123.

47. W.S.R.O. Probate Inventory E.P.I./29/134.

48. S.R.S., Vol. 32, p. 179.

49. W.S.R.O. Probate Inventory, E/29/139.

50. W.S.R.O., Admin., STC/III/Uf.10.

51. V.C.H., p. 81 (Bread's *Guide to Worthing*, 1859, p. 21).

52. Deeds, File A554, Worthing Borough Council.

53. V.C.H., p. 81 (S.A.C., lxxiv, 117-118; Dallaway & Cartwright, Hist. W. Sussex, ii(2) p. 36).

54. V.C.H., p. 81.

55. Extracts from the School's Log Book.

# *Index*